"There I grew up"

"There I grew up"

REMEMBERING ABRAHAM LINCOLN'S INDIANA YOUTH

WILLIAM E. BARTELT

Indiana Historical Society Press
Indianapolis 2008

© 2008 Indiana Historical Society Press. Reprinted 2009.

Printed in the United States of America

This book is a publication of the
Indiana Historical Society Press
Eugene and Marilyn Glick Indiana History Center
450 West Ohio Street
Indianapolis, Indiana 46202-3269 USA
www.indianahistory.org
Telephone orders 1-800-447-1830
Fax orders 1-317-234-0562
Online orders @ shop.indianahistory.org

The paper in this publication meets the minimum requirements
of American National Standard for Information Sciences—Permanence of Paper for Printed Library
Materials,
ANSI Z39. 48–1984

Library of Congress Cataloging-in-Publication Data

Bartelt, William E.
  There I grew up : remembering Abraham Lincoln's Indiana youth / William E. Bartelt.
     p. cm.
  Includes bibliographical references and index.
  ISBN 978-0-87195-263-9 (cloth : alk. paper)
  1. Lincoln, Abraham, 1809-1865—Childhood and youth. 2. Presidents—United States—Biogra-
phy. 3. Indiana—Biography. I. Title.
  E457.32.B218 2008
  973.7092—dc22
  [B]
                          2007051474

To Kathy
My wife, best friend, and personal librarian

Contents

Foreword

"My childhood home I see again," Abraham Lincoln wrote in February 1846, "And gladden with the view." It was the opening stanza of "a piece of poetry of my own making," as he described it almost boastfully to a friend. Even so, he admitted that he was encountering "a deal of trouble to finish it." Evidently it was more difficult than he realized to reimagine his childhood in Indiana. As his very next lines reveal, the thirty-seven-year-old Lincoln carried mixed memories about his years in the Hoosier State: "And still as mem'ries crowd my brain, / There's sadness in it too."

Here, "partly on account of slavery," as he would later remember, but "chiefly on account of the difficulty in land titles in Kentucky," his father had moved his family to "an unbroken forest" on Little Pigeon Creek across the Ohio River in the southwestern part of the region in 1816. That same year, Indiana became the nineteenth state in the American Union. The founding generation still ruled the infant nation: James Madison was president, and James Monroe had just been elected to succeed him. On the unsettled Indiana frontier, far away from the national capital, the seven-year-old future president helped his father clear the thick woods and build a crude, dirt-floor log cabin. Though "very young," Abe was big for his age, and as he later remembered, "had an axe put into his hands at once." Under his father's direction, he chopped wood, helped clear the land for planting, dropped seeds into the earth, and watched them grow. "It was a wild region," Lincoln later recalled, "with many bears and other wild animals still in the woods. There I grew up."

Life on the Indiana frontier proved not only arduous but also perilous—and at times, deeply traumatic. Two years after the family relocated to the promising new state, young Lincoln's mother fell mortally ill from drinking contaminated milk. Nancy Hanks Lincoln died in 1818, and her young son helped to build the coffin in which she was buried. Abe nearly died that year too, "kicked by a horse and apparently killed for a time," as he later described the incident. While he miraculously regained consciousness, he carried one mark of the Indiana injury for the rest of his life—a roving eye that floated upwards whenever he stared back at the many photographers who began taking his picture so often when he became famous.

Though he was born in Kentucky and gained his initial fame in Illinois, Indiana was in many ways Lincoln's true cradle. Here his hunger for knowledge first showed itself. Here he attended school, and here he began reading on his own—beginning with Aesop's fables and the bible—encouraged by a "good and kind stepmother," as he described Sarah Bush Johnston Lincoln, who came into his life in 1819. Yet otherwise, Indiana provided scant opportunity for education, and Lincoln forever rued his lack of formal schooling on the frontier. Nevertheless, the young man seized every opportunity, his stepmother marveled, to learn independently. "He read all the books he could lay his hands on" and became "a constant reader." Sarah remembered him as "the best boy I ever saw," even if his intellectual curiosity often interfered with his chores. "Abe was a good boy," Sarah insisted. Though "he didn't like physical labor," he "was diligent for Knowledge."

However limited the opportunities for education, Lincoln learned much by experience. It was as a Hoosier that Lincoln witnessed the cruelty of slavery for the first time, after a flatboat ride down the Mississippi to New Orleans. And here he scribbled the first surviving words written by a president who Harriet Beecher Stowe, Walt Whitman, and other great writers later judged to be the greatest writer of all presidents. The rhyme revealed a sly sense of humor and perhaps, even then, a longing to succeed in life: "Abraham Lincoln / his hand and pen / he will be good / but god knows When."

Lincoln accompanied his family out of "the old homestead in Indiana" in March 1830 and thereafter built a new life in neighboring Illinois. But he returned to Indiana as president elect in 1861, a favorite son who had comfortably won his old state in the recent election, and arrived in Indianapolis in triumph en route to his inauguration. "It is your business," he lectured the huge throng that greeted him at the train station with a thirty-four-gun salute, "to rise up and preserve the Union and liberty, for yourselves and not for me." Some twenty thousand admirers watched him parade through the streets that day, no doubt far more people than he had ever seen in the isolated backwoods in his entire decade and a half in residence. Significantly, Lincoln saw for himself how much his longtime home state had changed: the towns and cities he saw in Indiana on this, his last trip here, were "wonderfully different from the first scenes he witnessed in the State of Indiana." The state had matured—as had its most famous son.

Yet for all of the time Lincoln spent in Indiana—fourteen years in all, about a quarter of his life—much too little has been written about his formative life here. New scholarship is not only welcome, but also long overdue. Indiana was Lincoln's laboratory in life, and his experience has long called for the kind of deep research and close analysis that William E. Bartelt has now provided.

His work should open both eyes and minds about Abraham Lincoln's "childhood home."

Harold Holzer
Senior Vice President, External Affairs
The Metropolitan Museum of Art
New York, New York

Acknowledgments

On a Sunday afternoon in the summer of 1951 I first saw the site where Abraham Lincoln spent almost a quarter of his life. I was only five when my parents took my two sisters and me to the Nancy Hanks Lincoln State Memorial. Although I was too young to fully appreciate its significance, I knew something special happened here.

My interest in Lincoln grew as I learned more about him in school. On February 12, 1962, I was one of many students at a rally held at the Lincoln cabin site memorial to show support for including the site in the National Park Service. On February 19 of that year President John F. Kennedy signed the bill creating the Lincoln Boyhood National Memorial.

For me, a dream came true when I was hired as a seasonal park ranger in the summer of 1969. I am deeply grateful to National Park Service professionals Albert Banton, John Tiff, Dennis Beach, Jerry Sanders, and especially Norman Hellmers for allowing me to actually get paid to study Lincoln in Indiana. My fellow seasonal employees—Stan Harris, Nancy Harris, Larry Schnuck, Patsy Bates, Dan Leraris, Wayne Roell, and Sharon Wertman, to name a few—and I told thousands of visitors the Lincoln story. Sometimes we were in uniform and at other times we portrayed pioneer farmers.

Although I am no longer an employee of Lincoln Boyhood, the staff has been extremely helpful in assisting my research and reviewing the text. I especially thank Superintendent Randy Wester and Chief of Operations Mike Capps.

The work of Douglas L. Wilson and Rodney O. Davis, *Herndon's Informants*, was invaluable in this project. I also thank them for their suggestions and encouragement. The University of Illinois Press generously granted permission to use selections from *Herndon's Informants* in this work. Cooperation of the Abraham Lincoln Association in using material from *The Collected Works of Abraham Lincoln* is greatly appreciated.

James Hevron, Barbara Michel Hevron, Joe Hevron, and Beverly Hevron Kaiser, all descendants of Lincoln's Indiana neighbors, shared family photograph collections and stories with me. James and Barbara, along with Jon Carl, also read the manuscript and made valuable suggestions.

The grandchildren of Spencer County resident Bess V. Ehrmann, Millicent Westerfield, Karolyn Voigt, and Calder Ehrmann, kindly allowed me to use selected illustrations from her 1938 book *The Missing Chapter in the Life of Abraham Lincoln*.

Terry Hughes assisted with computer advice. The staffs at the Indiana State Archives, the Indiana State Library, the National Archives, the Bureau of Land Management, the Abraham Lincoln Presidential Museum and Library, the Lincoln Museum, the Lilly Library at Indiana University, Bloomington, and the Evansville–Vanderburgh Public Library assisted me greatly in my research. Special thanks go to Becky Middleton at the Spencer County Public Library in Rockport, Pat Sides at the Willard Library in Evansville, Jill Larson of the Lewis Historical Library in Vincennes, David Kent Coy and Nancy Easter-Shick of Coles County, Illinois, and Tom Lonnberg of the Evansville Museum of Arts, History, and Science for their assistance in locating material.

Doctor Sherry Bevins Darrell of the University of Southern Indiana has spent numerous hours editing my drafts and making wonderful suggestions. Kathryn Lawson assisted in verifying the quotes.

I am indebted to the Indiana Historical Society for its willingness to publish the work. I thank Presidents Sal Cilella and John Herbst, and the Society's Press editors Tom Mason, Paula Corpuz, Kathy Breen, and Ray Boomhower. Steve Haller, Susan Sutton, and David Turk of the Society's library assisted in obtaining illustrations for this work.

Most importantly I thank my personal academic librarian, my best friend, and my wife Kathy for spending vacations at historic sites and libraries, for the suggestions, and the encouragement.

Part One

ABRAHAM LINCOLN
Remembers Indiana

1

"There I grew up"
Lincoln's Indiana in Context

By 1859 curiosity about the life and thoughts of Abraham Lincoln extended far beyond Illinois's boundaries. To a large extent, this interest in the Illinois lawyer resulted from citizens across the country reading transcripts of the 1858 Lincoln-Douglas debates. In 1859 Jesse W. Fell, like Lincoln an Illinois-Whig-lawyer-turned Republican, requested biographical material to share with friends in Pennsylvania—Fell's home state. Lincoln responded in December 1859 with a short autobiography that soon was widely printed in Pennsylvania newspapers.[1]

Lincoln introduced his modest "little sketch" with "there is not much of it, for the reason, I suppose, there is not much of me."[2] One paragraph and two sentences of the four-paragraph statement centered on his 1816 to 1830 Indiana years. Although his statement lacks specifics, Lincoln gives a context to understand his Indiana years:

> My father, at the death of his father, was but six years of age; and he grew up, litterally without education. He removed from Kentucky to what is now Spencer county, Indiana, in my eighth year. We reached our new home about the time the State came into the Union. It was a wild region, with many bears and other wild animals still in the woods. There I grew up. There were some schools, so called; but no qualification was ever required of a teacher, beyond *"readin, writin, and cipherin,"* to the Rule of Three. If a straggler supposed to understand latin, happened to sojourn in the neighborhood, he was looked upon as a wizard. There was absolutely nothing

Alexander Hesler's June 3, 1860, portrait captured Abraham Lincoln's appearance at the time he wrote his autobiographical statements in December 1859 and June 1860.

to excite ambition for education. Of course when I came of age I did not know much. Still somehow, I could read, write, and cipher to the Rule of Three; but that was all. I have not been to school since. The little advance I now have upon this store of education, I have picked up from time to time under the pressure of necessity.

I was raised to farm work, which I continued till I was twenty two. At twenty one I came to Illinois, and passed the first year in Illinois—Macon county.[3]

"We reached our new home about the time the State came into the Union."

It is not surprising that Lincoln used the admission of his new state into the Union to place his family history in a larger historical context. The 1859 reader would have been familiar with the political history of the Old Northwest Territory. On July 4, 1800, as authorized by Congress in May, the territory divided to create a new area known as the Indiana Territory. The orderly, three-stage, territorial system, established by the Confederation Congress in the Northwest Ordinance of 1787, resulted in formation of the state of Indiana by the time of Lincoln's arrival in 1816.

Stage 1 lasted from 1800 until 1804. During this stage the government, located in Vincennes, was comprised of a governor, a secretary, and three judges—all appointed by the president. Thus, in 1800 President John Adams appointed William Henry Harrison governor. Stage 2 allowed for adding an elected House of Representatives and an appointed Legislative Council. By 1809 the Indiana Territory was reduced in size to about that of the future state. In 1814–15 a special census determined the area held 60,000 inhabitants and was, therefore, ready for statehood.[4]

That census revealed a population of 12,081 white males twenty-one years or older and a total population of 63,897. Perry County, which included part of the future Spencer County to which the Lincolns moved, contained 350 white males over twenty-one and a total of 1,720 residents.[5] In April 1816 Congress passed an Enabling Act that allowed the residents to elect delegates to determine the statehood issue. Forty-three delegates—most came to Indiana from Kentucky—assembled at Corydon, the territorial capital, and nineteen days later completed their work. The delegates approved a resolution for statehood and wrote a state constitution—doing some of the work in the shade of a large elm tree. Congress adopted a resolution approving the admission of Indiana; and, on December 11, 1816,

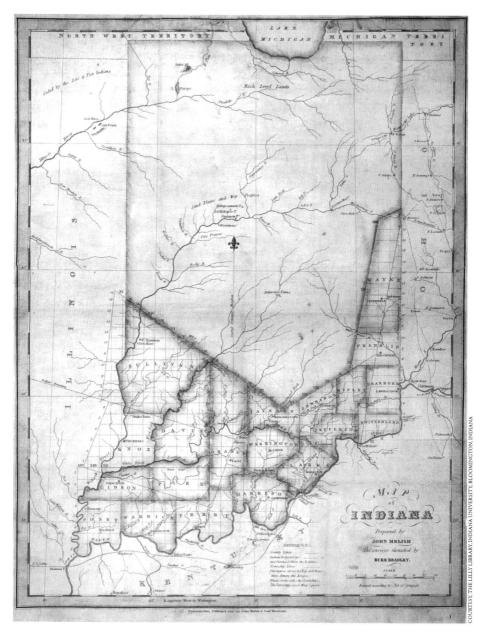

The Lincoln family moved to Perry County, Indiana, in 1816. This 1817 Indiana map, prepared by John Melish, shows the area before the creation of Spencer County in 1818. The Lincoln family located in the area just above the letter *P* in Perry. Little was known about the geographic details of northern Indiana, and Lake Michigan was placed in the center of the northern boundary.

President James Madison signed the legislation.[6] Lincoln, in fact, dates his family's arrival in Indiana to late November or early December 1816.

In 1817 the Vincennes Land Office led the country in land sales with 286,558 acres sold. By the completion of the 1820 federal census, the Indiana population had soared to 147,178.[7]

One reason for this rapid land-claim increase was the end of conflict with Native American tribes in the area.[8] Governor Harrison negotiated in Vincennes—some would say by intimidation—treaties with the Delaware on August 18, 1804, and with the Piankashaw on August 27, 1804. In these treaties the tribes agreed to "relinquishes [*sic*] to the United States forever, all their right and title to the tract of country which lies between the Ohio and Wabash rivers."[9] This tract was bounded on the north by the Vincennes tract negotiated in 1803 and a road from Vincennes to Clarksville. These treaties—along with another the next year in which the Miami and Potawatomi confirmed the right of the Delaware to relinquish the land—opened all of southwest Indiana to settlement.[10] Yet, as late as 1811 at least one group of Shawnee lived in the southern part of the Indiana Territory. This presence led to what became known as the "Meeks tragedy" in May 1811—some five and a half years before the Lincolns arrived and some fifteen miles

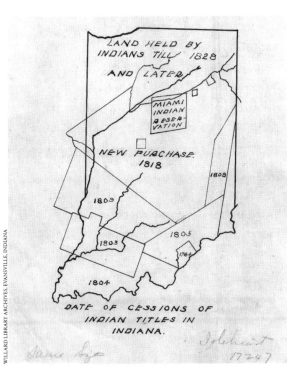

This hand-drawn map of "Date of Cessions of Indian Titles in Indiana" was made for the Southwestern Indiana Historical Society's Lincoln Inquiry project. The Lincoln neighborhood was part of the 1804 treaties with the Delaware and Piankashaw.

southwest of their future homesite. Not all accounts of the incident agree, and Lincoln probably heard several different accounts from his neighbors. Certainly the Meeks tragedy would prove a gripping tale for a boy.

Accounts generally agree that a group of Shawnee led by Setteedown continued to live near the present site of Boonville, Indiana, and hunted and trapped game along Little Pigeon Creek. The settlement of the Atha Meeks family on the east side of the creek resulted in the May 1811 confrontation. Early one morning Setteedown, his son, and another man referred to as Big Bones waited outside the Meeks cabin. As Atha Jr. left the cabin to bring water from the spring, the three Shawnee attacked. When Atha Sr. appeared at the cabin door, he was shot and mortally wounded. The gunfire brought a relative, William Meeks, to the scene from his nearby cabin; he shot and killed Big Bones, but Setteedown and his son disappeared into the woods. The Shawnee were pursued and one—possibly Setteedown—was captured and brought to the home of Justice of the Peace Uriah Lamar near present-day Grandview. Before the trial, however, the prisoner was killed in an apparent conspiracy designed to leave no witnesses. The remaining Shawnee left the area, and new settlers soon arrived.[11]

Some area residents remembered the conflict as a simple disagreement between two families; others blamed the teachings of Tecumseh and the Shawnee Prophet Tenskwatawa, who were attempting to unite the northwest tribes into a great confederation.[12] Residents of the Indiana Territory and Kentucky, fearing such a union, joined Harrison and the regular U.S. Army in defeating the confederation at the Battle of Tippecanoe on November 7, 1811. The county created in 1818, now remembered as the Indiana home of Lincoln, was named for Spier Spencer, a casualty at Tippecanoe.

"It was a wild region, with many bears and other wild animals still in the woods."

Lincoln remembered vividly the threat of bear attacks even in his later years. He mentioned the threat in his 1859 statement and in the 1846 poetry about his Indiana experiences. In one verse of that poetry Lincoln wrote:

> When first my father settled here,
>   'Twas then the frontier line:
> The panther's scream, filled night with fear
>   And bears preyed on the swine.[13]

The 1885 history of Spencer County relates how wild animals provided crude entertainment and adventure for residents in the Lincoln neighborhood:

> William Whittinghill caught a large black wolf in a wooden trap across the line in Warrick County, and brought it over to Gentryville, where it was disabled and made to fight the dogs. It could whip any of them singly. Whittinghill tanned deer, wolf, bear and other skins at his tannery. James Gentry, Sr., was one day hunting in Warrick County, when his dog startled a large bear which was soon brought to bay. The dog was courageous and approached so close to the bear that it was caught and killed by the latter. But Mr. Gentry put in an appearance about this time and sent a bullet crashing through the furious *Ursus*.[14]

"There was absolutely nothing to excite ambition for education."

In later years Lincoln always apologized about his lack of formal education. Answering an 1858 questionnaire for former members of Congress, Lincoln simply wrote "defective" in the line for education.[15]

John Rowbotham prepared this sketch titled "The Emigration from Kentucky" for Joseph Barrett's *Life of Abraham Lincoln*. The Lincolns might have used a wagon once they crossed the river, but certainly the land was much more heavily timbered than the sketch suggests.

While the 1816 Indiana Constitution and early state legislation en-
dorsed the establishment of schools, other concerns ranked much higher on
the frontier. Indiana historian Donald F. Carmony noted:

> Education developed slowly in pioneer Indiana, especially that
> under public auspices. Of necessity the pioneers gave high priority
> to meeting their basic needs for food, clothing, and shelter. At least
> until the 1830s they lived mainly in sparsely settled areas; hence,
> many neighborhoods had too few, if any, parents willing to help fi-
> nance either a private, denominational, or public school. Numerous
> families viewed education principally as the responsibility of parents
> or their respective religious denominations.[16]

In fact, the public school system in Spencer County developed years
after the Lincolns left the state. Schools in the 1820s were all subscription
schools; parents paid the teacher directly, oftentimes in grain or other produce. School buildings were constructed by such families and were abandoned and rebuilt frequently to meet the needs of students and teachers.[17]

Lincoln's characterization of the state's early teachers appears accurate.
Anyone fairly proficient at reading, writing, and working with mathematical
figures was capable of teaching children those skills. Frank Gilbert in his history of Evansville, Indiana, remembered, "the standard in those days seemed
to be the arithmetic and any one who could reach the rule of three, was
proficient and if he could reach the double rule of three, he was considered
an educated man. This rule of three meant that one must be able to multi-
ply, divide and subtract three figures and of course the double rule meant six
figures."[18] The rule of three was actually a method of using proportions to
find the fourth number when three were known.

Lincoln biographer David Herbert Donald concluded, "Though his
censure was largely deserved, a school system that produced Abraham Lincoln
could not have been wholly without merit."[19] And Hoosier historian James
H. Madison remarks, "Such meager schooling was not unusual; nor, as
Lincoln's life so nobly testifies, was formal education the sum and substance
of the individual's preparation for adulthood. Pioneer education must be
understood broadly to include socialization and learning outside the school-
room, all the more so because learning inside the classroom was so limited."[20]

Without doubt, the "wild country" of Indiana provided the young
Lincoln with many opportunities to receive a practical education.

2

"*The old homestead in Indiana*"
The Statement for John L. Scripps

John Locke Scripps of the *Chicago Press and Tribune* solicited Abraham Lincoln's longest autobiographical statement for a campaign biography of the newly nominated Republican presidential candidate. Written in the third person, this statement offers the most authoritative account of Lincoln's Indiana years.

   Below is the relevant portion of Lincoln's statement written in June 1860 for Scripps's biography that was published in July 1860.[1] The original spelling and grammar is retained.

> At this time his father resided on Knob-creek, on the road from Bardstown Ky. to Nashville Tenn. at a point three, or three and a half miles South or South-West of Atherton's ferry on the Rolling Fork. From this place he removed to what is now Spencer county Indiana, in the autumn of 1816, A. then being in his eigth year. This removal was partly on account of slavery; but chiefly on account of the difficulty in land titles in Ky. He settled in an unbroken forest; and the clearing away of surplus wood was the great task a head. A. though very young, was large of his age, and had an axe put into his hands at once; and from that till within his twentythird year, he was almost constantly handling that most useful instrument—less of course, in plowing and harvesting seasons. At this place A. took an early start as a hunter, which was never much improved afterwards. (A few days before the completion of his eigth year, in the absence of his father, a flock of wild turkeys approached the new log cabin,

and A. with a rifle gun, standing inside, shot through a crack, and killed one of them. He has never since pulled a trigger on any larger game.) In the autumn of 1818 his mother died; and a year afterwards his father married Mrs. Sally Johnston, at Elizabeth-Town, Ky—a widow, with three children of her first marriage. She proved a good and kind mother to A. and is still living in Coles Co. Illinois. There were no children of this second marriage. His father's residence continued at the same place in Indiana, till 1830. While here A. went to A.B.C. schools by littles, kept successively by Andrew Crawford, —— Sweeney, and Azel W. Dorsey. He does not remember any other. The family of Mr. Dorsey now reside in Schuyler Co. Illinois. A. now thinks that the agregate of all his schooling did not amount to one year. He was never in a college or Academy as a student; and never inside of a college or academy building till since he had a law-license. What he has in the way of education, he has picked up. After he was twentythree, and had separated from his father, he studied English grammar, imperfectly of course, but so as to speak and write as well as he now does. He studied and nearly mastered the Six-books of Euclid, since he was a member of Congress. He regrets his want of education, and does what he can to supply the want. In his tenth year he was kicked by a horse, and apparently killed for a time. When he was nineteen, still residing in Indiana, he made his first trip upon flat-boat to New-Orleans. He was a hired hand merely; and he and a son of the owner, with out other assistance, made the trip. The nature of part of the cargo-load, as it was called—made it necessary for them to linger and trade along the Sugar coast—and one night they were attacked by seven negroes with intent to kill and rob them. They were hurt some in the melee, but succeeded in driving the negroes from the boat, and then "cut cable" "weighed anchor" and left.

March 1st. 1830—A. having just completed his 21st. year, his father and family, with the families of the two daughters and sons-in-law, of his step mother, left the old homestead in Indiana, and came to Illinois. Their mode of conveyance was waggons drawn by ox-teams, or A. drove one of the teams.[2]

"From this place he removed to what is now Spencer county Indiana, in the autumn of 1816, A. then being in his eigth year."

Writers called 1816 the "Year Without a Summer," and "Eighteen-hundred-and-froze-to-death." C. Edward Skeen, in his work *1816: America Rising*, concludes that although much of the year had near normal temperatures, three cold spells during June, July, and August—each lasting a week—gave the year its reputation. In Washington, Kentucky, some 125 miles northeast of the Lincolns' home, killing frost occurred twice in August.[3]

The Lincolns' move from Kentucky was, no doubt, planned for some time. Thomas Lincoln visited the Indiana Territory earlier that year to select a suitable homesite—perhaps the unusual weather freed him from crop work. Family member Dennis Hanks remembered that this trip involved a flatboat loaded with many of the family's possessions and a large quantity of whiskey, the cash of the frontier. According to Hanks, much of the cargo sank when the boat capsized, but Lincoln saved some of his tools and whiskey.[4] After selecting his land, Lincoln unofficially marked the claim with piles of brush at each corner but did not register the claim for over a year.[5] Although the exact date of the Lincoln family's arrival in the new state is not known, it is believed that they came about the time Indiana joined the union—December 11, 1816. In his early work on the Lincolns in Kentucky, Louis A. Warren concluded that the trip occurred sometime between November 11 and December 20 because a Kentucky legal document states Thomas appeared before the justice of the peace in person on November 11. Then, Warren concludes from another court document dated December 20 that the Lincolns had left the Commonwealth by that date.[6]

Freezing temperatures and light snowfall are common during southern Indiana Novembers and Decembers. But apparently November and December 1816 were actually warmer than normal.[7] Although at first glance winter might seem an unusual time for a journey into an unsettled area, in an agricultural society this time is understandable: the crops are harvested, much of the underbrush has died out for the year, the soil is solid, and the settler has time to clear land at a new site for spring planting. Lincoln was seven years, nine months old at the time of the trip—hence the reference to his eighth year.

"This removal was partly on account of slavery."

In 1864 Lincoln wrote, "I am naturally anti-slavery. If slavery is not wrong nothing is wrong. I cannot remember when I did not so think and feel."[8] Indeed, Lincoln probably gained this view from his parents. In 1816 in Hardin County, Kentucky, there were 1,238 slaves. The issue of slavery divided the religious community. In fact, the South Fork Baptist Church, near the Lincolns, had split over slavery in 1808. By the time the Lincolns joined the Little Mount Baptist Church, it clearly proclaimed an antislavery stand.[9]

This antislavery feeling was not only a religious or moral issue, but also an economic one. In Kentucky the presence of slavery affected free laborers such as Thomas, workers who competed with slaves "hired out" by their masters to do farm work, split rails, and perform other menial labor. As a result, the wages paid to free workers stayed low. Therefore, a state without slavery offered more economic opportunity to men who needed to supplement their farm income.[10]

Indiana was such a state—at least on paper. The Northwest Ordinance of 1787 prohibited slavery. Nevertheless, slavery was practiced in the French settlement of Vincennes long before 1787 and continued in the territory, with slaves designated indentured servants. Later prominent citizens, led by Governor William Henry Harrison, believed it necessary to allow slavery in order to attract the numbers and kinds of settlers to make the territory successful. In 1802 this proslavery group petitioned Congress to repeal the prohibition. The slave prohibition remained, though, to the delight of an equally vocal antislavery group. Although the 1816 Indiana Constitution outlawed both slavery and involuntary servitude, questions remained about the legality of earlier indentures.[11]

The 1820 federal census lists 190 slaves in the supposedly free state of Indiana. While there are no slaves listed in Spencer County, there are 2 in Warrick and 16 in Perry, counties adjacent to Spencer County on the Ohio River. In the early 1820s the Indiana Supreme Court ruled illegal any slavery or involuntary servitude in the state.[12] Therefore, though slavery did exist in the area that the Lincolns settled in 1816, it legally ended within the next decade. The 1830 census, however, still lists 1 slave in Warrick County.[13]

"but chiefly on account of the difficulty in land titles in Ky."

Few legal concerns mattered to pioneer farmers as much as knowing their land claims were secure. This concern was especially true in Kentucky, which continued to use the antiquated metes and bounds system of land description. Land deeds used natural features such as streams, rocks, and roads to describe the land claimed. As a result, there was always uncertainty about the land description, especially when those natural features changed

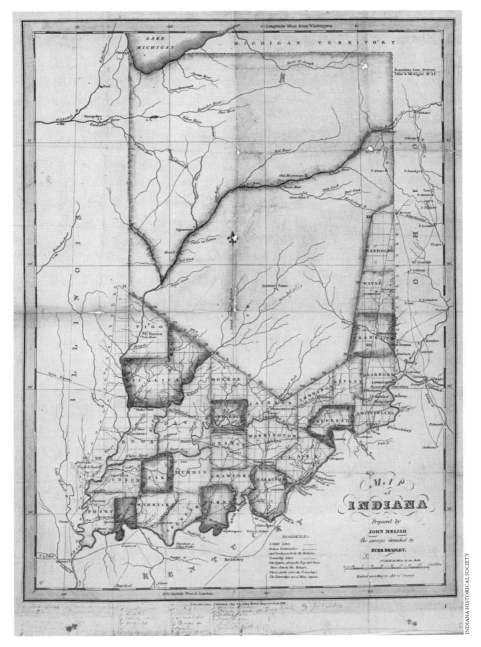

Spencer County was created in 1818 as shown in this 1819 map of Indiana.

over the years. This survey system, along with confusing colonial grants and previous purchasers not living up to agreements, resulted in constant land-ownership lawsuits. Thomas was party to such suits and, as a result, lost land and improvements. In all these cases Thomas acted in good faith, but was a victim of the system.[14]

Thomas believed he would find different circumstances across the Ohio River in the Northwest Territory—the area that eventually comprised Ohio, Indiana, Illinois, Michigan, Wisconsin, and part of Minnesota. Between 1781 and 1802, the states with western land claims—all but Maryland, Delaware, Pennsylvania, Rhode Island, and New Jersey—ceded land to the U.S. government to foster national unity. By 1802 the federal government claimed 170,000,000 acres in the Old Northwest and began the process of creating treaties with the Native Americans and developing an efficient system of making the treaty lands available for settlement.[15]

Congress, under the Articles of Confederation, developed the United States's first public-land policy by passing the Northwest Ordinance of 1785. Once the land was ceded through the treaty process, surveyors divided the land into six-mile by six-mile townships. These townships contained thirty-six sections of one square mile each. Since the United States owned all the property and the survey system provided for clear descriptions of the land claimed, the problems plaguing Thomas Lincoln and his neighbors in Kentucky were not to arise in the Northwest Territory.

"He settled in an unbroken forest; and the clearing away of surplus wood was the great task a head. A. though very young, was large of his age, and had an axe put into his hands at once; and from that till within his twentythird year, he was almost constantly handling that most useful instrument—less of course, in plowing and harvesting seasons."

In late 1804, or early 1805, David Sanford and Arthur Henrie surveyed the land on which the Lincolns eventually settled in 1816. Their field notes describe the pristine area. Within several miles of what became the Lincoln farm, the surveyors noted white oak, dogwood, hickory, black oak, cherry, sassafras, elm, and black walnut trees, as well as areas covered with brush, briers, and spice wood. While some terrain was "glady" or swampy, the surveyors assessed other areas as good for farming.[16]

The description for Section 32—Thomas claimed the southwest quarter—was "land level, oak and hickory, medium growth is hazel and other brush very thick. The timber on this mile is chiefly destroyed by fire."[17]

"The Youth of Abraham Lincoln." The two items most linked to Lincoln's Indiana years—an axe and a book—are evident in this 1889 engraving by Ernest F. Hubbard based on a painting by Morgan J. Rhees.

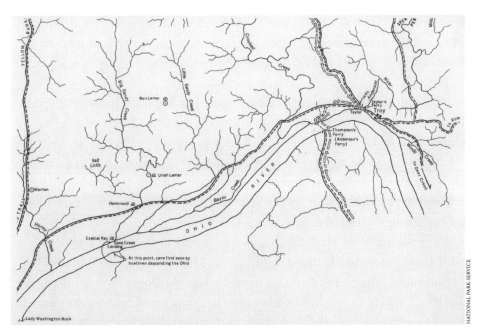

The Ohio River portion of the "Historical Base Map Spencer County, Indiana, 1816–1830" prepared by the National Park Service shows the location of Thompson's Ferry, where the Lincolns reportedly crossed the river. The arrows indicate the Lincoln route.

Twelve years later, this parcel might have contained less timber and more underbrush than surrounding forest, making it easier to clear. Family member Dennis Hanks said of the area, "it was the Brushes Cuntry that I have Ever Seen in any New Cuntry." He continued that "all Kinds of undegroth Spice wod Wild privy Shewmake Dogwood grape vines matted to Geather So that as the old Saying gowes you could Drive a Butcher Knife up to the Handle in it."[18]

There are many local legends about exactly where the Lincoln family—Thomas, Nancy, Sarah, and Abraham—crossed the Ohio River to enter Indiana.[19] Most of these locations lie near Troy, Indiana, where the Anderson River flows into the Ohio.[20] The site most frequently cited by early residents and accepted by historians is Thompson's Ferry down river from Troy.[21] Local records and river-navigation aids document that Thompson's Ferry (also known as Anderson's Ferry) operated, at the time, from the Kentucky side of the river approximately one and a half miles downriver from the mouth of the Anderson River.[22]

After the river crossing, the Lincolns traveled to Troy, at that time the county seat of Perry County. The land Thomas selected was located about sixteen miles from the river in Perry County (until Spencer County was created in 1818). Troy sat at the terminus of the Vincennes-Troy road, which came within four miles of the Lincoln farm, running northwest from the river over rolling hills and flowing streams toward present-day Santa Claus, Indiana.[23]

Possibly Abraham was remembering the last leg of the journey from Kentucky when he wrote about the unbroken forest and the axe used to clear it. There was no road for the last four miles except the one Thomas and Abraham cut while making their way to the new homesite. Abraham apparently commented that "he never passed through a harder experience" than cutting that road, and he might well have thought the same about his first three years in the Hoosier State.[24]

Tax records show that Thomas owned horses in Kentucky and, no doubt, used them in the move to Indiana.[25] Hanks informed William H. Herndon that the family came on horseback to the Posey farm on the Indiana shore, where they borrowed a wagon to convey their possessions, including items stored with Mr. Posey from Thomas's preliminary trip to their new site.[26] As difficult as it was to clear a road and ford the streams over which a wagon could travel, the real work began after the Lincolns arrived on their claim.

Thomas chose a hilltop on the western side of his claim as the site for the family's home. The Lincolns' immediate concern involved shelter from winter weather. In fact, Thomas may have anticipated this need during his first visit by constructing a three-sided or half-faced camp. Herndon, using information provided by Hanks, gave this description of the camp: "The structure, when completed, was fourteen feet square, and was built of small unhewn logs. In the language of the day, it was called a 'half-faced camp,' being enclosed on all sides but one. It had neither floor, door, nor windows."[27]

A fire burned constantly on the open side of the slanted-roof structure. The fire provided warmth, heat for cooking, and protection from wild animals. Although some biographers describe this camp as very flimsy, it not only provided shelter for the Lincoln family during its first Indiana winter but also served as home for extended family members in succeeding years. Even though Thomas built crude furniture and beds for the family, the Lincolns lived in unimaginably primitive conditions in those first few months.[28]

The family's next concern was clearing land for spring planting. To expedite the clearing, only trees of less than eighteen inches in diameter were cut, underbrush cleared, and roots dug or "grubbed" out. The larger trees were cut for logs for a cabin or later "girdled." To girdle a tree meant cutting a ring around the tree bark with an axe, cutting off the sap, and thus eventually killing the tree. Crops were planted around the dead trees, which did not block sunlight from the plants.[29] Thomas may have cleared six acres by spring 1818.[30]

"At this place A. took an early start as a hunter, which was never much improved afterwards. (A few days before the completion of his eigth year, in the absence of his father, a flock of wild turkeys approached the new log cabin, and A. with a rifle gun, standing inside, shot through a crack, and killed one of them. He has never since pulled a trigger on any larger game.)"

It sounds odd that, in a short autobiographical statement, Lincoln included this anecdote. Certainly this lack of interest in hunting was atypical in mid-nineteenth-century America. To a later audience, it seems unbelievable that the president who conducted the bloody Civil War was so moved by killing a turkey. One biographer, Charles B. Strozier, has found psychological significance in this memory. Strozier concludes the placement of the story suggests "an association between the wild turkey and his dead mother," and that Lincoln somehow felt responsible for the death of both.[31] But the obvious importance to a study of Lincoln's Indiana years is not the turkey at all, but rather the reference to "a few days before the completion of his eigth year" and "the new log cabin."

Despite disagreement about how long the Lincolns lived in the half-faced camp, Herndon and early Lincoln biographers concluded that the camp was the family's home for an entire year.[32] Benjamin Thomas, in his respected 1952 work, used the turkey story as proof that a new cabin was built "at once," illustrating that Thomas quickly provided permanent shelter for the family.[33] Thomas's interpretation seems valid.

"In the autumn of 1818 his mother died."

Lincoln used this simple clause to describe one of the most written about events of his Indiana years. A simple and abundant plant with a delicate white flower, white snakeroot caused Nancy Hanks Lincoln's death. Nancy died on October 5, 1818, a victim of milk sickness. The illness was well known to Indiana pioneers as witnessed by the words of Dennis Hanks, speaking of one reason the family moved to Illinois in 1830: "We war perplext By a Disese Cald Milk Sick."[34]

This sickness perplexed not only the Little Pigeon Creek community, but also many Lincoln biographers. Since colonial time, deaths from milk sickness occurred in isolated areas with few residents, drawing little interest from the medical profession. That changed as the frequency of such deaths increased with the settlement of Ohio, Indiana, and Illinois in the early 1800s. The illness in animals was called *the trembles*; in human beings it was called *sick stomach, puking fever, bilious fever, swamp fever, tires,* or *the slows.* By 1811 the population generally believed that human beings fell ill after drinking milk, and the name *milk sickness*—or *milk sick*—became the term most often used.[35]

Even if the Lincolns and their neighbors knew of the milk connection in 1818, no one knew what caused the milk to become poisoned—and that mystery made it difficult to prevent the deaths. An article from the *Providence Rhode Island Journal*, "The Milk Sicknesses at the West," was reprinted in the *Evansville Journal* on October 14, 1840:

> There is no announcement which strikes the members of a Western community with so much dread, as the report of a case of Milk Sickness. The uncertainty and mystery which envelopes its origin, and its fearful and terrible effects upon its victims, and the ruinous consequences upon the valuable property which follow in its train,

make it, in the eyes of the inhabitants of a district the worst looking foe which can beset their neighborhood.

The article specifically mentions Perry County, Indiana, but concludes, "the herb or mineral imparting the poison has not yet been detected."[36]

In 1841 Daniel Drake, a respected Louisville doctor and professor, conducted a detailed study of the illness in Ohio. After examining many cases, Drake concluded that animals with the sickness frequented "densely timbered table-land, which from its flatness abounds in wet places and ponds, indicated by the presence of lofty white elms, black walnuts, maples, burr oaks, and other trees, which delight in rich and moist soil." He concluded that most cases occurred from August to November and that clearing the forest destroyed the cause.[37]

This picture of a white snakeroot plant in bloom was taken very near the reconstructed Lincoln cabin in the Lincoln Boyhood National Memorial on October 5, 2006—the 188th anniversary of Nancy Hanks Lincoln's death.

Drake investigated several possible causes of the illness. He dismissed a mineral origin and one from decaying organic matter, but accepted vegetable poison as the cause. John Rowe, an Ohio farmer, proposed to Drake white snakeroot as the cause, but Drake's "professional scrutiny" found Rowe's work "defective and inconclusive."[38] Drake seemed to favor poison oak and poison ivy as causes.[39] Another early white snakeroot proponent was Anna Pierce Hobbs, a southern Illinois doctor, who learned the cause from a Shawnee medicine woman in 1834.[40] Finally the cause was conclusively established in 1928. At that time, James Fitton Couch determined that the white snakeroot plant contained a poison he named *tremetol*. This chemical was indeed the cause of milk sickness—perhaps the most deadly illness on the Indiana frontier.[41] But in 1818 no one knew that the slender, erect, perennial herb with its opposite, three- to five-inch serrated, ovate leaves and white cluster of flowers was a deadly killer in the Little Pigeon Creek settlement.[42]

Most farm animals on the frontier fed by grazing in unfenced, wooded areas. In the autumn most forage plants had dried, leaving vegetation only in wet areas as a source of food. Animals fed on white snakeroot only when other food was unavailable. Such appears to be the case in the autumn of 1818 in southwest Indiana. The milk might be poisoned before the cow showed the trembling signs of the illness, thus making the identification of the source more difficult.[43]

As foliage began to show fall colors in 1818, milk sickness was brutal in the Little Pigeon Creek community. One victim was a Lincoln neighbor. Peter and Nancy Brooner, along with their family, settled in the community before the Lincolns, possibly in 1814. When Nancy Brooner began to show signs of the illness—weakness, nausea, and vomiting—Nancy Lincoln called on her frequently. According to the Brooners' son Allen, during one visit his mother questioned whether she would recover. Nancy Lincoln replied, "Oh, you may outlive me."[44] Within a couple of weeks they lay buried side by side—along with Thomas and Elizabeth Sparrow, Nancy Lincoln's aunt and uncle—all victims of the milk sickness.

The Sparrows came to the Lincoln farm in 1817 and lived in the old three-sided camp. The Sparrows had reared Nancy in Kentucky, and many Indiana neighbors referred to them as her parents. Although Nancy certainly welcomed the company of her kinfolk, the new arrivals added burdens because they expected to live off the Lincolns' generosity. The Sparrows' ward

Dennis Hanks, a cousin of Nancy, became Abraham's constant companion. Later Hanks became the source of much information—some say misinformation—about Lincoln's Indiana stay.[45]

Thomas Sparrow was the first to fall ill with symptoms, as described by chemist Couch in 1933:

> weakness, dizziness, and loss of appetite, followed by nausea and persistent vomiting. There is pain in the region of the stomach and great thirst. The tongue is swollen and coated white, and the skin is dry. There is an odor of acetone on the breath, no peristalsis, obstinate constipation, weak pulse, slow respiration, subnormal temperature, great prostration, and frequently collapse. As the disease progresses coma develops and continues until death, which is quiet.[46]

Sparrow, anticipating his doom, prepared a will on September 21, 1818, with Nancy Lincoln as one witness. Within a week Sparrow was dead, and his wife soon followed.[47]

Thomas Lincoln stayed busy that autumn building coffins for the community's dead. Because the settlement lacked a churchyard, a hilltop on John Carter's farm became the cemetery. The Carter farm lay adjacent to the Lincoln farm on the south, and the hilltop could be seen from the Lincoln cabin door. A sled pulled by horses carried the bodies to the burial site.[48]

Nancy Lincoln soon developed the symptoms and died on October 5, 1818. The only account of Nancy's death comes from Hanks, who lived with the Lincolns after the Sparrows died. Despite Hanks's possible inaccuracy, it is the only record of the event that brought the first great sorrow to Abraham.

> She struggled on, day by day . . . a good Christian woman, and died on the seventh day after she was taken sick. Abe and his sister Sarah waited on their mother, and did the little jobs and errands required of them. There was no physician nearer than thirty-five miles. The mother knew she was going to die, and called the children to her bedside. She was very weak, and the children leaned over while she gave her last message. Placing her feeble hand on little Abe's head she told him to be kind and good to his father and sister; to both she said, "Be good to one another," expressing a hope that they might live, as they had been taught by her, to love their kindred and worship God.[49]

To another interviewer Hanks remembered (in his dialect),

> O Lord, O Lord, I'll never furgit the mizry in that little green-log
> cabin in the woods when Nancy died!
>   Me 'n' Abe helped Tom make the coffin. He tuk a log left over
> from buildin' the cabin, an' I helped him whipsaw it into planks an'
> plane 'em. Me 'n' Abe held the planks while Tom bored holes an' put
> 'em together, with pegs Abe'd whittled. Thar wasn't sca'cely any nails
> in the kentry an' little iron, except in knives and guns an' cookin'
> pots. Tom's tools was a wander to the hull deestrict. 'Pears to me like
> Tom was always makin' a coffin fur some one. We laid Nancy close
> to the deer-run in the woods. Deer was the only wild critters the
> women wasn't afeerd of. Abe was some'er's 'round nine years old,
> but he never got over the mizable way his mother died.[50]

There is no doubt that neighbors came to help prepare the body before
placing it in the coffin. A sled bore the coffin about three hundred yards
from the Lincoln cabin to the cemetery on the Carter farm. There Nancy's
body was buried near those of Nancy Brooner and the Sparrows. After the
burial, Peter Brooner "extended his hand to Thomas Lincoln and said, 'We
are brothers, now,' meaning that they were brothers in the same kind of sorrow."[51]

If a ceremony occurred at the burial, it would have been simple. Perhaps
a local Baptist leader such as Young Lamar said a few words, and maybe
some neighbors contributed some remarks. Sometime later, Reverend David
Elkins, a Baptist preacher the Lincolns knew in Kentucky, conducted a
funeral. One tradition is that young Abraham wrote Elkins asking him to
come and conduct the ceremony. Though Hanks agrees that Elkins did appear, he said the visit was not in response to a letter.[52]

The next fourteen months proved some of the most difficult of Abraham's life. The family now consisted of Thomas aged forty, Dennis Hanks
aged nineteen, Sarah aged eleven, and Abraham aged nine. The Lincoln
children lost not only their mother, but also their surrogate grandparents.
And no one felt assurance that milk sickness would not claim another member of the family.[53]

Each family member felt his or her own grief. Certainly Thomas
mourned and, in all probability, failed to offer much emotional support to
his children. But perhaps Sarah suffered most during this time because she

assumed duties as the woman of the house.[54] Hanks remembered,

> She was the only woman in the cabin that year, an' no neighbors fur
> miles. Sairy was a little gal, only 'leven, an' she'd git so lonesome,
> missin' her mother, she'd set by the fire an' cry. Me 'n' Abe got'er a
> baby coon an' a turtle, and tried to git a fawn but we couldn't ketch
> any. Tom, he moped 'round. Wasn't wuth shucks that winter. He
> put the corn in in the spring an' left us to 'tend to it, an' lit out fur
> Kaintucky. Yes, we knowed what he went fur, but we didn't think
> he'd have any luck, bein' as pore as he was, and with two children to
> raise.[55]

Hanks's statement that Thomas left the family for Kentucky shortly after
"he put the corn in" seems questionable. In southern Indiana farmers usually
plant in late April or May. It seems unlikely therefore that Thomas, who
returned in December 1819, would leave his family for five or six months.
As will be discussed later, Thomas conducted a land transaction with a
neighbor on July 3, 1819. It is understandable that by mid-1819 Thomas realized his family could not continue in its present condition, and he needed
to find a companion for himself and a mother for his children. In order to
assure success in his venture, he returned to his former place of settlement in
Kentucky.

"A year afterwards his father married Mrs. Sally Johnston, at Elizabeth-Town, Ky—a widow, with three children of her first marriage."

Daniel Johnston died in Elizabethtown, Kentucky, sometime before
July 8, 1816, leaving his widow, Sarah Bush Johnston, with three children
ranging from ages five to nine. The Lincolns knew the Bushes and certainly
knew of Daniel's death before they moved to Indiana. Possibly Thomas
returned to Kentucky with Sarah (Sally as she was called) in mind.[56]

Thomas apparently approached the situation practically and expedi-
ently. According to a Bush relative, Thomas's candid proposal reminded
Sally that she was a widow with three children and he was a widower with
two children and both families would be better off if the two married. Sally
hesitated because of some debts she incurred after her husband's death;
but Thomas paid the debts, and on December 2, 1819, Reverend George
L. Rogers, a Methodist minister, married the two.[57] Once again Thomas
prepared to move a family from Kentucky to Indiana. This time he obtained
the help and a wagon from his brother-in-law Ralph Crume. A wagon

was necessary to transport Sally's possessions—chairs, a table, a bureau, a clothespress, and other household goods—that would make the Indiana home more comfortable.[58] Sometime in December 1819, the Lincoln-Johnston families, and Hanks, began to merge. The new family included Thomas aged forty-one, Sally aged thirty-one, Dennis Hanks aged twenty, Elizabeth Johnston and Sarah Lincoln both aged twelve, Matilda Johnston and Abraham Lincoln both aged ten, and John D. Johnston aged nine.[59]

In 1865 Sally remembered that the Indiana area was "wild and desolate" and Thomas "had erected a good log cabin—tolerably Comfortable." Sally also remembered she "dressed Abe & his sister up [so they] looked more human."[60]

"She proved a good and kind mother to A. and is still living in Coles Co. Illinois. There were no children of this second marriage."

Certainly Sarah welcomed her stepmother and the companionship of two stepsisters. And Abraham especially bonded quickly with his stepmother, who recognized and encouraged his desire to learn and read. She shared with Abraham three books she brought to Indiana: *Webster's Speller, Robinson Crusoe,* and *The Arabian Nights.* Later, of course, Abraham paid tribute to her in his statement, and she told Herndon that "He was the best boy I ever saw."[61]

"His father's residence continued at the same place in Indiana, till 1830."

Although the Lincolns arrived in Indiana in late 1816, Thomas did not begin the legal process of buying the land until the following fall. On October 15, 1817, he filed for the southwest quarter of Section 32, Township 4 South, Range 5 West, at the Land Office in Vincennes, Indiana. Applicants were required by the U.S. government to purchase a minimum of 160 acres at a price of two dollars an acre, with one-twentieth down, one-fourth in forty days, another one-fourth due in two years, another one-fourth due in three years, and the final payment within four years of the sale date. A one-year grace period was allowed before forfeiture could occur.[62]

Thomas began to comply with regulations to pay the $320 for this land. At his initial appearance he paid sixteen dollars (one-twentieth) and received receipt number 8499. He received receipt number 9205 at his next payment of sixty-four dollars on December 26, 1817. The receipts record the name as "Linkorn" or "Linkern," an error that continued throughout the history of the transaction. By the end of 1817 he had paid a total of eighty dollars—one-fourth of the total as required.[63]

Thomas, and thousands of others who used the credit system, failed to meet his future obligations when cash became very scarce following the panic of 1819. As a result, the federal government ended the credit option for purchasing new land and granted additional time to those still owing. An additional provision allowed settlers to relinquish some of their land in payment for the remainder.

On September 12, 1821, Thomas traveled to Vincennes to apply for an extension and received declaration number 1964. To take advantage of the relinquishment provision, he needed either to pay more or to obtain additional land from another debtor to dispose of. Although details remain unclear, Thomas did obtain a claim on eighty acres in Posey County, Indiana. His most complicated action occurred on April 30, 1827, when he relinquished the eastern half of his Spencer County land and all of the Posey County land. By returning these parcels he had enough equity to pay for the western eighty acres of the Spencer County land, the plot where his cabin sat. On June 6, 1827, Thomas was granted a patent giving him a clear title to eighty acres of land. Before he left Indiana in 1830, he acquired an additional twenty acres of land adjacent to this property.[64]

Thomas Lincoln traveled to the Vincennes Land Office to file for his 160 acres on October 15, 1817. He made a second payment on the land on December 26, 1817, and received receipt number 9205. The name is spelled the way it was pronounced. He received a Land Patent from the United States on 80 acres of the land in 1827.

Examining Thomas's land activity in Indiana reveals him as a resourceful man far different from the shiftless one of legend. In fact, he participated in an additional land transaction not known before. On July 3, 1819, Luther Greathouse assigned to Thomas the 139.36-acre "short section" described as the northeast quarter of Section 6, Township 5 South, Range 5 West. This land lies adjacent to the southwestern tip of the Lincoln farm. Significantly, this transaction occurred less than a year after Nancy's death and shortly before his return to Kentucky to find a new wife. He held that land until September 11, 1821, when he assigned the land to James Gentry. Although the financial details of these actions are unknown, it is obvious that Thomas actively attempted to improve his and his family's condition.[65]

"While here A. went to A.B.C. schools by littles, kept successively by Andrew Crawford, ——— Sweeney, and Azel W. Dorsey. He does not remember any other. The family of Mr. Dorsey now reside in Schuyler Co. Illinois. A. now thinks that the agregate of all his schooling did not amount to one year. He was never in a college or Academy as a student; and never inside of a college or academy building till since he had a law-license. What he has in the way of education, he has picked up. After he was twentythree, and had separated from his father, he studied English grammar, imperfectly of course, but so as to speak and write as well as he now does. He studied and nearly mastered the Six-books of Euclid, since he was a member of Congress. He regrets his want of education, and does what he can to supply the want."

Obviously presidential candidate Lincoln felt embarrassed that "the agregate of all his schooling did not amount to one year." Indeed, he regretted his lack of schooling, and he wanted the public to know that he attempted to compensate by continuing his education well into his adult years—even studying and mastering Euclid.

Lincoln's education began in Kentucky, where education was more available than in frontier Indiana. At age six he attended Zachariah Riney's school, and at age seven his teacher was Caleb Hazel. Both schools were conducted within a couple of miles of the Lincoln home, each met for a few months, and Lincoln was introduced to the ABCs. By the time the Lincolns left Kentucky, he could read and write and, in the words of Kentucky historian Lowell Harrison, was "able to start learning largely on his own."[66]

For the first couple of years in Indiana, there were no schools for Abraham and Sarah to attend, and probably the only book available was the family King James Bible. When Herndon corresponded with and interviewed several of Lincoln's former schoolmates forty years later, he gathered the basic information about their education. Nathaniel Grigsby gave Herndon the most detail about schools on Little Pigeon Creek and listed the order of teachers as Crawford, Dorsey, and Swaney. Grigsby dates the first school to 1818 or 1819 and describes it as a round (unhewn) log building with greased-paper windows. It lay about a mile and a quarter south of the Lincoln farm and two hundred to four hundred yards east of where the Little Pigeon Baptist Meetinghouse would be built in 1821.[67] Parents in the community built the structure and hired Andrew Crawford as teacher. Crawford, a respected citizen of Spencer County, was commissioned justice of the peace in 1818 and, thus, was more educated than most local residents.[68]

The curriculum focused on reading, writing, and ciphering. Lincoln's former schoolmates remembered studying from books such as *Dilworth's Spelling* and *Ray's Arithmetic*. While in the White House, Lincoln supposedly told a story to a couple of Senators that questioned the availability of books:

> The only schooling I ever had, . . . was in a log school-house when reading-books and grammars were unknown. All our reading was done from the Scriptures, and we stood up in a long line and read in turn from the Bible. Our lesson one day was the story of the faithful Israelites who were thrown into the fiery furnace and delivered by the hand of the Lord without so much as the smell of fire upon their garments. It fell to one little fellow to read the verse in which occurred, for the first time in the chapter, the names of Shadrach, Meshach, and Abed-nego. Little Bud stumbled on Shadrach, floundered on Meshach, and went all to pieces on Abed-nego. Instantly the hand of the master dealt him a cuff on the side of the head and left him wailing and blubbering as the next boy in line took up the reading. But before the girl at the end of the line had done reading he had subsided into sniffles, and finally became quiet. His blunder and disgrace were forgotten by the others of the class until his turn was approaching to read again. Then, like a thunderclap out of a clear sky, he set up a wail which even alarmed the master, who with rather unusual gentleness inquired: "What's the matter now?"
>
> Pointing with a shaking finger at the verse which a few moments later would fall to him to read, Bud managed to quaver out the

answer:

"Look there, marster—there comes them same damn three fellers again."[69]

Although it cannot be determined if this event actually happened, there is another account that Lincoln told the same story later, only this time the main character was a "poor little boy out West who had lost his mother" and was taught by a clergyman.[70]

Spelling bees reinforced reading and writing skills, and according to several accounts Lincoln helped other students spell their words. Anna Caroline Roby Gentry told Herndon in 1865 that one day the class had difficulty spelling the word *defied*. Crawford decided the class would not be released until the word was spelled correctly. Anna was about to spell the word with a *y* when she saw Lincoln at the window pointing to his eye. She changed the letter *y* to *i* and the class was dismissed.[71]

Crawford also taught proper manners to the frontier children. Grigsby remembered that "he [Crawford] would ask one of the schollars to retire from the School room—Come in and then some schollar would go around and introduce him to all the schollars—male & female."[72]

Azel W. Dorsey, a resident of Spencer County before the Lincolns arrived and a county official and local businessman, probably taught the second school Lincoln attended. The school sat near the meetinghouse, and Dorsey appears well educated. Grigsby remembered Lincoln being fourteen or fifteen years old at this school, probably during 1823 or 1824. He also remembered that Lincoln wrote poetry and a composition against cruelty to animals.[73]

The teacher that Lincoln identified as Sweeney was James Swaney. Lincoln probably attended Swaney's school for a term between 1825 and 1827. More than four miles from the Lincoln home, the school was built of hewn logs with a chimney on each end and a spring nearby. It was on the road from Gentryville to Rockport and probably served a community larger than the Little Pigeon Creek settlement. But because of the four-mile distance, Lincoln attended erratically, and he probably was more advanced than his teacher at this point.[74]

No records exist that describe the interior of the schools Lincoln attended. There is, however, a description of a school of the era in the southern part of Spencer County.

It was a round log building 22 feet by 18 feet with a clapboard roof fastened on with poles and a first class dirt floor with nothing between the floor and the roof. There was a fireplace in each end and a door in one side near the middle. One end of the school was for girls, the other for boys. The seats were made by splitting a log in two, hewing the split side and boring four holes for the legs in the round side. These legs were set at such an angle that they would not turn over very easily. The desks were made the same way only the legs were longer. These desks set round the room against the wall and the seats in front of them. When using the desk the pupils faced the wall, when not using it they faced outward. The door was made of clapboards and hung on wooden hinges. The window was made by cutting out one of the logs for nearly the whole length of the house. This space was left open and not only admitted light but air, rain, snow, bats, owls, wild oats and other things that went with frontier life. . . .

The teacher's desk set in the center of the room was a rude home made affair. It was not a specimen of art or a thing of beauty but it answered the purpose. Here the teacher spent much of his time making goosequill pens and writing copy across the "headline" of fools-cap paper. The teacher was equipped with a good pen knife and a bundle of goose quills and had to manufacture pens for all of his pupils who were practicing writing. He also had for his own use a bottle of store ink. Most of the pupils used home made ink, generally made from polk berry juice which made a very fair quality of red ink. At least the ink was about as good as the pupils writing.

Then there was the water bucket that usually stood on a block of wood near the door and the gourd which hung on the wall near by it. The water was brought from a nearby branch and had to be carried quite a distance, so that to save labor in carrying the water the pupil who dipped up more water in the gourd than he could drink always poured the rest back into the bucket.[75]

Lincoln's schools may have contained more conventional windows. Grigsby described greased-paper windows in the first school he and Lincoln attended.

Lincoln once told his friend Joshua Speed, "I am slow to learn and slow to forget that which I have learned—My mind is like a piece of steel, very

mpound Multiplication

2 What is Compound Multiplication

A When several numbers of divers Denomination
are given to be multiplied by one common multiplier
this is called Compound multiplication

£	S	D		lb	℔	dwt	gr
17	3	4½		17	5	12	16
							3
2)34	6	2½	3)52	4	18	0
17	3	1¼		17	5	12	16

567 at 8 cents   4567 at 9 cents
                                    9
                          4T 1/03
                                              6543:6 at 89 cts ℔ Barrel
                                                    89
                                                  58887

Bought 26 yards at   6 – 4 – 6 ¼

        6 – 4 – 6 – 4
                26
    38 – 7 – 5 – 4
  129 – 2 – 8
  168 – 0 – 6 – 4

An army of a 10000 men having plundered a
City took so much money that when it was
shared among them each man had £ 27 9 denars
how much money was taken in all

              10000
                27
              70000
            20000
          27000 10000
            27 0000

The most significant artifacts associated with Lincoln's Indiana years are the few pages
from his sum book. On this page Lincoln learned compound multiplication.

To Exercise Multiplication

There were 40 men Concerned in payment
a sum of money and each man paid 12/71£
how much was paid in all —

12/71
40
40) 508/40
12/71

If 1 foot contain 12 inches I demand how there ^many
are in 126 feet —

126
12
12/52
12) 15/1/2
126

# of Compound Division

Q What is compound Division

A When several numbers of Divers Denomination
are given to be divided by 1 common divisor this called
Compound Division —

	£	S	D	
2	13	12	6½	
	24	6	3¼	
			2	
	48	12	6½	

	llo	dz	dr	
7	16	12	13	
	9	5	5	
	16	12	10	

Abraham Lincoln His Book

On this page of his sum book Lincoln claims his book.

hard to scratch any thing on it and almost impossible after you get it there to rub it out."[76] His stepmother remembered him as "diligent for Knowledge" and "what he learned and Stowed away was well defined in his own mind—repeated over & over again & again till it was so defined and fixed firmly & permanently in his Memory."[77]

During his interview with Sally, Herndon discovered the most valuable artifacts of Lincoln's Indiana period—his sum book pages. She told Herndon:

> He had a copy book—a kind of scrap book in which he put down all things and this preserved them. He ciphered on boards when he had no paper or no slate and when the board would get too black he would shave it off with a drawing knife and go on again: When he had paper he put his sums down on it. His copy book is here now or was lately.[78]

Most students in the community used copybooks, and Grigsby recalled that old copybook pages were greased and used to cover schoolhouse windows.[79]

Only a few pages torn and tattered remained in Lincoln's sum book. Today ten extant pages provide the earliest known handwriting of Lincoln. Most of the pages contain "ciphering" from 1824 and 1826. In addition, we find a few lines such as

> Abraham Lincoln
> his hand and pen
> he will be good but
> god knows When

and

> Abraham Lincoln is my name
> And with my pen I wrote the same
> I wrote in both haste and speed
> And left it here for fools to read.[80]

It cannot be determined if Lincoln did the "cipherings" while attending school—perhaps Dorsey's school—or as he tried to teach himself new knowledge, he told a friend years later:

> My father . . . had suffered greatly for the want of an education, and he determined at an early day that I should be well educated. And

what do you think he said his ideas of a good education were? We had a old dog-eared arithmetic in our house, and father determined that somehow, or somehow else, I should cipher clear through that book.[81]

According to his son, then, Thomas was interested in education, at least education that could help a frontier farmer and carpenter with the mathematical calculations necessary to succeed.

Even if Lincoln's schooling amounted to only a year, his education was lifelong. His curiosity led him to learn everything he could from people, books, and newspapers.

"In his tenth year he was kicked by a horse, and apparently killed for a time."

This sentence is the most intriguing in Lincoln's autobiographical statement. Why did he consider such an event important enough to include, and what does it mean? The best answer may come from his law partner Herndon. Lincoln "considered this one of the remarkable incidents of his life. He often referred to it and we had many discussions in our law office over the psychological phenomena involved in the operation," Herndon said.[82] The best description of the event, complete with a negative assessment of Thomas, appears in the Herndon-Weik biography:

One day, taking a bag of corn, he mounted the old flea-bitten gray mare and rode leisurely to Gordon's mill. Arriving somewhat late, his turn did not come till almost sundown. In obedience to the custom requiring each man to furnish his own power he hitched the old mare to the arm, and as the animal moved round, the machinery responded with equal speed. Abe was mounted on the arm, and at frequent intervals made use of his whip to urge the animal on to better speed. With a careless "Get up, you old hussy," he applied the lash at each revolution of the arm. In the midst of the exclamation, or just as half of it had escaped through his teeth, the old jade, resenting the continued use of the goad, elevated her shoeless hoof and striking the young engineer in the forehead, sent him sprawling to the earth. Miller Gordon hurried in, picked up the bleeding, senseless boy, whom he took for dead, and at once sent for his father. Old Thomas Lincoln came—came as soon as embodied listlessness could move—loaded the lifeless boy in a wagon and drove home. Abe lay unconscious all night, but towards break of day the attendants noticed signs of returning consciousness. The blood beginning to flow normally, his tongue struggled to loosen itself, his frame jerked for an instant, and he awoke, blurting out the words "you old hussy," or the latter half of the sentence interrupted by the mare's heel at the mill.[83]

"When he was nineteen, still residing in Indiana, he made his first trip upon flat-boat to New-Orleans. He was a hired hand merely; and he and a son of the owner, with out other assistance, made the trip. The nature of part of the cargo-load, as it was called—made it necessary for them to linger and trade along the Sugar coast—and one night they were attacked by seven negroes with intent to kill and rob them. They were hurt some in the melee, but succeeded in driving the negroes from the boat, and then 'cut cable' 'weighed anchor' and left."

Although it is often assumed that the Lincolns and their frontier neighbors were isolated from the American economic and social mainstream, in reality they resided less than twenty miles from what one historian called "our first interstate highway"—the Ohio River.[84] The river provided contact with persons who proved a constant source of news and made the Little Pigeon Creek settlement a part of an expanding market economy.

During the Lincoln years in Indiana, the most significant southern Indiana agricultural activity was "hogs and hominy." That is, by raising hogs and planting corn, settlers provided for their own subsistence; and by trading the "surplus produce" they could obtain commodities such as sugar and coffee from local merchants.[85] In his study of southern Indiana, historian Richard Nation concludes, "One cannot really understand antebellum southern Indiana—and probably much of the United States—if one does not understand hogs."[86]

The Lincolns appear to authenticate this conclusion. Hanks remembered that they raised corn and enough wheat for a cake on Sunday morning.[87] According to Hanks, from 1824 to 1830 the family farm consisted of ten acres of corn, five acres of wheat, two acres of oats, and one acre of meadow.[88] Perhaps the best documentation for the Lincoln hog and hominy farming came from David Turnham. Turnham told Herndon that he bought about one hundred hogs and four hundred or five hundred bushels of corn from the Lincolns before they moved to Illinois.[89]

The Little Pigeon Creek community used "surplus production" to barter with local storekeeper James Gentry for items they could not produce for themselves. Gentry disposed of the grain and animals he collected by sending them, profitably, down the Ohio and Mississippi rivers.

Merchants and some farmers used flatboats as an inexpensive way to send produce to New Orleans. Louis A. Warren discovered in the county records specifications for an 1833 Spencer County flatboat to be built at the cost of $97.50. The boat was to be

> 65 feet long the gunwales to be of good poplar 2 feet in width and nine inches thick . . . the said boat to be 18 ft. wide the bow of said boat to be very strong with a good solid piece of timber to strengthen the bow, . . . the bottom plank to be of gum or poplar 2 inches thick substantially put on . . . the cabin to be of gum or oak 1½ inches thick 7 inches wide the studding to be three feet apart . . . the roof to be first-rate and not to leak . . . the boat is to be on each side 4½ feet high in the middle.[90]

Gentry hauled the produce and herded the hogs he collected in trading with his customers to his land on the Ohio River near Rockport. There his workers butchered the hogs and cured the meat for shipment. Butchering hogs, a seasonal job, began in November when cold weather could chill the carcasses and prevent meat from spoiling during curing.[91]

Gentry's son Allen, two years older than Abraham, was in charge of the flatboat trip. Allen married Anna Caroline Roby on March 20, 1828. Anna informed Herndon in 1865 that the trip lasted from April to June 1828.[92] Warren, however, accepts Spencer County resident Bess V. Ehrmann's conclusion that the Gentrys sent flatboats down river in December. Allen's grandson, years later, told Ehrmann that the family made its trips in late fall or early winter. The family assumption was that Allen and Lincoln delayed their departure in order for Allen to be present at the birth of his first child, born on December 18, 1828. In that case, the trip probably began before the end of the month.[93] On the other hand, surely Anna would remember whether her husband was absent for over two months within a month after her marriage or within days after bearing a child.

Furthermore, Lincoln himself gave credence to the spring date. A copy of William Dean Howells 1860 campaign biography of Lincoln, with corrections in Lincoln's handwriting, is in the Abraham Lincoln Presidential

Library in Springfield, Illinois. Of three corrections in the chapter on his life in Kentucky and Indiana, two deal with incorrect names, and the third corrects, with regard to the New Orleans trip, when the Lincolns left Indiana. Howells said the move occurred four years after the flatboat journey. Lincoln struck out *four* and wrote *two*. If we accept the December 1828 date, the return would have occurred only a year before the family moved to Illinois.[94] The evidence supports an April date for the trip.

How natural that Lincoln included this adventure in his autobiographical statement for Scripps. He was a curious nineteen-year-old who had never traveled outside Kentucky and Indiana. He read about adventures on the river, heard stories from those who had traveled the river, and studied the history of General Andrew Jackson's War of 1812 battle in the New Orleans area—and now he could visit and experience some of those same places.[95]

Perhaps Lincoln was also trying to escape memories of the second great sorrow of his Indiana years. On August 2, 1826, Sarah Lincoln married Aaron Grigsby, the oldest son of Reuben and Nancy Grigsby. Less than a year

Guiding a flatboat down the Ohio required maneuvering around steamboats, sandbars, and driftwood. Additionally the banks of the river were lined with clever thieves waiting to steal the cargo. Lincoln was not attacked by notorious thieves operating around Cave-In-Rock, Illinois, but was attacked farther downriver.

and a half later, on January 20, 1828, Sarah died in childbirth. One account says Abraham was working at Reuben's home when he was told of his sister's death. According to the story, "He sat down in the door of the smoke house and buried his face in his hands. The tears slowly trickled from between his bony fingers and his gaunt frame shook with sobs."[96] Now, three months after Sarah and her child—family tradition says a boy—were buried near the Little Pigeon Church, Lincoln was to go on a true adventure.

This flatboat journey was a huge responsibility for these two young men, aged twenty-one and nineteen, and involved maneuvering the flatboat in the river channel around sandbars and fallen trees, avoiding eddies, and dodging steamboats. Gentry and Lincoln had to be on guard to protect themselves and the cargo from bandits, such as the infamous pirates operating at Cave-In-Rock, Illinois, who lured unsuspecting river travelers to the riverbank, feigning an emergency, then robbed and killed them. Finally, the two had to negotiate the sale of the valuable cargo with veteran traders.[97]

Lincoln relates one close call along the sugar coast of Louisiana. Demand for pork, corn, and other products was great at towns and plantations along the river. Indeed, they sold much of their cargo before reaching New Orleans, the likely reason they tied the boat on shore over night. Anna told Herndon that the incident occurred at a plantation six miles below Baton Rouge. She also told Herndon that Gentry and Lincoln scared the attackers away by pretending to have guns. [98]

In New Orleans, the men sold the remaining cargo and the wood from the flatboat itself—and then explored the city. New Orleans was an education for young men from the Hoosier frontier. The city's bustling river wharves teemed with flatboats, steamboats, and ships from around the world, and physically the city looked and felt quite different from the Ohio River towns they knew. Biographer Albert J. Beveridge, in his 1928 work on Lincoln, said of New Orleans, "It was then a remarkable city of narrow streets, foreign-built houses, with colored stuccoes and iron railings, broad avenues lined by handsome houses, a cathedral, and immense warehouses for receiving, pressing, and storing cotton."[99]

Moreover, the people of New Orleans proved as interesting to Lincoln as the architecture; he experienced an ethnic mix unlike anything he imagined back in Indiana. The culture he observed surely shocked his Baptist upbringing, but intrigued him as well. Nevertheless, how much of the city Lincoln experienced remains open to speculation.

Most Lincoln biographers find the overwhelming presence of slavery along the route the most significant aspect of the trip. Undoubtedly Lincoln had seen slaves in Kentucky, but not as many as he saw in the Deep South. He probably saw the inhumane slave market in operation for the first time during this New Orleans visit. According to a Gentry family tradition, Lincoln told his companion, "Allen this is a disgrace. If I ever get a lick at the thing I'll hit it hard."[100] The importance of the experience on Lincoln's future view of slavery is debatable, but the experience was one he would always remember.

The return trip also proved an unforgettable experience. As a passenger on a northbound steamboat, a new and thrilling adventure, Lincoln observed a variety of passengers, and onboard activities gave him a wealth of stories to tell when he returned to Spencer County. Lincoln earned eight dollars a month plus steamboat passage for the return trip. The trip probably lasted two months.[101]

"March 1st. 1830—A. having just completed his 21st. year, his father and family, with the families of the two daughters and sons-in-law, of his step mother, left the old homestead in Indiana, and came to Illinois. Their mode of conveyance was waggons drawn by ox-teams, or A. drove one of the teams."

On his twenty-first birthday on February 12, 1830, Lincoln became an independent and a legal citizen of the country. No longer economically obligated to his father and now free to chart his own life, Lincoln, nevertheless, chose to join his extended family and move to Illinois.

As the autobiography for Scripps indicates, in 1830 the family was more Johnston than Lincoln. Only Thomas and Abraham remained from the Lincoln family that came to Indiana in 1816; the majority belonged to Sally's family. Thirteen of them left Indiana that March day. Thomas, Sally, John D., and Abraham constituted one family unit. The Hanks and Squire Hall families also made the journey.

Dennis Hanks married Elizabeth Johnston on June 14, 1821. The previous year, on September 27, 1820, Thomas Barritt "assigned" to Hanks a farm of 160 acres that bordered the eastern edge of the Lincoln farm. Here, within a mile of the Lincoln cabin, Dennis and Elizabeth lived and had four children, Sarah Jane, John Talbot, Nancy, and Harriet. Hanks's land dealings proved less successful than Thomas's. Hanks failed to meet his obligations and, consequently, "assigned" the land to James Gentry in 1826. The next

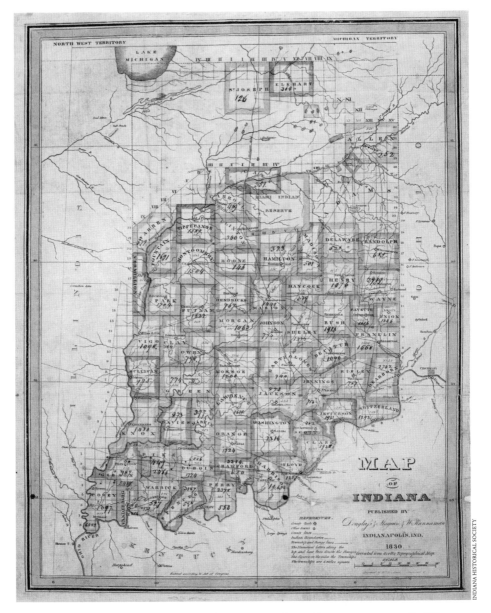

During the almost fourteen years Lincoln spent in Indiana, the state grew rapidly. When Lincoln arrived in 1816, approximately the southern third of the state was organized into counties. By the time Lincoln departed in 1830, it was true for more than two thirds of the state.

year Gentry relinquished the land that tradition says the Hankses lived on to the United States, and the Hankses remained as squatters on government land until they left in 1830.[102] Matilda Johnston married Squire Hall, a half brother of Dennis Hanks, on September 14, 1826; and by 1830 they had a son John Johnston Hall. Sally's unmarried son John D. Johnston joined the Lincoln, Hanks, and Hall families on the move to Illinois.[103]

Contrary to conclusions of some Lincoln biographers, Thomas probably did not initiate this move. He held free title to his land, was a respected member of the community, and had a comfortable lifestyle. Life in Spencer County had improved drastically in the fourteen years that the Lincolns resided in Indiana. According to neighbors, the Lincoln family had actually started building a new house in late 1829, a house that was not completed before the family left the county.[104]

The originator of the idea to leave southern Indiana may have been Hanks. He lost four cows to milk sickness, probably in 1829, and he was perplexed by the illness. He was "determed to Leve and hunt a cuntry whare the Milk was not."[105] That country lay in central Illinois where John Hanks, a cousin, had settled. Sally, according to Hanks, "Could not think of parting with hir [daughter Elizabeth] and we Riped up Stakes and Started to Illinois and Landed at Decatur."[106]

The Lincoln family entered Illinois by fording the Wabash River at Vincennes, Indiana. This early drawing shows the Wabash near Vincennes.

The families needed to take care of many details before leaving Spencer County. Thomas began to sell the eighty-acre portion of his land to Charles Grigsby on November 26, 1829. The deal was completed on February 20, 1830, with a warranty deed signed by Thomas and with Sally making her mark to sell the land to Grigsby for $125. As mentioned earlier, Thomas sold Turnham his hogs and several hundred bushels of corn.[107]

Thomas and Sally were granted a "letter of Dismission"—meaning they left in good standing—by the Little Pigeon Baptist Church on December 12, 1829. But, in January, Nancy Grigsby asked the church to recall the letter until she was satisfied about Lincoln's views on some doctrinal issue. It appears Nancy was satisfied and the family left in March in good standing with the church.[108]

Lincoln said that wagons, pulled by teams of oxen, carried the furniture, household goods, farm implements, and the other items the families needed to start a new life in Illinois. Since three family units traveled together, it is naturally assumed that they used three wagons. Indeed, Hanks's daughter Harriet, age four at the time, remembered "three covered wagons, two drawn by oxen, and one by horses, and two saddle horses."[109] According to one legend in the community, Abraham saw the move as an opportunity to become an entrepreneur; he bought a number of items from local storekeeper William Jones—or James Gentry—and peddled these goods to persons they met along the way.[110]

The exact route the Lincolns followed to leave Indiana in 1830 is as confusing as the one they used to leave Kentucky in 1816. The second Indiana commission to determine the Lincolns' 1816 and 1830 routes concluded "there is not available absolute proof as to the route traveled by the Lincolns during either one of the migrations."[111] The one area of agreement is that the families left Indiana by crossing the Wabash River at Vincennes. After examining support for at least five different routes from Spencer County to Vincennes, the commission accepted the Troy-Vincennes trail that passed near the present-day towns of Gentryville, Selvin, Stendal, Petersburg, and Monroe City before reaching Vincennes.[112]

One final Indiana Lincoln story should be mentioned. Vincennes, the oldest city in Indiana, has a fascinating history. One event of that history involves George Rogers Clark's capture of the town for the Americans during the Revolutionary War. Certainly Lincoln would have wanted to learn all he could about that episode, but, perhaps of more interest to the young man was the *Vincennes Western Sun* newspaper office. The *Western Sun* was one of the papers Lincoln read while living in Spencer County, and he naturally would want to know about newspaper printing. Therefore, it is not surprising that a Hanks family member related that Abraham told him that, while in Vincennes, "he saw a printing press for the first time."[113]

3

"My childhood's home I see again"
Lincoln's Poetry about Indiana

On February 24, 1846, Abraham Lincoln, "feeling a little poetic," wrote a letter to Quincy, Illinois, lawyer Andrew Johnston. Johnston had requested a copy of Lincoln's favorite poem "Mortality" by William Knox, and Lincoln enclosed a copy in this letter. Then Lincoln added, "By the way, how would you like to see a piece of poetry of my own making? I have a piece that is almost done, but I find a deal of trouble to finish it."[1] That ninety-six-line poem began with this quatrain:

> My childhood-home I see again,
> And gladden with the view;
> And still as mem'ries crowd my brain,
> There's sadness in it too.[2]

The poem ended with this stanza:

> The very spot where grew the bread
> That formed my bones, I see.
> How strange, old field, on thee to tread,
> And feel I'm part of thee![3]

On April 18, 1846, Lincoln wrote Johnston again on the subject of poetry. Presumably Johnston asked if Lincoln wrote the "Mortality" poem, and Lincoln responded, "I am not the author. I would give all I am worth, and go in debt, to be able to write so fine a piece as I think that is."[4] Then Lincoln described the circumstance under which he wrote the Indiana poetry:

> In the fall of 1844, thinking I might aid some to carry the State of Indiana for Mr. Clay, I went into the neighborhood in that State in which I was raised, where my mother and only sister were buried, and from which I had been absent about fifteen years. That part of the country is, within itself, as unpoetical as any spot of the earth; but still, seeing it and its objects and inhabitants aroused feelings in me which were certainly poetry; though whether my expression of those feelings is poetry is quite another question. When I got to writing, the change of subjects divided the thing into four little divisions or cantos, the first only of which I send you now and may send the others hereafter.[5]

During the next few months Lincoln sent Johnston three of the four cantos. Whether he wrote the fourth or if it is lost, is not known.[6]

The first section explores Lincoln's feelings on seeing the people and the places of his youth. For Lincoln, as for most people, such a visit proved bittersweet. As Douglas L. Wilson recounts, the returning Lincoln differed significantly from the twenty-one-year-old who left Indiana in 1830: "From his hardscrabble beginnings with nothing to encourage education, he had risen to surprising heights. He had become educated; he had gained a profession; and he had achieved by his political efforts, a measure of recognition."[7] Perhaps the returning thirty-five-year-old successful attorney and ambitious politician came to Spencer County filled with pride for his accomplishments. But in Wilson's words, "What this confident and self-reliant man encountered in his boyhood home in Indiana was probably as unexpected as it was unforgettable—the humbling fact of his own mortality."[8]

Whereas the first verse reveals minor changes from the quatrains sent to Johnston earlier, the final verse sounds much more fatalistic:

> My childhood's home I see again,
> And sadden with the view;
> And still, as memory crowds my brain,
> There's pleasure in it too.
>
> O Memory! thou midway world
> 'Twixt earth and paradise
> Where things decayed and loved ones lost
> In dreamy shadows rise,

And, freed from all that's earthy vile,
Seem hallowed, pure, and bright,
Like scenes in some enchanted isle
All bathed in liquid light.

As dusky mountains please the eye
When twilight chases day;
As bugle-notes that, passing by,
In distance die away;

As leaving some grand waterfall,
We, lingering, list its roar—
So memory will hallow all
We've known, but know no more.

Near twenty years have passed away
Since here I bid farewell
To woods and fields, and scenes of play,
And playmates loved so well.

Where many were, but few remain
Of old familiar things;
But seeing them, to mind again
The lost and absent brings.

The friends I left that parting day,
How changed, as time has sped!
Young childhood grown, strong manhood gray,
And half of all are dead.

I hear the loved survivors tell
How nought from death could save,
Till every sound appears a knell,
And every spot a grave.

I range the fields with pensive tread,
And pace the hollow rooms,
And feel (companion of the dead)
I'm living in the tombs.[9]

The second canto Lincoln sent Johnston in September 1846. Although Lincoln may have felt surprise that half the persons he knew in Indiana were dead, he felt more surprise that one still lived—the subject of the next part of his poem. Lincoln wrote Johnston:

> His name is Matthew Gentry. He is three years older than I, and when we were boys we went to school together. He was rather a bright lad, and the son of *the* rich man of our very poor neighbourhood. At the age of nineteen he unaccountably became furiously mad, from which condition he gradually settled down into harmless insanity. When, as I told you in my other letter I visited my old home in the fall of 1844, I found him still lingering in this wretched condition. In my poetizing mood I could not forget the impression his case made upon me. Here is result—

> > But here's an object more of dread
> > Than ought the grave contains—
> > A human form with reason fled,
> > While wretched life remains.

> > Poor Matthew! Once of genius bright,
> > A fortune-favored child—
> > Now locked for aye, in mental night,
> > A haggard mad-man wild.

> > Poor Matthew! I have ne'er forgot,
> > When first, with maddened will,
> > Yourself you maimed, your father fought,
> > And mother strove to kill;

> > When terror spread, and neighbours ran,
> > Your dange'rous strength to bind;
> > And soon, a howling crazy man
> > Your limbs were fast confined.

> > How then you strove and shrieked aloud,
> > Your bones and sinnews bared;
> > And fiendish on the gazing crowd,
> > With burning eye-balls glared—

And begged, and swore, and wept and prayed
With maniac laugh[ter?] joined—
How fearful were those signs displayed,
By pangs that kill thy mind!

And when at length, tho' drear and long,
Time soothed thy fiercer woes—
How plaintively thy mournful song
Upon the still night rose.

I've heard it oft, as if I dreamed,
Far distant, sweet, and lone—
The funeral dirge, it ever seemed
Of reason dead and gone.

To drink it's strains, I've stole away,
All stealthily and still,
Ere yet the rising god of day
Had streaked the Eastern hill.

Air held his breath; trees, with the spell
Seemed sorrowing angels round,
Whose swelling tears in dew-drops fell
Upon the listening ground.

But this is past; and nought remains,
That raised thee o'er the brute.
Thy piercing shrieks, and soothing strains,
Are like, forever mute.

Now fare thee well—more thou the *cause*,
Than *subject* now of woe.
All mental pangs, by time's kind laws,
Hast lost the power to know.

O death! Thou awe-inspiring prince,
That keepst the world in fear;
Why dost thou tear more blest ones hence,
And leave him ling'ring here?[10]

How long Gentry lived after the Lincoln visit is not known; family histories merely mention he lies buried in Spencer County.

For the third section of his poem Lincoln remembered the violent, manly bear hunts of his youth. He provided Johnston no background for this—the longest of his poems. But no doubt it describes an actual event he recalled on his return visit:

> A wild-bear chace, didst never see?
> Then hast thou lived in vain.
> Thy richest bump of glorious glee,
> Lies desert in thy brain.
>
> When first my father settled here,
> 'Twas then the frontier line:
> The panther's scream, filled night with fear
> And bears preyed on the swine.
>
> But wo for Bruin's short lived fun,
> When rose the squealing cry;
> Now man and horse, with dog and gun,
> For vengeance, at him fly.
>
> A sound of danger strikes his ear;
> He gives the breeze a snuff:
> Away he bounds, with little fear,
> And seeks the tangled *rough*.
>
> On press his foes, and reach the ground,
> Where's left his half munched meal;
> The dogs, in circles, scent around,
> And find his fresh made trail.
>
> With instant cry, away they dash,
> And men as fast pursue;
> O'er logs they leap, through water splash,
> And shout the brisk halloo.
>
> Now to elude the eager pack,
> Bear shuns the open ground;
> Th[r]ough matted vines, he shapes his track
> And runs it, round and round.

The tall fleet cur, with deep-mouthed voice,
Now speeds him, as the wind;
While half-grown pup, and short-legged fice,
Are yelping far behind.

And fresh recruits are dropping in
To join the merry *corps*:
With yelp and yell,—a mingled din—
The woods are in a roar.

And round, and round the chace now goes,
The world's alive with fun;
Nick Carter's horse, his rider throws,
And more, Hill drops his gun.

Now sorely pressed, bear glances back,
And lolls his tired tongue;
When as, to force him from his track,
An ambush on him sprung.

Across the glade he sweeps for flight,
And fully is in view.
The dogs, new-fired, by the sight,
Their cry, and speed, renew.

The foremost ones, now reach his rear,
He turns, they dash away;
And circling now, the wrathful bear,
They have him full at bay.

At top of speed, the horse-men come,
All screaming in a row.
"Whoop! Take him Tiger. Seize him Drum."
Bang,—bang—the rifles go.

And furious now, the dogs he tears,
And crushes in his ire.
Wheels right and left, and upward rears,
With eyes of burning fire.

But leaden death is at his heart,
Vain all the strength he plies.
And, spouting blood from every part,
He reels, and sinks, and dies.

And now a dinsome clamor rose,
'Bout who should have his skin;
Who first draws blood, each hunter knows,
This prize must always win.

But who did this, and how to trace
What's true from what's a lie,
Like lawyers, in a murder case
They stoutly *argufy*.

Aforesaid fice, of blustering mood,
Behind, and quite forgot,
Just now emerging from the wood,
Arrives upon the spot.

With grinning teeth, and up-turned hair—
Brim full of spunk and wrath,
He growls, and seizes on dead bear,
And shakes for life and death.

And swells as if his skin would tear,
And growls and shakes again;
And swears, as plain as dog can swear,
That he has won the skin.

Conceited whelp! we laugh at thee—
Nor mind, that not a few
Of pompous, two-legged dogs there be,
Conceited quite as you.[11]

The second verse is the most quoted portion of this poem, likely Lincoln's most graphic account of the Indiana frontier. Because Lincoln is rarely portrayed as a hunter, this offers a unique account of an event in his youth.

Lincoln uses the same rhythm (iambic), meter (lines 1 and 3 in tetrameters; lines 2 and 4 in trimeters), rhyme scheme (*abab*), and stanza pattern (quatrain) in all three poems. The poems suggest the ballad. And Lincoln would be familiar with ballads, both sung and recited, simply because the form is easy to learn and remember. Moreover, the form and uses of apostrophe and personification indicate Lincoln's familiarity with some of the poets of the Federalist Age and of the Early American Romantic Period.

As for figurative language and imagery, Lincoln avoids metaphors, rarely uses even a simile, and occasionally includes hyperbole. Lincoln enjoys using imagery—visual, tactile, auditory. Auditory imagery dominates in much of the bear hunt: deep-mouthed voice, yelping, yelp and yell, mingled din, woods in a roar, cry, full at bay, screamin', whoop, bang, dinsome clamor, growls. A bear hunt, according to Lincoln's poem, is filled with noise.[12]

Johnston arranged to publish the first two cantos in the *Quincy* (IL) *Whig* on May 5, 1847, under the heading "The Return" with subtitles "Part I—Reflection" and "Part II—The Maniac." Evidently, Johnston regarded the "Bear Hunt" as inappropriate for printing.[13]

The journey that served as the catalyst for Lincoln's poetry was chiefly political. In 1844 John Tyler was president of the United States, the "Tyler Too" of the 1840-election slogan, "Tippecanoe and Tyler Too." In 1840 the Whig candidate, William Henry Harrison, "Old Tippecanoe," won election but died after serving only one month. As a consequence, Tyler became the first vice president to assume the presidency, and he quickly alienated Whig Party leaders. Thus, in 1844 the party turned to its leader, Henry Clay of Kentucky, as its candidate. The Democratic Party selected dark horse James Knox Polk of Tennessee, and a spirited campaign followed.

An Illinois Whig presidential elector, Lincoln actively campaigned for Clay—perhaps at the expense of his legal practice. Shortly before the election Lincoln "took to the stump" in Indiana. As near as can be determined, the trip probably occurred from October 24 to near or shortly after Election Day, Monday, November 4, 1844. (Congress established a national election day in 1845. Prior to that time, each state chose electors any time within a thirty-four-day period before the first Wednesday in December. Indiana and Illinois both selected November 4 for the 1844 election.)[14]

Lincoln stopped first in Vincennes, Indiana, and then traveled to nearby Bruceville. Vincennes resident Anna O'Flynn, who found residents of the area still remembered the night nearly fifty years later, collected most of what is known about the Bruceville stop. Democrat and Whig followers tried to disrupt the other's rallies, and "the night was made hideous with the rattle of tin pans and bells and the blare of cow-horns."[15]

One story O'Flynn collected may lack accuracy, but certainly Lincoln would love this story, which captures the campaign fervor. The symbol of the Democratic Party was a rooster; the Whig Party's icon was a raccoon. According to the legend, after the Bruceville speech, as Lincoln walked to the home of the town's founder,

> Mr. Bruce said, "Lincoln, that old box up on the pole has a rooster in it, and that rooster gets out every morning and proclaims a Democratic victory." [Lincoln replied] "Don't worry about that; wait until tomorrow morning." In the morning when they pulled the string the rooster didn't come out but the feathers flew away in every direction. Then a coon came out on the board where the rooster had previously proclaimed his victory. The people thought that Abe Lincoln had put that coon in the box to devour the Democratic rooster.[16]

Next, Lincoln traveled to Washington, Indiana, where, legend holds, he delivered a speech under an elm tree at what is now Third and Main streets. From there he rode to Spencer County. Although the sequence of events in his old county remains unclear, he apparently made at least three speeches there. The best documented he delivered at the county seat of Rockport on Wednesday, October 30. A page of the *Rockport Herald*, a Whig paper, dated November 1, 1844, survives:

> Mr. Lincoln, of Springfield, Ill., addressed a large and respectable audience at the court house on Wednesday evening last, upon the whig policy. His main argument was directed in pointing out the advantages of a Protective Tariff. He handled that subject in a manner that done honor to himself and the whig cause. Other subjects were investigated in a like manner. —His speech was plain, argumentative and of an hour's duration.—When he closed, Mr. J. Pitcher arose and delivered a speech in his forcible and powerful manner.—He exhibited the democratic policies in an unenviable light, at least we thought so.[17]

According to one account, the next day Lincoln accompanied his former employer, William Jones, to the Jones home west of Gentryville, where he spent the night, saw old neighbors, and made another speech. He also spoke at a schoolhouse, east of the old farm, that served as the polling

FOR PRESIDENT:
HENRY CLAY.
FOR VICE PRESIDENT:
T. FRELINGHUYSEN.

For State Electors.

_____ B. Lane, of Montgomery,
_____ B. _____, of Jefferson,

District Electors.

John A. _____, of Franklin,
_____ W. Payne, of Fayette,
_____ O'Neal, of Marion,
George G. Dunn, of Lawrence,
Richard W. Thompson, of Vigo,
8. Albert L. Holmes, of Carroll,
9. Horace P. Biddle, of _____,
10. Lewis G. Thompson, of Allen,

THE HERALD

JAMES C. VEATCH, EDITOR.

ROCKPORT, IA.

FRIDAY, NOVEMBER 1, 1844.

The great conflict is drawing to a close: and on Monday next the great question, "who shall be the next President—Henry Clay or J. K. Polk?" is to be decided. The merits of these men have been presented repeatedly; and the principles which each advocate are well

that no fraudulent votes are polled —be active, and preserve peace and order at the ballot boxes.

Mr. Lincoln, of Springfield, Ill., addressed a large and respectable audience at the court house on Wednesday evening last, upon the whig policy. His main argument was directed in pointing out the advantages of a Protective Tariff. He handled that subject in a manner that done honor to himself and the whig cause. Other subjects were investigated in a like manner.— His speech was plain, argumentative and of an hour's duration.— When he closed, Mr. J. Pitcher arose and delivered a speech in his forcible and powerful manner.— He exhibited the democratic policies in an unenviable light at least we thought so.

Through the politeness of Mr. Wicks, of the Fawn, we are in possession of late Louisville papers, from which gather several important items of news.

The Harrisburg Union gives the official vote of every county in the State of Pennsylvania, as received at the office of the Secretary of State, showing the following result:
Shunk, loco   160,403
Markle, whig   155,114
                     _____
Locofoco majority   4,289

No return was made from the sixth ward of the northern liberties which would add about one hundred to this majority. The vote for Lemoyne, the Abolition candidate, is not given, but said to be over five thousand.

PENNSYLVANIA.—Many influential Locofocos said, before the election, that unless Shunk carried Pennsylvania by 10,- 000 majority, there was no hope of its

we beg leave
irregularities
unavoidable
had for procu
been cut off
consequence
But now, a
Packet Fawn
Henderson a:
procure pape
that we shall
ogies for the

IMPORTANC
St Louis New
tion in Misso
lature of Lev
majority of
Clarke by 5
votes; one
one from Pe
Carroll by tw
vices by five
bers from H
by 10 votes,
Audrian, Gro
majorities
was elected b
and the Sena
ity of eight vo
Benton by ni

Laboring u
tle; it is a wa
the argument
approach the
next Monday
now before the
didates for
that one is a
borer; the oth
him. That f
opponent is J

LET THE
There is no c
which is so m
tive Tariff a
Locofoco pre
or to excite a
tive tariff, th
to benefit the

The only known document related to Lincoln's 1844 campaign trip to Indiana is a copy of a page from the *Rockport Herald* for November 1, 1844. Lincoln's speech was "plain, argumentative and of an hour's duration."

Lincoln's Rockport speech was delivered at the Spencer County Courthouse on October 30, 1844.

Lincoln is reported to have stayed at this inn or tavern built in 1836. The building stood northeast of the courthouse for many years but is no longer extant.

place—perhaps on Election Day. At this time he likely walked over the old fields, visited his mother's grave, and memory crowded his brain.[18] In 1865 residents told William H. Herndon additional stories about events of this 1844 visit, which will be discussed later.

The Illinois lawyer visited Boonville and made another typical Whig speech. Shortly after Lincoln received the presidential nomination in 1860, a Boonville correspondent for the *Evansville Journal* remembered, "Mr. Lincoln passed through our town some years ago, and made a speech in our Court House. All who heard him (without distinction of party) concur in saying he made one of the best speeches ever delivered in this place. His speech was mainly on the Tariff question."[19] Evansville is also mentioned as a Lincoln destination in 1844, but no solid evidence is available to support such a visit.

The impact of the Lincoln campaign trip is debatable. While three of the four counties where Lincoln spoke voted for Clay in 1844, the state and nation elected Polk.[20]

Part Two

THE LINCOLN FAMILY
Remembers Indiana

4

"The inner life of Mr. L."
William Henry Herndon Collects the Memories

In late summer of 1865 William H. Herndon began the trip that produced the cache of information on Abraham Lincoln's Indiana years. Herndon had corresponded earlier in the year with some of the informants on Lincoln's youth and viewed his interviews with these persons as a means for immediate responses to questions. Most important, in the words of David Herbert Donald, "He could closely watch his informants as they talked and could at last determine where lay truth and where error."[1]

Herndon was born in Kentucky in 1818, but in 1820 his father brought the family to Illinois. He attended Illinois College in Jacksonville for a year and in 1837 began to clerk in Joshua Speed's Springfield store, where he became acquainted with another man born in Kentucky—Abraham Lincoln.[2]

In 1844 Herndon was admitted to the Illinois bar and began his partnership with Lincoln, an association that lasted until Lincoln's death. Donald concludes, "Lincoln's death was the most important event in Herndon's life. For the first time Herndon became front-page news. He found himself described and quoted and characterized."[3] This new fame, along with the view that other biographers were not revealing the real Lincoln story, convinced Herndon that he should research and write a book on "the inner life of Mr. L."[4] He certainly knew Lincoln's Springfield history, but he needed to collect information on the Kentucky, Indiana, and New Salem years.

While the work began in 1865, the book, *Herndon's Lincoln: The True Story of a Great Life*, was not published until 1889, and then only after he arranged with Jesse W. Weik to write the text. The book and the material collected by Herndon are often challenged, but in Donald's words, "Whether or

Most of what is known of Lincoln's life in Indiana comes from the interviews and correspondence of William H. Herndon.

not scholarly critics approve, Herndon's lectures, letters, and books have largely shaped current beliefs and traditions about Abraham Lincoln."[5] Indeed, that is true for the Indiana years of Lincoln.

Most of what is written about those 1816 to 1830 years of Lincoln's life results from the memories found in Herndon's interviews and letters. Granted, questions are raised in using this material: Can memory be trusted? Was Herndon crafting the questions to obtain the answers he wanted? Did he record only the responses that supported his views? Did he interview the most significant individuals? However, nothing validates the importance of the material more than the realization that even Herndon's critics make extensive use of his work.[6]

In 1998 this important collection was published in its entirety for the first time as *Herndon's Informants: Letters, Interviews, and Statements about Abraham Lincoln*, edited by Douglas L. Wilson and Rodney O. Davis, codirectors of the Lincoln Studies Center at Knox College in Galesburg, Illinois.

The memories of Lincoln's family, friends, and neighbors, collected by Herndon in September 1865, comprise most of the remainder of this work. The most significant interviews chosen to examine in depth are:

Sarah (Sally) Bush Johnston Lincoln (1788–1869), Lincoln's stepmother
Matilda Johnston Hall Moore (1809–1878), Lincoln's stepsister
Dennis Friend Hanks (1799–1892), Lincoln's cousin
Nathaniel Grigsby (1811–1890), schoolmate and friend
David Turnham (1803–1884), schoolmate and friend
Anna Caroline Roby Gentry (1807–1883), schoolmate
Elizabeth Crawford (1806–1892), neighbor and wife of employer
Nancy Castleman Richardson (1783–1868), neighbor
John Romine (1806–1888), neighbor and employer
William Wood (1784–1867), neighbor and friend
Joseph Richardson (1816–1892), acquaintance
Silas Richardson (1812–1884), acquaintance
Green B. Taylor (1814–1899), son of employer[7]

Here then is the history of Lincoln's youth as remembered by those who were there.

5

"He was the best boy I ever saw"
Sarah (Sally) Bush Johnston Lincoln

On his first stop William H. Herndon visited the remaining Lincoln family members in Coles County, Illinois. No interview proved more moving or sentimental than the September 8, 1865, visit to Lincoln's stepmother, Sarah (Sally) Bush Johnston Lincoln.

Sally was born in Kentucky in 1788, making her about seventy-seven years old at the time of the interview—she told Herndon she was about seventy-five. Her father, Christopher Bush, had migrated to Hardin County, Kentucky, in about 1780. He became a successful landowner of more than two thousand acres in two different Kentucky counties. Another resident of the Elizabethtown, Kentucky, area, Thomas Lincoln, knew the Bush family well. In fact Thomas was on a New Orleans flatboat trip with Sally's brother Isaac when she married Daniel Johnston on March 13, 1806, in Elizabethtown.[1]

After studying extant Kentucky records, Louis A. Warren concluded, "Daniel Johnston was far from successful in his finances."[2] Johnston constantly owed money, at least until he became Hardin County jailer in 1814. The Johnston family, including three children, lived in a part of the stone jail, and Sally prepared the prisoner meals. Johnston continued to hold this position until his death in the summer of 1816. Following her husband's death, Sally and her children purchased a cabin in Elizabethtown, and there Thomas persuaded her to marry him and move to Indiana.[3]

When members of the Lincoln family left Indiana in 1830, they first settled in Macon County, Illinois. After a very difficult winter—known as the "winter of the deep snow"—the family decided to return to Indiana.

The only known photograph of Sarah Bush Johnston Lincoln was taken late in her life.

The group of eleven (minus twenty-two-year-old Abraham and twenty-one-year-old John D. Johnston) began the return journey late in spring 1831. Plans changed, however, when, according to family legend, Sally's niece's husband John Sawyer convinced the party to settle in Coles County, Illinois, some thirty miles west of the Indiana border. Thomas and Sally lived the rest of their lives in Illinois.[4]

Herndon found Sally living with her grandson's family approximately eight miles south of Charleston, Illinois. Herndon little expected a successful interview with the elderly Sally, writing in his notes:

> When I first reachd the House of Mrs Lincoln and was introduced to her by Col A H. Chapman her grandson by marriage — I did not Expect to get much out of her — She seemed to old & feeble —: She asked me my name 2 or 3 times and where I lived as often — and woud say — "Where Mr Lincoln lived once his friend too" She breathed badly at first but She seemed to be struggling at last to arouse her self— or to fix her mind on the subject. Gradually by introducing simple questions to her — about her age — marriage — Kentucky — Thomas Lincoln — her former husband Johnston her children — grand children She awoke — as it were a new being — her Eyes were clear & calm: her flesh is white & pure — not Coarse or material — is tall — has bluish large gray Eyes: Ate dinner with her — sat on my west side — left arm — ate a good hearty dinner she did[5]

Indeed Sally did "arouse her self" and "fix her mind on the subject." The transcript of Herndon's notes follows:

> Friday — Old Mrs Lincolns Home — 8 m South of Charleston
> — Septr 8th 1865
>
> Mrs Thomas Lincoln Says—
>   I Knew Mr Lincoln in Ky — I married Mr Johnson — he died about 1817 or 18 — Mr Lincoln came back to Ky, having lost his wife — Mr Thos Lincoln & Myself were married in 1819 — left Ky — went to Indiana — moved there in a team — think Krume movd us. Her is our old bible dated 1819: it has Abes name in it. Here is Barclay's dictionary dated 1799 —: it has Abe's name in it, though in a better hand writing — both are boyish scrawls — When we

landed in Indiana Mr Lincoln had erected a good log cabin — tolerably Comfortable. This is the bureau I took to Indiana in 1819 — cost $45 in Ky Abe was then young —so was his Sister. I dressed Abe & his sister up — looked more human. Abe slept up stairs — went up on pins stuck in the logs — like a ladder — Our bed steds were original creations — none such now — made of poles & Clapboards — Abe was about 9 ys of age when I landed in Indiana — The country was wild — and desolate. Abe was a good boy: he didn't like physical labor — was diligent for Knowledge — wished to Know & if pains & Labor would get it he was sure to get it. He was the best boy I ever saw. He read all the books he could lay his hands on — I can't remember dates nor names — am about 75 ys of age — Abe read the bible some, though not as much as said: he sought more congenial books — suitable for his age. I think newspapers were had in Indiana as Early as 1824 & up to 1830 when we moved to Ills — Abe was a Constant reader of them — I am sure of this for the years of 1827–28–29–30. The name of the Louisville Journal seems to sound like one. Abe read histories, papers — & other books — cant name any one — have forgotten. Abe had no particular religion — didnt think of that question at that time, if he ever did — He never talked about it. He read diligently — studied in the day time — didnt after night much — went to bed Early — got up Early & then read — Eat his breakfast — go to work in the field with the men. Abe read all the books he could lay his hands on — and when he came across a passage that Struck him he would write it down on boards if he had no paper & keep it there till he did get paper — then he would re-write it — look at it repeat it — He had a copy book — a kind of scrap book in which he put down all things and this preserved them. He ciphered on boards when he had no paper or no slate and when the board would get too black he would shave it off with a drawing knife and go on again: When he had paper he put his sums down on it. His copy book is here now or was lately (Here it was shown me by Mr Thos Johnson) Abe, when old folks were at our house, was a silent & attentive observer — never speaking or asking questions till they were gone and then he must understand Every thing — even to the smallest thing — Minutely & Exactly —: he would then repeat it over to himself again & again — sometimes in one form and then in another & when it was fixed in his mind to suit him he became Easy and he never lost that fact or his understanding of it. Sometimes he seemed pestered to give Expression to his ideas and got mad almost at one who couldn't Explain plainly what he wanted to convey. He would hear sermons preached — come home — take the children out — get on a stump or log and almost repeat it word for word — He made other Speeches — Such as interested him and the children. His father had to make him quit sometimes as he quit his own work to speak & made the other children as well as the men quit their work. As a usual thing Mr Lincoln never made Abe quit reading to do anything if he could avoid it. He would do it himself first. Mr. Lincoln could read a little & could scarcely write his name: hence he wanted, as he himself felt the uses & necessities of Education his boy Abraham to learn & he Encouraged him to do it in all ways he could — Abe was a poor boy, & I can say what scarcely one woman — a mother — can say in a thousand and it is this — Abe never gave me a cross word or look and never refused in fact, or Even in appearance, to do any thing I requested him. I never gave him a cross word in all my life. He was Kind to Every body and to Every thing and always accommodate others if he could — would do so willingly if he could. His mind & mine — what little I had seemed to run together — move in the same channel — Abe could Easily learn & long remember and when he did learn anything he learned it well and thoroughly. What he thus learned he stowed away in his memory which was Extremely good — What he learned and Stowed away was well defined in his own mind — repeated over & over again & again till it was so defined and fixed firmly & permanently in his Memory. He rose Early — went to bed Early, not reading much after night. Abe was a moderate Eater and I now have no remembrance of his Special dish: he Sat down & ate what was set before him, making no complaint: he seemd Careless about this. I cooked his meals for nearly 15 years —. He always had good health — never was sick — was very careful of his person — was tolerably neat and clean only — Cared nothing for clothes — so that they were clean & neat — fashion cut no figure with him — nor Color —nor Stuff nor material — was Careless about these

things. He was more fleshy in Indiana than Ever in Ills —. I saw him
Every year or two — He was here — after he was Elected President
of the US. (Here the old lady stopped — turned around & cried
— wiped her Eyes — and proceeded)   As Company would Come
to our house Abe was a silent listener — wouldn't speak — would
sometimes take a book and retire aloft — go to the stable or field or
woods — and read —. Abe was always fond of fun — sport — wit
& jokes — He was sometimes very witty indeed. He never drank
whiskey or other strong drink — was temperate in all things — too
much so I thought sometimes — He never told me a lie in his life
— never Evaded — never Equivocated never dodged — nor turned
a Corner to avoid any chastisement or other responsibility. He never
swore or used profane language in my presence nor in others that
I now remember of — He duly reverenced old age — loved those
best about his own age — played with those under his age — he
listened to the aged — argued with his Equals — but played with
the children —. He loved animals genery and treated them Kindly:
he loved children well very well —. There seemed to be nothing unusual in his love for animals or his own Kind — though he treated
Every body & Every thing Kindly — humanely — Abe didnt Care
much for crowds of people: he choose his own Company which
was always good. He was not very fond of girls as he seemed to me.
He sometimes attended Church. He would repeat the sermon over
again to the children. The sight of such a thing amused all and did
Especially tickle the Children. When Abe was reading My husband
took particular Care not to disturb him — would let him read on
and on till Abe quit of his own accord. He was dutiful to me always
— he loved me truly I think. I had a son John who was raised with
Abe Both were good boys, but I must Say — both now being dead
that Abe was the best boy I Ever Saw or Ever Expect to see. I wish
I had died when my husband died. I did not want Abe to run for
Presdt — did not want him Elected — was afraid Somehow or
other — felt it in my heart that Something would happen him and
when he came down to see me after he was Elected Presdt I still felt
that Something told me that Something would befall Abe and that I
should see him no more. Abe & his father are in Heaven I have no
doubt, and I want to go there — go where they are — God bless Abm[6]

Sally refutes all myths about stepmothers. Few stepmothers, or even birth mothers, can say their child "never gave me a cross word or look and never refused in fact, or even in appearance, to do any thing I requested of him." Granted, this memory comes from an elderly woman remembering her assassinated, famous stepson. Yet without question he was "dutiful" to her and cared for her deeply.

Although Lincoln visited his Coles County family infrequently, often when he came to the area for legal business, he cared about Thomas and Sally's comfort, providing some financial support. His most significant contribution came in 1841 when he purchased forty acres of land from Thomas for two hundred dollars. The land, now in Abraham's name, was protected from Thomas's creditors while Thomas and Sally enjoyed "use and entire control" of the land for the remainder of their lives.[7] Lincoln's concern for his stepmother grew after Thomas died in 1851. In a letter to his stepbrother, John D. Johnston, on November 25, 1851, Lincoln said of his "mother," "I want her to have her living, and I feel that it is my duty, to some extent, to see that she is not wronged."[8] Those Lincoln felt Sally needed protection from included her own family, especially John D. and his financial dealings. The most famous Lincoln journey to Coles County occurred on January 30, 1861, just weeks before he left Illinois to become president. It was their last visit; Sally outlived her stepson by four years, dying in 1869.[9]

Sally offered a sound explanation for her close bond with Lincoln when she told Herndon, "His mind & mine . . . seemed to run together." Much of what she remembered—perhaps at Herndon's probing — she summed up in the comment, "He didn't like physical labor—was diligent for knowledge." Indeed the young man revealed in her comments wanted to understand the world by reading books and newspapers; and Sally and Thomas encouraged him. John Hanks remembered, "When Lincoln, Ab & I returned to the house from work, he would go to the Cupboard — Snatch a piece of Corn bread — take down a book — Sit down on a chair — Cock his legs up as high as his head and read."[10] The reference to Abraham's not caring about his appearance, not caring about girls, and being temperate in all things contrasts starkly with her son, John D., who was the direct opposite.[11]

It is more difficult to explain the relationship between Abraham and Thomas, than that between Abraham and Sally. Although early biographers described Thomas as a shiftless drifter, recent scholarship has revised that view, especially for the Kentucky and Indiana years, focusing attention on a

Thomas Lincoln died in 1851 and was buried in the Gordon or Shiloh Cemetery in Coles County, Illinois. Sarah was buried next to Thomas in 1869. His grave was unmarked until local poet George Bell Balch, believed to be the man in this photo, wrote a poem drawing attention to the grave in 1876. The monument seen here was erected in 1880. This monument was moved to another part of the cemetery after 1924 when the current tombstone marking both of their graves was placed.

new consideration. Perhaps John Y. Simon best illustrates this focus by saying that Louis A. Warren's search of contemporary documents

> revealed a man more nearly typical of his time: a man who owned horses and livestock, paid his share of taxes, assembled cash and credit to acquire farmland, served the county when necessary, and maintained his standing in the local Baptist church. Based upon records rather than recollections, a portrait of Thomas as sturdy pillar of a frontier community rather than shiftless drifter provides more solid ground for interpretation. Yet neither portrait alone will illuminate the tangled relationship of father and son. The importance of Thomas Lincoln lies less in who he was than in what his son thought about him.[12]

Not surprisingly, Sally portrays her husband as someone supportive of Abraham. Thomas "never made Abe quit reading to do anything if he could avoid it. He would do it himself first." Family member Dennis Hanks responded to Herndon's question about Thomas's treatment of Abraham by saying, "He [Thomas] loved him   I Never Could tell whether Abe Loved his farther Very well or Not I Don't think he Did for Abe was one of those forward Boys I have Seen his farther Nock him Down of the fence when a Stranger would Call for information to neighbour house."[13]

Just as Sally formed a strong bond with her stepson, Abraham, Thomas developed a close relationship with his stepson, John D., and they shared similar views of life. John D. and Abraham maintained a close relationship during the Indiana years as evidenced in stories of boyish pranks and mischief; of course, there may have existed some sibling rivalry as well.[14]

Whatever the relationship between father and son while they lived together, the relationship between Abraham and Thomas became more strained as years passed in Illinois. It is difficult to explain Lincoln's refusal to visit his dying father in 1851 and his failure to take his sons to visit their grandparents. Lincoln's reasons for neither visiting his father nor attending his funeral—a demanding workload and a sick wife—sound disingenuous.

Rodney O. Davis concludes that Lincoln's attitude toward his father was greatly influenced by his success as a middle-class lawyer and becoming the husband of a woman from a patriarchal family. Each man failed to understand the other's world.[15]

6

"He loved us all"
Matilda Johnston Hall Moore

Matilda Johnston Hall Moore joined the Lincoln family at age ten when Thomas Lincoln married her mother, Sarah (Sally) Bush Johnston, and brought the family to Indiana in late 1819. Matilda lived with the family until she married Dennis Hanks's half brother Squire Hall in 1826 and then lived as a close neighbor. Matilda and her family were part of the extended Lincoln family that moved to Illinois in 1830. After Squire Hall died in 1851, she married a widower, Reuben Moore, in 1856. He died in 1859. Her second marriage was apparently unhappy.[1]

Sarah Lincoln lived with Matilda in Farmington, south of Charleston, Illinois, on January 31, 1861, when the president-elect paid his last visit to his stepmother and stepsister. Because Matilda was not prepared to provide dinner for the special guest and others who wanted to visit the president elect, she asked her neighbor, Mrs. N. S. Freeman, for help. One who attended the repast remembered, years later, that an appropriate meal resulted when the neighbors "brought their nicest cakes and pies, baked turkeys and chickens."[2]

No wonder William H. Herndon insisted on speaking with Matilda Moore:

Sept 8th 1865 — at Mrs Lincolns House
Mrs More — once Mrs Hall — once Miss Johnson —

I am the youngest Step Sister of A Lincoln — remember Coming from Ky — remember Ohio River — My Earliest recollection of Abe is playing — Carrying water about one mile — had a pet cat that would follow him to the spring went to school — about 2 miles or more — Abe was not Energetic Except in one thing — he was active & persistant in learning read Everything he Could — Ciphered on boards — on the walls — read Robinson Crusoe — the bible — Watts hymns —. When father & Mother woud go to Church, they walked about 1 ½ miles — Sometimes rode — When they were gone — Abe would take down the bible, read a verse — give out a hymn — and we would sing — were good singers. Abe was about 15 years of age —: he would preach & we would do the Crying — sometimes he would join in the Chorus of Tears — One day my bro John Johnston caught a land terrapin — brought it to the place where Abe was preaching — threw it against the tree — crushed the shell and it Suffered much — quivered all over — Abe preached against Cruelty to animals, Contending that an ants life was to it, as sweet as ours to us — Abe read I think Grimshaws History of the U.S — and other books — Cant now remember what — Abe would go out to work in the field — get up on a stump and repeat almost word for word the sermon he had heard the Sunday before — Call the Children and friends around him — His father would come and make him quit — send him to work — Often Abe would make political speeches such as he had heard spoken or seen written &c —. He never forgot anything — was truthful, good to me — good to all — Once when he was going to the field to work I ran — jumped on his back — cut my foot on the axe — we said — "What will we tell Mother as to how this happened: I said I would tell her "I cut my foot on the axe" that will be no lie — said Lincoln, but it won't be all the truth — the whole truth — will it Tilda — Tell the whole truth and risk your Mother Abe seemed to love Every body and Every thing: he loved us all and Especially Mother — My Mother, I think has given Abes character well — I am about 50 years of age —

    This was taken down by me from the lips of Mrs Moore at Mrs Lincoln's House as she Spoke it at the time — Done in the Presence of Mrs Lincoln and the family — including Col Chapman who took me out W H Herndon[3]

Moore's comments are consistent with ones Herndon hears from other Lincoln contemporaries. Many mentioned Lincoln's desire to read and his kindness to animals. The reference to mimicking preachers, complete with a crying congregation, not only illustrates Lincoln's retentive memory, but also documents the practice that children did not always accompany parents to church services. The reference to carrying water for a mile parallels the account by Dennis Hanks that no source of water lay close by on the Lincoln farm.[4]

LEFT: Matilda Johnston Hall Moore was Lincoln's stepsister and was visited by William H. Herndon in 1865.
ABOVE: It was in this house in Farmington, Illinois, that the dinner for President-Elect Abraham Lincoln was held on January 31, 1861. Sarah Lincoln and other family members and friends attended this event.

COURTESY OF THE COLES COUNTY HISTORICAL SOCIETY

WILLIAM E. BARTELT

7

"[I] knew him intimately and well"
Dennis Friend Hanks

No one living in 1865 knew more intimately the story of Abraham Lincoln's Indiana years than Dennis Friend Hanks. Hanks was Lincoln's mother's cousin, Lincoln's foster brother, and Lincoln's stepsister's husband. In the selection that follows, Hanks says of Lincoln, "[I] knew him intimately and well from the day of his birth to 1830."[1]

Hanks came to Indiana in 1817 with his foster parents, Thomas and Elizabeth Sparrow, to live in the abandoned, three-sided camp Thomas Lincoln built. Nevertheless, Hanks speaks of the Lincoln move and the early days in Indiana as if he had been present. Hanks could have visited the Lincolns in Indiana before he moved there permanently. Even though Hanks probably heard this information secondhand, most likely from the stories the Lincolns told of their move and difficulties establishing a home on the Indiana frontier, his stories cannot be discounted.

Hanks was in Abraham's company constantly from 1818 until 1830. After the Sparrows and Nancy Hanks Lincoln died, Hanks joined the Lincoln household. He continued to live with the Lincolns even after Thomas married Sarah (Sally) Bush Johnston and brought her family to the cabin. Legally Hanks became a member of the family when, in 1821, he married Sally's daughter Elizabeth Johnston. The Hanks family lived on a neighboring farm east of the Lincolns, and they moved in the caravan to Macon County, Illinois, in 1830. Furthermore, Hanks and his family accompanied Thomas and Sally Lincoln to Coles County in 1831. The Hankses and their children remained closely associated with Thomas and Sally for the rest of the Lincolns' lives.

Hanks, no doubt, enjoyed the notoriety of the close association with the president of the United States during the Civil War. But his real celebrity status developed after Lincoln's assassination. In the summer of 1865 the Lincoln cabin from Macon County, Illinois, was exhibited at the Chicago Sanitary Fair, and here Hanks found an audience for his tales of the martyred president.[2]

At that Sanitary Fair William H. Herndon initiated his association with Hanks. On June 8, 1865, Erastus Wright of Springfield, Illinois, interviewed Hanks and his cousin John Hanks for Herndon. Herndon, finding the interview both intriguing and confusing, traveled to Chicago from Springfield so he could continue the interview with Dennis.[3]

Herndon visited Hanks at the Sanitary Fair on June 13, 1865, to obtain answers to questions Herndon had earlier written to Hanks. Hanks readily shared his memories while Herndon wrote comments in letter form and requested that Hanks sign the document.[4] Herndon, a lawyer, surely realized that oral history, especially that offered by Hanks, like testimony, must be carefully scrutinized. In fact, some who knew the Lincoln cousin warned Herndon "to be careful about what Hanks said."[5] Eventually Herndon concluded that Hanks was "a blow-exag[g]erator—not a wilful liar."[6]

Lincoln's cousin Dennis Hanks married Lincoln's stepsister Elizabeth Johnston on June 14, 1821, in Spencer County. This undated photo shows the couple. Elizabeth died in 1864, one year before William H. Herndon started interviewing family members.

The interview begins with a tedious section on the Lincoln and Hanks genealogies. It is confusing and inaccurate. Hanks was not knowledgeable about the Lincoln family history, and, although he was more familiar with the Hanks family, it is unclear if he was willing to be completely honest. One of the most debated Lincoln topics remains the Hanks genealogy, specifically, was Lincoln's mother, Nancy, born out of wedlock? Hanks dismissed that assertion, blaming such rumors on political enemies, telling Herndon her name was actually Nancy Sparrow, not Nancy Hanks, as Lincoln himself said. One researcher, Paul H. Verduin, concluded that Nancy's mother, Lucey Hanks, did marry Henry Sparrow, but not until years after Nancy's birth. Herndon's interest in the topic resulted from a conversation with Lincoln in which Lincoln implied his grandfather was "a well-bred Virginia planter."[7] After further questioning, Herndon concluded that Hanks was covering information to protect the family image.[8] This debate continues today.

Next Hanks discussed his memory of the Lincolns before the move to Indiana and the physical and personality traits of Thomas and Nancy.

> Her memory was strong — her [perception?] was quick — her judgement was accute almost. She was Spiritually & ideally inclined — not dull — not material — not heavy in thought — feeling or action. Her hair was dark hair — Eyes bluish green — keen and loving. Her weight was one hundred-thirty —. Thomas Lincoln Abrahams father — was 5 — 10 ½ high — very stoutly built and weighed 196 pounds — His hair dark — his Eyes hazel. He was a man of great streght & courage — not one bit of Cowardice about him — He could [*illegible*] fatigue for any length of time — was a man of uncommon Endurance.

And later adds:

> Thomas Lincoln the father of Abraham could beat his son telling a story — cracking a joke — Mr Thomas Lincoln was a good, clean, social, truthful & honest man, loving like his wife Evry thing & every body.[9]

Hanks claims to have been Lincoln's first teacher in spelling, reading, and writing. This may be one of those exaggerations Herndon mentioned. Ten years older than Abraham, Hanks may have helped the boy with his studies; but soon the student advanced beyond the teacher.

Whereas much of Hanks's information is unreliable, Herndon soon realized that Hanks's comments on life in pioneer Indiana—the Lincolns' day-to-day life—were valuable.[10] Those Indiana years are the topic of the last two-thirds of the June 13, 1865, interview. Since Hanks's comments are so extensively quoted in Lincoln literature, this part of the interview must be examined in its entirety. Here then is the "raw stuff of history" as recorded by Herndon at the Sanitary Fair:

> At about the year 1818 [*sic*] Thomas Lincoln — the father of Abraham had a notion in his head — formed a determination to sell out his place and move to Indiana, then a new State where he could buy land as said before at $125 per. He sold out to_____ Mr Lincoln got $300 — and took it— the $300 — in whisky. The 30 acre farm in Ky was a knotty — knobby as a piece of land could be — with deep hollows — ravines — cedar trees Covering the parts — knobs — knobs as thick as trees could grow. Lincolns hous was in a hollow — high — tall & peaky hills & borded with cedar. Stood up against the sky all around — Mr Lincoln as stated before sold his farm for whisky. He cut down trees — made a kind of flat boat out of yellow poplar. He made the boat on the Rolling fork at the mouth of Knob Creek Hardin Co Ky — loaded his household furniture — his tools — whisky and other Effects, including pots — vessels — rifles. &c. &c on the boat. He took no dogs — chickens — cats — geese or other domestic animals. He floated on awhile down the Rolling Fork and upset — and lost the most of the tools &c and some of his Whisky. He went along by himself not taking his family. From the Rolling Fork he ran into the Beach fork and thence into the great Ohio. He landed at Thompsons Ferry at *Poseys* — house or farm. He started out from this ferry in search of a place and found one and located it by making blazes — brush heaps &c to make a location, which he afterwards bought at $2.00 per acre — purchased it under the $2.00 act. This was an 80 a tract, and Mr Lincoln not being able to pay for it, lost his $80 which he paid to the government and which the government kept and has to-day —. When he had Cornered the land — blazed it off — marked the boundaries he proceeded on horse back, with his own food & his horses fodder behind him to Vincennes where he paid the $200

Although a character and perhaps an exaggerator, Lincoln's cousin Dennis Hanks became the best source of information on the early years of the future president.

per acre as stated before. Mr Lincoln never owned the land — more than a kind of preemption right & sold it when he moved to Ills. I fared like him in all these particulars.[11]

Hanks reported correctly that he himself held only a preemption right to his Indiana land, but he was incorrect when he reported the same for Thomas. The transaction resulting in Thomas's receiving a land patent for eighty acres from the United States government has already been discussed. Hanks's references to "$125 per" land should actually be $1.25 per acre. When the Lincolns arrived in Indiana land cost $2.00 an acre, but could be purchased on credit. That price dropped when the U.S. government eliminated the credit option after the panic of 1819.

In 1817 Thomas Barritt filed for the quarter section adjacent on the east to the quarter section Thomas claimed. On September 27, 1820, Barritt assigned the land to Hanks for an unknown amount, and Hanks and his family lived there. Hanks assigned the land to James Gentry on May 9, 1826, but probably continued to live on the land until the move to Illinois. Also from 1823 to 1825 Hanks had a claim on land south of the Lincoln farm. He owned no land at the time of the Illinois move.[12]

The final part of this interview reveals details about Lincoln's youth that only someone who lived in the same cabin could testify to. Hanks said:

> He then returned to the State of Kentucky from Spencer Co Indiana, then Perry Co — since divided — as Hardin Co Ky was — as Sangamon Co —. From the old homestead in Ky Hardin — now Lareau Co Thomas Lincoln — Nancy father & mother of Sarah & Abe ther two children, & two feather beds —clothing &c mounted 2 horses and went back to Spencer Co — then Perry Co Indian where said land was located on a little Creek Called pigeon Creek — about north of the Ohio — & about 70 miles north west of Hardin Co Ky — & across & north of the Ohio —. They had no waggons — no dogs — cats — hogs — cows — chickens or such like domestic animals. Abe was at this time 7 years of age. — Abe read no books in Ky — Abe was a good boy — an affectionate one — a boy who loved his father & mother dearly & well always minding them well — Sometimes Abe was a little rude. When strangers would ride along & up to his fathers fence Abe always, through pride & to tease his father, would be sure to ask the strang-

er the first question, for which his father would sometimes knock him a rod. Abe was then a rude and forward boy Abe when whipped by his father never bawled but dropt a kind of silent unwelcome tear, as evidence of his sensations — or other feelings. The family landed at Thompson's Ferry on the Ohio & on the other side crossed the Ohio, and landed at Poseys Farm on the Indiana side. Hence 17 miles northwest of the ferry. I went myself with them backwards & forwards — to Indiana — & back to Ky & back to Ky & back to Indiana and know the story & all the facts well. We all started from Ky in Septr 1818 & was three or four days to the ferry & one day from the Ferry out to the place of location — Here they stopt — Camped — erected a little two face Camp open in front, serving a momentary purpose. Lincoln saw a wild turkey near the Camp on the second day after landing and Mrs Lincoln — Abs good mother loaded the gun — Abe poked the gun through the crack of the camp and accidentally killed one, which he brought to the Camp house. Thomas Lincoln then went to cutting trees for the logs of his house — cutting down the brush and underwood — Indiana then being a wilderness and wholly a timbered Country. I assisted him to do this — to cut timber — hawl logs. &c and helped him erect his log Cabin — & Camp — one story high — just high Enough to stand under — no higher. This took only one day. Abe Could do little jobs — such as Carry water — go to the springs — branches &c, for water which was got by digging holes — This was a temporary affair. This was in 1818. We — Lincolns family, including Sally & Abe & my self slept & lodged in this Cabin all winter & till next Spring. We in the winter & spring cut down brush — under wood — trees — cleared ground — made a field of about 6. acres on which we raised our crops —. We all hunted pretty much all the time, Especially so when we got tired of work — which was very often I will assure you. We did not have to go more than 4 or 5 hundred yards to kill deer — turkeys & other wild game. We found bee trees all over the forests. Wild game and were our [fir?] We ate no wild locust, like John The Babtist. We had to go to the Ohio river 17 miles to mill and when we got there the mill was a poor Concern: it was a little bit of a hand horse mill the ground meal of which a hound could Eat as fast as it was ground. Yet this was a God

Send. The mill was close to Posey's. The Country was wild full of game — dense with vegetation —swampy —. We could track a bear — deer — wolf or Indian for miles through the wild matted pea vines. Indians — wild bears — wolves — deers were plenty. We had no trouble with the Indians in Indiana, they soon left and westward. In the fall & winter of 1819 & 20 we Commenced to cut the trees — clear out the brush and underwoods & forest for our new grand old log cabin, which we Erected that winter: it was one Story — 18 by 20 feet — no passage — on window — no glass in it. The lights were made from the leaf Coming off from the hog's fat. This was good mellow light & lasted well. The house was sufficiently high to make a kind of bedroom over head — a loft. This was approached by a kind of ladder made by boring holes in the logs, forming [*illegible*] one side of the house and this peg over peg we Climed aloft, the pegs creaking & screching as we went. Here were the beds — the floor of the loft was clap boards & the beds lay on this. Here I and Abe slept & I was married there to Abes stepsister — Miss Elizabeth Johnston —not Johnson. During this fall Mrs Lincoln was taken sick. with what is known with the Milk sick: she struggled on day day by day — a good Christian woman and died on the 7th day after she was taken sick. Abe & his sister did some work — little jobs — Errand & light work. There was no physician near than 35 miles —She knew she was going to die & Called up the Children to her dying side and told them to be good & kind to their father — to one an other and to the world, Expressing a hope that they might live as they had been taught by her to love men — love — reverence and worship God. Here in this rude house, of the Milk Sick, died one of the very best women in the whole race, known for kindness — tenderness — charity & love to the world. Mrs Lincoln always taught Abe goodness — kindness — read the good Bible to him — taught him to read and to spell — taught him sweetness & benevolence as well. From this up to 1821 — Mr Lincoln lived single, Sarah cooking for us, she then being about 14 years of age. We still Keept up hunting — and farming it Mr Lincoln — Ab's father was a Cabinet maker & house joiner &c —: he worked at this trade in the winter at odd times, farming it — in The summer. We always hunted it made no difference what came for we more or less de-

pended on it for a living — nay for life. We had not been long at the
log Cabin before We got the usual domestic Animals, Known to
Civilization. These were driven out from near the Ohio river or
halled in a cart pulled by one yoke of oxen. Mrs Lincoln was buried
about one fourth of a mile from the log cabin and the babtist
Church, the Pastor was [Lamar?]. Abraham learned to write so that
we could understand it in 1821 —. David Elkin of Hardin Co Ky
— called Parson Elkin whose name has been mentioned before paid
a visit — I do not think Elkin Came at the solicitation & letter
writing of Abe, but Came of his own accord or through the solicitation of the Church to which Mrs Lincoln belonged She being a
hard shell Babtist Abe was now 12 years old. Elkin Came over to
Indiana in about one year after the death of Mrs Elkin — and
preach a funeral sermon on the death of Mrs Lincoln. Parson Elkin
was a good — true — man and the best preacher & finest orator I
Ever heard. I have heard his words distinctly & clearly one fourth of
a mile. Some little time before this funeral service he Thomas
Lincoln went to Kentucky and married Johnson whose maiden
name was Bush. When Thomas Lincoln married her she had 3
children — 2 daughters — & 1 son. The family Came to Indiana
with their Step-father and their own mother. There was now 5
Children in the family — Sarah — & Abe. Lincoln — Elizabeth,
John D — & Matilda Johnston —. I married the Elizabeth. I was
just 21 — She was 15. Thos Lincoln now hurried his farming — his
Calling & business, always remember hunting. Now at this time
Abe was getting hungry for book, reading Evry thing he could lay
his hands on. The marriage of Thomas Lincoln & the widow
Johnson was in 1821 — Abraham being now 12 years old. Websters
old Spelling Book — The life Henry Clay. Robinson Crusoe —
Weems Life of Washington — Esops fables — Bunyan's Pilgrim's
progress —. I do not Sy that Lincoln read thse books just then but
he did between this time & 1825. He was a Constant and I my Say
Stubborn reader, his father having Sometimes to slash him for
neglecting his work by reading. Mr Lincoln — A bs father — often
Said I had to pull the old sow up to the trough — when speaking of
Abes reading & how he got to it, then and now he had to pull her
away" From the time of the marriage Thos Lincoln & Mrs Johnson,

Mrs Lincoln proved an Excellent Step mother: When she Came into Indiana Abe & his sister was wild — ragged & dirty. Mrs Lincoln had been raised in Elizabethtown in somewhat a high life: She Soaped —rubbed and washed the Children Clean so that they look pretty neat — well & clean. She sewed and mended their Clothes & the Children onc more looked human as thir own good mother left them. Thomas Lincoln and Mrs Lincoln never had any Children, accident & nature stopping things short. From 1820 to 1825. Mr Lincoln & Mrs Lincoln Each worked a head at their own business — Thomas at farming — Cabinet making — & hunting: She at Cooking — washing — sewing — weaving &c. &c — About the year 1825 or 1826, Abe borrowed of Josiah Crawford Ramseys life of Washington — which got spoiled as specified generally in The Presidents life and paid as therein described —: he pulled fodder at 25c per dy to py for it. He worked 3 or 4 dys —. Abe was then growing to be a man and about 15 or 16 ys of age. He was then just the Same boy in Evry particular that he subsequently Exhibited to the world from 1831 — to the time of his death — at this Early age he was more humerous than in after life — full of fun — wit — humor and if he Ever got a new story — new book or new fact or ideia he never forgot it. He was honest — faithful — loving truth, Speaking it at all times — & never flinching therefrom. Physically he was a stout & powerful boy — fat round — plump & well made as well as proportioned. This Continued to be so up to the time he landed in Salem. Sangamon County. In 1825 or 1826 he then Exhibited a love for Poetry and wrote a piece of humorous Rhyme on his friend Josiah Crawford that made all the neighbors, Craw-ford included burst their sides with laughter. I had it was lost in the fire. He was humorous funny — witty & good humored in all times. Sarah married a man (Aaron Grigsby): she married him in 1822 and died in about 12 mo in childbed. About 1826 & 7 myself and Abe went down to the Ohio & cut Cord wood at 25c per Cord & bought stuff to make Each a shirt. We were proud of this — It must have been about this time that Abe got kicked by a horse in the mill and who did not Speak for several hours and when he did speak — he ended the sentence which he Commenced to the horse as I am well informed & blieve. From this last period 1825–6 & 7 Lincoln was Constantly reading, writing — cipher a little in Pikes Arithmatic. He Excelled any boy I ever saw, putting his opportunities into Conversation,. He then Some had or got Barclay's English Dictionary — a part of which I have now & which can be seen now at my house — and which I am to give to W H Herndon of the City of Springfield. During these years the ports of Mr Lincoln were hunting — shooting squirrels — jumping — wrstling — playing ball — throwing the mall over head — The story about his Carrying home a drunken man is not true as I think or re cellect. He was good Enough & tender Enough & Kind Enough to have saved Any man from Evil — wrong — difficulties or damnation. Let his claim nothing but what is true — Truth & Justice — & Mankind will make him the great of the world: he needs no fictions to back him. Lincoln sometimes attempted to sing but always failed, but while this is true he was harmony & time — & sound. He loved such music as he knew the words of. He was a tricky man and sometimes when he went to log house raising — Corn shucking & such like things he would say to himself and sometimes to to others — I don't want thes fellows to work any more and instantly he would Commence his pranks — tricks — jokes — stories — and sure Enough all would stop — gather around Abe & listen, sometimes Crying — and sometimes bursting their sides with laughter. He sometimes would mount a stump — chair or box and make speeches — Speech with stories — anecdotes & such like thing: he never failed here. At this time Abe was Somewhat He was now and well as before a kind of forward boy & sometimes forward too when he got stubborn: His nature went an Entire revolution. One thing is true of him — always was up to 1830 when our intimacy ended, because he went to Sangamon & I went to Coles Co.: he was ambitious & determined & when he attempted to Excel by man or boy his whole soul & his Energies were bent on doing it — and he in this generally — almost always accomplished his Ends. From these years 1826 — & 7 what has been said of other years is applicable up to 1830 — working — chopping — toiling — woman child & man —. The plays & sports were the Same. In 1829 (March) Thomas Lincoln moved from Spencer Co Indiana and landed in Macon Co Ills, ten miles west of Decatur. In that spring & summer the log cabin which I now have on Exhibition at the Sanitary fair in Chicago was Erected. Lincoln helped Cut the logs — so did John Hanks — Abe halled them & I hewed them all in & raised it the next day we raised the Cabin. Abraham & his neighbors had a mall, [railing?] party 1830 and he & they then split the rails to fence the ten acres of land which was done. In the Spring & Summer of 1830 the ten acres of land were broken up with the place —. This was on the north fork of Sangamon River in Macon Co Ills — Lincoln was 20 years of when he left Indiana, not 21 — as said in the Books. In the fall of 1830 he went down the Sangamon, he then being 21 years of age with John Hanks in a boat of some kind.

I now have told you all I recollect & think worthy of being told. I hope this will put history right, as I have taken time to reflect & to refresh my memory by Conversations — times of well authenticated date — by records — friends & papers. All of which I do hereby certify to be true in substance — time & fact — knowing what is said to be true personally, as I was an actor pretty much all my life in the scene —

Your Friend

D. F. Hanks[13]

Hanks witnessed both the good relationship between Sally and the developing rift between Thomas and his son. Hanks's quotation from Thomas about Abraham's reading—"I had to pull the old sow up to the trough . . . then and now [I] had to pull her away"—indicates Thomas's attitude toward education: he wanted Abraham to learn to read, but not to become obsessed with reading. Abraham's devotion to reading, however, led his father to "slash" him for neglecting work. Hanks described Thomas's manner of discipline, which included "knocking [Abraham] a rod" for acting rude or forward. And Hanks notes that Abraham never cried when whipped by his father.

Herndon visited Hanks a second time on his September 1865 visit to Coles County, Illinois. By now Herndon had analyzed earlier information and brought specific questions, especially about Lincoln's political, oratorical, and educational development and the general living conditions in early Indiana. Here is the second interview with Hanks:

Charleston Ills Sept 8th 1865

— (Hon. O. B. Ficklin — and others told me to be careful about what Hanks said)

Dennis Hanks says he is [blank space] years old — Knew Thos Lincoln — Abe & Sister in Ky — think Miss Lincoln went to school in Ky — says that the Lincoln family came from England about 1650 — Two Lincoln's came to Virginia — think on the head waters of the Roanoke — probably in Halifax Co — were not Puritans — were not Quakers — never were in Penn. I opposed Abe in Politics when he became whig — was till 20 years of age a Jackson Democrat — turned whig — or whiggish about 1828–9 — think Col Jones made him a whig — dont know it — The two original Lincolns had [blank space] children — (Here I closely & critically Examined Hanks and he confessed he knew nothing — Except as above stated — backed down from his Chicago letter to me. Dennis gets gloriously tight — drinks to hard — is not to be relied on always —) — think Abe Lincoln's grandfathers name was Mordacai He was born in Virginia about 1740 — Mordecai the grandfather of Abe, had 3 sons — Mordecai — Thos — & Josias — & 2 daughters — Krume married one of them — Abe was born in 1809 on the farm his father sold to [blank space] — the farm is about 4 ½ SE of Hodgensville Ky — Hardin Co — or now La Rue. The farm is on Knob Creek — Abe used to go with me down the branch to shoot fish in puddles & holes washed by the water — killed a fawn — Abe was tickled to death — Abe Exhibited no special traits in Ky, Except a good kind — somewhat wild nature — Thos Lincoln moved to Indiana about 1816 in what was Called Perry Co — now Spencer Co Indiana — moved on 2 horses — not a waggon — Abe rode with his mother & Sally with her father — Lincolns farm in Indiana is about 15 north of the Ohio River— and about 80 miles NW of Hodgensville. The Illinois farm of Thos Lincoln is worth about $1200 — Knew all these farms well — the Ky farm when Thos Lincoln left it contained in cultivated land only six acres running up & down the branch — about 40 feet wide on either side — Hills 300 or 400 feet high — Covered once with heavy timber — some ceder on the Knobs — Shrubs — &c. up the hills sides — Vallys narrow and deep —

When we landed in Indiana in 1817 I think there were lots
of bears — deer — turkeys — ate them as meat — water & bread
— the Country was full of chestnuts — Pawpaws — wild pea vines
— or wild [lusty?] peas &c — Could track bears — wolves — horses — cattle & men for miles through and by the pea vine — would
direct People by the tracks thus made when they wanted to find
a place to go — got hogs in Ky — took them to Indiana — bears
got among them — scared them — swam the Ohio went back to
old homes in Ky — Saw them —knew them —: Abe could when
15 years of age or in the year 1824, could hear a Sermon — Speech
or remark and repeat it accurately — He would go home from the
church say to the boys & girls that he could repeat the Sermon
— got on Stumps — logs — fences and do it well and accurately
— Old People have heard him do it o'er & o'er again — have told
me so — Could do the Same in what he heard and read. Lincoln
would frequently make political and other Speeches to the boys
— he was calm — logical & clear alwys — He attended trials
— went to Court — read the Rev. Statutes of Indiana dated 1824
— Heard law Speeches & listened to law trials &c &c — Lincoln
was lazy — a very lazy man — He was always reading — scribbling
— writing — Ciphering — writing Poetry &c. &c — He was a head
& shoulders above us all — would learn us — set our Copies — The
school only taught reading — writing and Ciphering — Ciphered
up to single rule of three, never got up to the double rule of three
—. Thomas Lincoln Entered the farm in Ills in 1834 — Mortaded
it to the School Comms — Abe paid the debt $200 — Thos Lin-
coln conveyed the farm to Abe reserving in the land a life Estate
for him & his wife — and at their death the fee goes to Abe —Abe
gave a bond to — Jno D Johnson — saying that if Johnson & his
heirs woud on the death of Thos Lincoln & wife and in one year
thereafter pay said $200 — that he Lincoln would convey to them
— if they would pay interest to L at the rate of 6 per ct from the
death of Thos L & wife — deed dated Octr 25th 1841 — Bond or
agreement of Abe to Johnson about same date — (see Records in
Charleston Ills — Book C.E.G — &c).

    To the question put by me to Hanks — "How did Lincoln &
yourself learn so much in Indiana under such disadvantages" he

replied — "We learned by sight — scent & hearing — We heard
all that was said & talked over & over the questions heard — wore
them slick — greasy & threadbare — Went to political & other
speeches & gathering as you do now — we would hear all sides &
opinions — talk them over — discuss them agreeing or disagreeing
— Abe as I said before was originally a Democrat after the order of
Jackson — so was his father — so we all were — Abe turned whig
in 1827–8. — He preached Made Speeches — read for us — Explained to us &c — sang from Watts hymns — from Dupay's —.
Abe was a cheerful boy — a witty boy — was humorous always —
sometimes would get sad — not very often — He would Joke — tell
stories — run rigs — &c on the boys — Didn't love the Company
of girls — didn't love crowds as a general rule — was a *retired* boy
— & a good listener to his Superiors — bad to his inferiors — that
is he Couldn't Endure Jabber — Could good [sense?] while he was
learning —

One day a Yankee came round and said to Thomas Lincoln that
he could find water on his farm — would do so by a divining rod
&c. for the sum of five dollars — Old Man Lincoln couldnt beleive
such stuff — Thos Lincoln had dug his hill to find water with a
honey Comb as it were — wanted water badly — but said to the
Yankee this — "Do you suppose I am going to give you $5 — for a
pig in the polk." In Gentryvill about 1 m west of Thomas L's farm
Lincoln would go and tell his jokes — stories &c. and he was so odd
— original and humorous & witty that all the People in town would
gather around him — He would keep them there till midnight or
longer telling stories — cracking jokes — & running rigs — &c—. I
would get tired — want to go home — cuss Abe — &c. most hearty
Lincoln was a great talker — a good reader & was a kind of news
boy — Hanks went to Indiana about the time of the 2 marriage in
1819 of Thos Lincoln. Abe was so attatched to reading that we had
to buy him — hire him to work — bought him, I think the Colum-
bian Orator or American Preceptor. We were Excellent bow shots
— a squirrel couldnt Escape unless he got in his hole and then if
Abe took the notion he would pull him or it out of his hole — Abe
was born on Knob Creek which runs into the rolling fork — thence
into & then into the Ohio River —. Abe made no mark in Ky

worthy of being Known: when he left there he was only 7 ys old
— The date of the Copy book which you have got or a leaf of which
&c — is dated 1824 — one part & the 2d pt 1826 — This book he
made in Indiana — I bought the paper — gave it to Abe — Barclay's
dictionary is dated 1799 — & the family Bible 1818 — Abe used
both — his hand writing is in both — in a rough School boy's hand
— Hall brought the Dictionary to Indiana in [blank space] & Thos
Lincoln brought the Bible in 1818 — or 19 — Lincoln didnt read
the Bible half as much as said: he did read it — I thought he never
believed it and think so still —

This I copied from notes taken on the Spot nearly in Hanks
own words — copied this the 20th dy of Sept 1865 — in my office
in presence of Zane & our Student Johnson read it to him — I say it
is correct

On the Copy book of Mr Lincoln — a part of which is given
me is this Expression

"Abraham Lincoln is my name
I'll be a good boy — God knows when"

This is in his hand writing and I think I give the Exact words.
W H Herndon[14]

As if to remind himself later, Herndon recorded in this interview others' assessments of Hanks and remarked that "Dennis gets gloriously tight
— drinks to hard—is not to be relied on always." Herndon also observed
that, when challenged on some issues, Hanks "backed down," which perhaps
explains why these notes seem more general with fewer dates and specifics
than the earlier interview.

Not surprisingly Herndon wanted to know the young Lincoln's political views, and Hanks's statements certainly were clearer to Herndon than to
readers today. When the Lincolns arrived in Indiana, the country was in the
midst of the "era of good feelings." But when the Federalist Party collapsed
following the election of 1816, the first American political party system
also ended. Generally the citizens of the country saw this development as
being positive, and an aversion to political parties emerged. The new system
involved "personal politics," voters supporting individual political leaders
rather than party organizations. By the time Lincoln was twenty years old,
a new political party system—the one Lincoln became a player in—had

begun evolving.[15]

The presidential election of 1824 concluded with the House of Representatives selecting John Quincy Adams. Andrew Jackson of Tennessee won more popular and electoral votes than Adams, but not the majority of electoral votes needed. Jackson and his followers felt robbed and began a campaign to capture the presidency in 1828. By that election, political parties assisted the leaders' chances of election. Henry Clay became leader of the National Republicans, supporting Adams's reelection, while Jackson became the leader of the Democratic Party. The parties disagreed on issues such as internal improvements, tariffs, and the Bank of the United States. Political tension escalated, and by 1834 anti-Jackson supporters founded the Whig Party.

Certainly these developments energized political discussion in Spencer County, and residents doubtless heard, in Hanks's words, "all sides & opinions" and debated the views. Hanks maintained that early on he, Abraham, and Thomas all favored Jackson, and there is no good reason to doubt this statement. In fact, Nathaniel Grigsby supported that view, "We were all Jackson boys & men at this time in Indiana."[16]

Unfortunately the township election results for the 1820s were lost in the 1833 Spencer County Courthouse fire. However, aggregate results for the county are illustrative of the views of Lincoln and his neighbors. In 1824 electors for Clay received 33 votes, Jackson 10, and Adams 5.[17] Obviously, in this "election of favorite sons" many transplanted Kentuckians supported Clay. But the 1828 results differed significantly: electors for Adams received 74 while Jackson's electors won 173.[18] Without Clay on the ballot, Spencer County citizens obviously felt their interests lay with westerner Jackson, not easterner Adams.[19]

As Lincoln heard the views expressed, read the newspapers, and discussed the issues—such as higher tariffs, funds for roads and canals, and aid to manufactures—with men such as William Jones, he came to support the views that emerged, within a decade, as the Whig Party. Jones, a merchant, naturally favored the pro-economic development ideas. Jones was not born in Kentucky, but in Vincennes, Indiana, and his father had worked actively in Indiana territorial politics as a political ally of William Henry Harrison.[20]

Herndon's second interview with Hanks stresses Lincoln's curiosity and his ability to learn from the world around him. In fact Hanks credits Lincoln's education not to schooling but to his ability to reflect upon the ideas and sensory perceptions he heard around him and to use this knowledge to understand his world. By implication, schools taught students to read and figure, but individuals educated themselves.

The story about the Yankee and the divining rod introduces a topic historians have long pondered: Why would Thomas locate his homestead on a hill without a reliable water supply? His family needed water for survival, and livestock needed even more water. Ward Hill Lamon quotes Hanks as stating that Thomas "riddled his land like a honeycomb" in search of water, and the Lincoln children carried water from a spring a mile away.[21] Matilda Johnston Hall Moore, Lincoln's stepsister, also told Herndon about carrying water for a mile after she came to live with the family. Today, however, the Lincoln spring, located at the base of the hill about three hundred feet from the cabin site at the Lincoln Boyhood National Memorial is identified as the source for the Lincolns' water. How can this incongruity be explained?

Thomas purchased a tract of land that originally belonged to David Casebier and was just west of the Lincoln property. The spring near the cabin flowed on the eastern edge of the Casebier property. Thus, the Lincolns settled near a water supply, but it was not on their land. One explanation is that when Thomas failed to find his own water, he simply purchased the tract with the spring.

Herndon never interviewed Hanks again, although he corresponded with him from December 12, 1865, to September 20, 1866. Herndon posed questions, and Hanks responded in sixteen letters. Most letters were brief with specific answers to questions raised. Hanks's answers raised more questions, and the two men repeated the process. At times, the comments are funny, such as when Herndon noted that Hanks wrote his previous letter in pencil. Hanks responded on December 24, 1865, "you Speake of My Letter written with a pencil the Reason of this was My Ink was frose."[22]

The first letter Hanks addressed to "Der Sir," but by December 27 the salutation became "Friend Billy." The following is an example of Dennis Hanks's diction, grammar, and spelling:

January the 6th 1866

Friend Billy

I Received your Letter January the 3d
    The first question that you ask is this what has Be Cum of John

BESS V. EHRMANN, *THE MISSING CHAPTER IN THE LIFE OF ABRAHAM LINCOLN* (CHICAGO: WALTER M. HILL, 1938)

William Jones was born in Vincennes, Indiana, and witnessed the development of the Indiana Territory. He came to Spencer County around 1828. Lincoln worked for Jones and also read his newspapers and discussed the events of the day with Jones. Jones became a merchant, state legislator, and was a lieutenant colonel when he was killed in the Civil War.

Hall   he was in town to Day   You Say that have writen 3 or 4 Letters to him and got No answer   what was it Billy that you wanted to No of him   I can answer all that he can he cant write very well he Does Not No Much a Bout the Old Man Lincoln for he was a Boy at his Death   he has Nothing to Do with writing to any one a Bout the Life of Lincoln it Dependes on Me to Do all this   I have writen a Letter to Josiah Crofford in Spencer County Indiana Concerning Books that Abe Read   I have No answer yet

Next question   how many people was at Mrs Lincoln furnel at hir Beriel   Thare was a Bout 20 persons the hole Nabour hood   Do you Mean hir funerl preaced or hir interment in the grown   I have jest Seen John Hall   he Says that he got your Letters But Could Not answer any of them   ask Me the questions   I will Answer them Satisfacttory   at Mrs Lincoln furnel preched was By David Elkins of Hardin County Ky   Cum to pay us a Visit and preacht hir furnel   the Customs of the people at time was very Ruff Drinking a Little whisky Corn Shuckings Log Rolings &c — No Dancing as Sum Did — Shooting Maches throwing the Mall over head.

Size of the fields from. 10. 12 16 20 acors Raised Corn Mostly Sum wheat a Nuf for a Cake a Sundy Morning

Hogs and Venison hams was a Legal tender and Coon Skins all so

we Raised Sheep and Cattle But they Did not fecth Much Cows and Calfes was onely worth 6 Dollars Corn 10 cts wheat 25 at that time

I think I will Be able to tell you all a Bout these things   I take plesure in Doing

Yours Respectfuly
D. F. Hanks
Not well at this time
Now a Bout the timber   it was Black walnut and Black oake hickory and Jack oake Elm and white oake under grooth Dogwood in a Bundance grape vines and Shewmake Bushes and Milk Sick plenty   all of My Relitives Died with that Disease on Little pigeon Creek Spencer County

this all at this time[23]

John Hall, the man Hanks says "cant write very well," was the son of Matilda Johnston and Squire Hall and was born the year before the family left Indiana.

Undoubtedly major problems occur in information obtained from Hanks. Nevertheless, as eminent historian David Donald concludes, "his two interviews with Herndon constitute one of the best accounts of Lincoln's Indiana years. Dennis was boastful and sometimes he made mistakes, but most of his statements have the authentic ring of truth."[24]

Part Three
THE NEIGHBORS
Remember Lincoln
in Indiana

8

"Old friends of my boyhood"
The Little Pigeon Creek Community

On October 23, 1860, Abraham Lincoln wrote his Indiana friend David Turnham, concluding his letter with these words: "I would much like to visit the old home, and old friends of my boyhood, but I fear the chance for doing so soon, is not very good."[1]

The Indiana region where Lincoln lived was indeed frontier, but it was not unpopulated. It was a community, and Lincoln left many friends there in 1830. To appreciate Lincoln's Indiana years, more must be known about the community he lived in and the people he met daily.

After the War of 1812, Indiana beckoned Americans eager to move west for new opportunities. The main obstacle to settling the Indiana Territory—Indian resistance—had been removed by the war. The U.S. government surveyed the land and enticed settlers with a land-credit-purchase system. Some of these new residents moved from New England, a larger number from the Mid-Atlantic States, but most from the upland South—in the case of the Lincoln community, from Kentucky.[2]

It is not possible to determine exactly how many inhabitants lived in the Lincoln neighborhood because early settlers did not immediately—or ever—officially claim land from the U.S. government. Early claims lay along the Ohio River with few inland near the Lincoln land. But dramatic change occurred quickly in this sparsely settled region. For instance, a study for the National Park Service of land entries for eight townships around the Lincoln farm before 1830 found that 80 to 90 percent of entries were recorded from 1817 to 1819.[3]

Springfield, Ills. Oct 23. 1860

David Turnham, Esq

My dear old friend:

Your kind letter of the 17=ᵗʰ
is received. I am indeed very glad
to learn, you are still living and
well— I well remember when you and
I last met, after a separation of
fourteen years, at the Cross-road
voting place, in the fall of 1844.
It is now sixteen years now and
we are both no longer young men—
I suppose you are a grand-fa-
ther; and I, though married
much later in life, have a son
nearly grown—

I would much like to visit the
old home, and old friends of my
boyhood, but I fear the chance
for doing so soon, is not very good.

Your friend & sincere well-wisher A. Lincoln

Lincoln refers to "old friends of my boyhood" in this October 23, 1860, letter to former neighbor David Turnham.

The Original Land Claims in the Indiana Lincoln Neighborhood before 1830

T4S-R6W	T4S-R5W			
25	**30** Michael Wood 1817	**29**		**28**
			Thomas Turnham 1819	William Whitman 1817
36 Peter Brunner 1817 / James Gentry 1818	**31** John Jones 1817 / David Casebier 1817	**32** **Thomas Lincoln 1817** / Thomas Barritt 1817	**33** Thomas Carter 1817	

T5S-R6W	T5S-R5W			
1 William Whittenhill 1818 / James Gentry 1818 James Gentry 1824 / James Gentry 1818	**6** Luther Greathouse 1817 Samuel Howell 1817	**5** John Carter 1817 / John Carter 1818 Noah Gorden 1818	**4** J. & E. Davidson 1817 / Moses Randel 1817	
12 Noah Gorden 1821	**7** Noah Gorden 1818	**8**	**9** Amos Richardson 1817 David Edwards 1817	
13 Benoni Hardin 1818	**18** Reuben Grigsby 1816	**17** Reuben Grigsby 1818 / J. Crawford 1826 William Barker 1824	**16**	
24 Benoni Hardin 1818 / Henry Gonterman 1818 Benoni Hardin 1818	**19** Reuben Grigsby 1818	**20**	**21**	

This map shows the land claimed before 1830 in the area traditionally known as the Little Pigeon Creek community. About one-third of the land was claimed at this time, with most of the claims being made from 1817 to 1819. The shaded area shows the eighty acres for which Thomas Lincoln received a patent from the U.S. government in 1827.

The immediate Lincoln neighborhood, known as the Little Pigeon Creek community, developed south of a stream that originated five miles northeast of the Lincoln farm. The stream flowed across Spencer County a mile north of the Lincoln farm, and then turned southward. West of Gentryville the creek became the boundary between Warrick and Spencer counties until it flowed into the Ohio River.

The Lincoln neighbors at the time probably did not use Little Pigeon Creek to describe their community. The creek flowed across the very northern edge of the Lincoln neighborhood. Most students of the community define that area as a twenty-four-section or twenty-four-square-mile area, with the Lincoln farm in the northern third. The area most associated with Lincoln extends two miles north, two miles east and west, and four miles south of his home.[4] Federal land records reveal that by 1830 settlers had claimed a third of the land in this twenty-four-square-mile area. Of this third, about 82.8 percent was claimed in 1817 or 1818. Only four new land claims occurred in the area following the panic of 1819.[5]

One Kentucky historian contended that "The Kentucky influence was so pervasive in southern Indiana that one could almost suggest that the youthful Lincoln had never left the farm at Knob Creek."[6] Although Lincoln grew up surrounded by former Kentucky residents, it must be remembered that these new Hoosiers chose a nonslavery environment that afforded more economic opportunity and land-ownership security than did Kentucky.

According to federal land records before 1830, thirty-three men claimed land or were assigned land by the original claimant in the twenty-four-section area identified as the Lincoln neighborhood. With government land records and genealogical files, the origins of twenty-two of these men can be documented. All but one—Thomas Turnham—came to Indiana from Kentucky, and he lived in Kentucky for most of his life before moving briefly to Tennessee. Furthermore, thirteen of these men came from either Hardin or neighboring Nelson County. An additional four men came from adjoining Kentucky counties of Breckinridge, Green, and Washington. Others came from Daviess, Ohio, Muhlenberg, and Allen counties. All of these counties—with the exception of Allen—lie in north-central Kentucky. In addition, there is strong evidence that many of the eleven other men came from this area, too.[7] What emerges then is a transplanted Kentucky neighborhood where many people knew one another before arriving in Indiana; and, in fact, several were kin to one another.

The 1820 federal census offers a community snapshot. Because the 1820 census lists no township or community divisions, to determine the Lincoln neighbors, it is necessary to look at names of people who claimed land in the Lincoln region. Of course, some of the landowners held claims in other parts of the county, and it cannot always be determined where their homes were located. Additionally, residents who lived in the area, but did not claim land (squatters), cannot be identified. There is also the possibility that the census taker missed some of the residents. The following chart describes landowners who probably lived in the twenty-four-section Lincoln neighborhood in 1820.

1820 Federal Census Showing Men Claiming Property in the Lincoln Neighborhood in That Year. (Spellings are as recorded by the census taker.)

Name of household	Male -10	Male 10-15	Male 16-18[1]	Male 16-25	Male 26-44	Male 45+	Female -10	Female 10-15	Female 16-25	Female 26-44	Female 45+	Total
Thomas Lincoln	1	1	0	1	1	0	1	2	0	1	0	**8**
Thomas Caster	3	1	1	1	0	1	1	2	0	1	0	**11**
Thomas Barret	1	0	0	0	1	0	3	0	0	1	0	**6**
John Carter	2	2	0	0	1	0	4	0	0	1	0	**10**
David Edwards	1	0	0	1	2	1	2	2	1	1	0	**11**
James Gentry	2	2	0	0	1	0	2	1	0	1	0	**9**
Henry Gontraman	0	2	0	0	1	1	1	2	0	0	1	**8**
Noah Gorden	1	2	0	1	1	0	4	0	1	1	0	**11**
Reuben Grigsby	3	2	1	1	0	1	2	1	0	1	0	**12**
Samuel Howel	2	0	0	0	1	0	2	2	0	1	1	**9**
Amos Richardson	2	1	0	0	1	0	2	1	0	1	0	**8**
William Whittinghill	2	0	0	1	0	0	1	1	1	0	0	**6**
Thomas Turnham	0	0	3	0	0	1	0	0	0	0	1	**5**
Wm Wood[2]	2	0	0	0	1	0	1	1	0	1	0	**6**
TOTAL	**22**	**13**	**5**	**6**	**11**	**5**	**26**	**15**	**3**	**11**	**3**	**120**

Source: Willard Heiss, comp., *1820 Census for Indiana* (Indianapolis: Genealogy Section of the Indiana Historical Society, 1975)

1. Instructions advise figures in this column were to be repeated in the next column and thus not included in totals, but the Spencer County census taker frequently violated instructions so that both columns were counted.
2. William Wood's name does not appear in land records at this time, but documents testify he lived in the neighborhood.

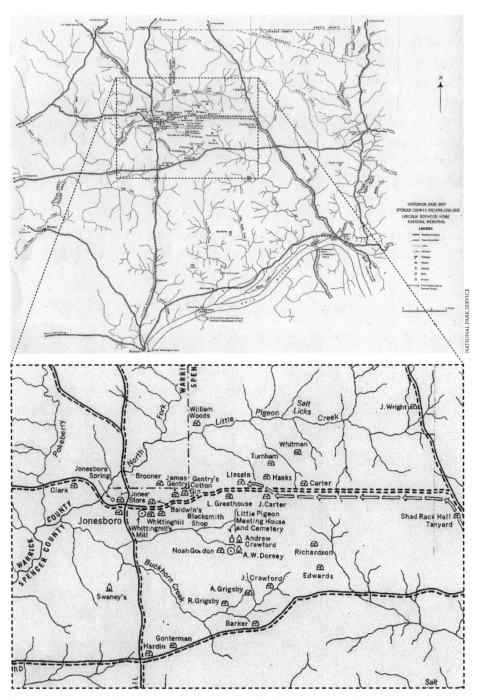

This portion of the "Historical Base Map Spencer County, Indiana, 1816–1830" prepared by the National Park Service shows the approximate locations of neighbors, schools, businesses, and the church in the Little Pigeon community. Jonesboro was probably a later development.

Though likely incomplete, these figures certainly reveal the neighbor-hood demographics, a developing area, and a community of large, young families. The average household comprised about eight people—the same number as the Lincolns. Of the 120 total, 76 (63.3 percent) were under age fifteen. Thus, the eleven-year-old Abraham Lincoln had ample opportunity to make friends near his own age. Only eight (6.6 percent) in the community were over age forty-five. The gender mix of the community was approxi-mately even with sixty-two males and fifty-eight females.[8]

Comparing names in the 1820 and 1830 censuses reveals the commu-nity's fluidity. Of the fifteen head of household names listed in 1820, fewer than half appear in 1830. Only David Edwards Sr. is believed to have died during the decade. Thus, Thomas Lincoln, the man sometimes portrayed as a drifter, was typical for the time he spent in Indiana. In fact, family histories reveal that many settlers spent fewer than the nearly fourteen years he spent in the state.[9]

These new Hoosiers brought with them their upland-southern dialect, values, customs, and beliefs. J. Edward Murr, a Methodist minister in Spen-cer County in the 1890s, became acquainted with some of the Lincolns' neighbors and many of their families. He reported that

> To the pioneer in Lincoln's day the carrying of an edged tool, such as a hoe or ax, through the house was an omen of bad luck, foretell-ing a death in the family during the year. The breaking of a mirror was also another sign of death within that period. The plaintive howling of a dog meant that the morrow would tell of death some-where. The crossing of the hunter's path by a dog meant bad luck in the chase unless the hunter locked his little fingers until the dog was out of sight; or, what was regarded better still, if he returned to the point of starting and began his journey anew, all ill fortune occasioned by the bad start would not be reckoned against him. The writer has frequently witnessed these circumstances.
>
> Friday was a day in the calendar to be avoided in instituting any new departure; that is to say, beginning anything new such as plowing, sowing or reaping in the fields, or the making of a garment, unless the labor could be completed during the day. A bird alighting on the window or coming into the house was a sure sign of sorrow. All planting, sowing, fencing and preparation for the same was to be governed by certain signs of the moon. Plants, such as potatoes, ma-

turing beneath the surface of the soil must be planted in the dark of the moon. And in like manner tomatoes and beans must be planted in the light of the moon.[10]

Sounding superstitious or strange today, these ideas were not unique to residents of the Lincoln neighborhood. Nevertheless, some Lincoln biographers have used Murr's words to unjustly characterize the residents. For example, Albert Beveridge, U.S. senator from Indiana (1899–1911), in his 1928 biography concluded, "In common with most people of the Western country, those on and about Pigeon Creek were very ignorant, rough mannered, vividly superstitious."[11]

Of course, these residents' lives were not governed totally by superstition. Both symbolically and geographically, the Little Pigeon Primitive Baptist Church served as the community's center. Little Pigeon Baptist Church began in neighboring Warrick County in 1816. Finally, in 1819 the congregation decided to build a meetinghouse, and on December 11, 1819, the members selected a site on Noah Gorden's property. In 1821 a committee was selected to make plans for a building "30 x 26 feet, hewed logs, 8 feet in the under story and 6 feet above the joists."[12]

The most valuable extant record of the community is the Little Pigeon Baptist Church's minute book for 1816–40. The original, deerskin-covered book—measuring 34 cm. by 22 cm., with the inner sheets 33.3 cm. by 19.8 cm.—is now at the Abraham Lincoln Presidential Library in Springfield, Illinois.[13] It is a record of beliefs, membership, and monthly business meet-

THE ABRAHAM LINCOLN PRESIDENTIAL LIBRARY, SPRINGFIELD, ILLINOIS

The Minute Book of the Little Pigeon Baptist Church is a record not only of the church but also a glimpse into the dialect and values of the community. Shown here is the entry for Thomas "Linkhon." Sarah joined the same day.

ings. The book remained the property of the church until the members sold it in 1943 to Hilbert Bennett of Rockport for $1,000.[14]

Although Lincoln was not a member of the church—it appears most young people did not join until near their marriage—his father, stepmother, and sister were. Not all members of the community belonged to the church, and not all members of the church came from the Lincolns' immediate neighborhood. Significantly, though, over half of the men who at some time before 1830 claimed land in the community held membership in the church, or some member of their family did. The percentage rises when only those families documented living in the community are considered. Naturally even nonmembers frequently attended the services.

The minute book of the church records the following beliefs of the congregation:

1. we believe in one god the Father the word & the holliest who haith created all things that are created by the word of his power for his pleasure.
2. we believe the old & new testaments are the words of god thare are everry thing Contained thare in nessessary For mans salvation & rule of faith and pracktice
3. We believe in the fall of man in his public head & that he is Encapable of recovery un less restorired by Christ
4. we be live in Election by grace given us in Christ Jessus Before the world began & that God Cawls regenerates & and santifies all who are made meat for Glory by his special grace
5. we believe the righteous will preservere throw grace to glory & none of them fineley fawl away
6. we believe in a general ressurection of the Just and unJust and the Joys of the righteous and the punishment of the wicked are Eturnel
7. We believe that Good works are the fruits of Grace and follow fter Justification
8. We belive that babtism and the lords supper are ordenances of Jesus Christ and the true belivers are the only proper subjects and the only proper mode of babtism is immertion
9. We belive the washing of feet is a command to be complide with when opportunity serves
10. we belive it is our duty severally to seport the lords table and that we orght to administrer the lords supper at lest twise a year

11. We belive that no minister ought to preach the gospel That is not
Calld and sent of god and they are to be proven By hiering them & we
allow of none to preach A Mongst us but such as are well recommend-
ed and that we aurght to Contribute to him who Faithfully Labors a
mongs us in wird and Docttrin According to our several abilities of our
temporal [manuscript torn]¹⁵

Furthermore, participation in Little Pigeon Baptist Church extended
beyond the Sunday experience. The minute book provides many examples of
addressing a member's inappropriate behavior. For instance, the November
1826 meeting minutes record that "the Shurch Say they are hurt with Br.
Wm. Whittinghill for pieching Dollars and Drinking too much Spirituous
Luiquers in using profan language." Then the members appointed a committee to cite Whittinghill to come to the next meeting to answer charges. He
appeared at the December meeting, and the minutes read, "Brither whiten-
hill attende and arose and from his Confession and Sorrow for his Conduct
that he has bin Charged with the church aquits and for gives him and he
Retains his seat." Whittinghill's case followed typical procedure: a charge, a
confession, a plea for forgiveness, and forgiveness granted. If the individual
did not answer the charge or ask for forgiveness, the member's name could
be removed from the society.

The monthly business meetings where these issues arose usually occurred the second Saturday of each month and were attended by members
only. Those coming from a distance spent the night, perhaps the men in the
church and the women at a nearby home. The services on Sunday were open
to everyone.

The congregation attempted not only to regulate the members' behavior
but also to control their beliefs. This same William Whittinghill announced
on November 7, 1829, that he no longer believed in the doctrine of election
and predestination and wished to not remain a member of the church. But
the church delayed accepting his decision and in March 1830 appointed a
group of five men "to labour" with him on the issue. Finally, in May 1830
the church decided "We deny a fellowship with Br. Wm Whittinghill for
deneying the doctrins of election & predistination & refusing to obey the
voice of the church."

Mission activity and Sunday Schools so divided this congregation that
in 1840 some members, including the Grigsbys, Barkers, and Crawfords,
broke away and formed a new Little Pigeon Baptist Church farther south.

Today the congregation of the original Little Pigeon Baptist Church, now called "Old Pigeon," still meets once a month in a building surrounded by Lincoln State Park.[16]

The church also provided important social activities—especially for women, allowing them to temporarily escape the hardship of frontier life to discuss daily concerns and joys with other women. Despite the lack of gender equality, women were important in the proceedings. Women could, and frequently did, charge other members with wrongdoings. For example, on January 10, 1830, "Sister nancy grigsby informe the Church that She was not Satisfied with Br. and Sister LinColn the church agreed and called back their Letters untill Satisfaction Could be attained. the partys Convend at Wm Hoskins and agreed and Settled the DiffiCulty." We do not know what concerned Nancy Grigsby, but it was probably some church doctrine.[17]

Two of the schools held during the Lincoln years sat near the church. Thus, spelling bees and recitations provided entertainment for local families. But much of the social activity centered on attempting to make frontier work more enjoyable—log rollings, house raisings, quilting bees, and corn huskings. Competitions and shared meals helped make work seem like fun.[18] Dennis Hanks remembered enjoying shooting matches and contests such as throwing a mall (mallet) overhead.[19]

Other gathering places in the community were strictly for males. Perhaps the best example of this was the blacksmith shop. Few today can appreciate the importance of this frontier artisan. Here the men came to have their farm implements repaired or fabricated, their horses shod, and their tools made.[20] Residents gravitated to the blacksmith not only for their metalworking needs but also for their chance to swap stories and catch up on politics and current affairs. Hanks informed William H. Herndon that the first blacksmith in the Lincoln neighborhood, John Baldwin at Gentryville, was "Abes pertickler friend" and "a great hand at telling stories."[21]

Citizens also gathered in local stores. Probably the first store for the Little Pigeon Creek community was located upstairs in John Jones's log cabin, north of the creek. A merchant from Rome, Indiana, stocked sugar, coffee, and other items the residents could not produce. James Gentry met the need shortly after his arrival in 1818 by opening a store first at his home and then at the crossroads of the east-west and north-south roads.[22]

At these stores the settlers traded their farm produce—meat, grain, butter, eggs—for goods such as coffee, tea, utensils, and gunpowder. With cash scarce in the premarket economy of early Indiana, most residents bartered routinely.[23] Perhaps the best-documented example for the Little Pigeon Creek community appeared as an entry in the church minute book listing what produce was acceptable to support the church: "Corn Wheat wiskey pork Lainen wool or any other article or material to the Worth." A list of individual contributions followed:

> James Gentry pork 400
> Henry Gontiman in trade Cow Brute $10
> Robert Hoskins in Corn Bushels 20
> Ruben grigsby in pork hundred 500
> Noah gorden wheat bushels 20
> John B. Turnham ~~for givin~~ in Corn Bushels 15
> Charles Harper in Corn Bushels 20
> Jacob oskins on Corn Bushels 20
> Jesse Hoskins a Cow Brute in trad $5-00
> ~~Wm. W Bronir Corn Bushels in Smith work~~ $3.00 paid
> Thomas Lincoln the Case (?) manfactored pounds 24
> amos Hodge in gin'd cotton pounds 25
> Wm. Barker in Bading (?) of the hands Dollars $8-00
> John Worth (?) killans Days 5
> moses Lamar in pork 150 pounds
> Jeseph weller in pork pounds 100
> Wm. Hoskins pork pounds 200
> Wm. Whittinghill ~~Corn~~ Bacon pounds 25
> David Turnham gr back work $2
> Josset west Do $1[24]

Although no individuals contributed whiskey to the church, it remained on the list as an acceptable contribution, and it may have been one of the most convenient bartering commodities. According to one legend, Thomas, a carpenter and cooper, chose the Little Pigeon Creek community as his Indiana home because he was hired to make barrels for the Reuben Grigsby still.[25] More likely, Thomas had the same arrangement with his old friend from Kentucky and now Indiana neighbor, Thomas Carter. One Spencer County history recorded that "Thomas Carter . . . erected a distillery a short time after locating on his place, having brought the still with him. He conducted it about three years, beginning in 1817."[26] That same history mentioned that another neighbor, Noah Gorden, operated a distillery.[27] As a consequence, Thomas's skills surely proved valuable in this bartering economy.

Beyond his distillery, Gorden's most important economic activity for the community was his horse-drawn mill, where the horse kicked Lincoln.[28] By 1825 Peter Whittinghill operated a mill or "corn cracker" west of Gentryville. Nearly every family grew an acre or two of cotton, and Gentry opened a cotton gin to expedite processing the fiber.[29]

Another important economic activity on the frontier involved tanning hides. William Whittinghill had such a tannery at Gentryville, and Shadrack Hall conducted one just east of the twenty-four-section community. The work required soaking the hides in several solutions (including manure-treated water) and scraping with stones and knives. This unpleasant, stinking procedure probably fascinated young boys of the area.[30]

This was the community where Lincoln grew from a boy of seven to a man of twenty-one. Herndon realized that to understand the Lincoln he knew in Illinois, he had to know the Lincoln of Indiana. In September 1865 the quest to find that Lincoln began, and the neighbors remembered Abraham Lincoln.

9

"The man soared above us"
Nathaniel Grigsby

William H. Herndon initiated contact with his Indiana informants with a shot in the dark on June 5, 1865, when he addressed a letter to "Some good *Union* Lawyer" in Rockport. Judge L. Q. DeBruler received the letter and handed it to attorney J. W. Wartmann. On June 8 Wartmann wrote Herndon that two of Lincoln's old Hoosier friends, Josiah Crawford and William Jones, had recently died; however, Wartmann agreed to visit the Lincoln neighborhood and report his findings to Herndon. He assured Herndon that he himself was an ardent "Lincoln man."[1]

On June 19 Wartmann responded to another Herndon letter by suggesting he write Silas Richardson, Nathaniel Grigsby, John W. Lamar, John Romine, David Turnham, and Mrs. Allen Gentry (Anna Roby).[2] Following Wartmann's advice, on June 25 Herndon sent a letter to Nathaniel Grigsby, and Grigsby responded on July 4 saying, "Anything that I can do for the history of that good and great man, I shall be happy to do it."[3]

Grigsby proved the sort of person Herndon hoped to find: he knew the young Abraham Lincoln and strongly supported Lincoln during his presidential years. Born in Nelson County, Kentucky, on October 11, 1811, Grigsby was two years, eight months younger than Lincoln. In 1815 his father, Reuben Grigsby, moved the family to Spencer County, a year before the Lincolns arrived. The Grigsby farm lay approximately two miles southwest of the Lincoln farm. The two families attended the same schools and Little Pigeon Baptist Church, and Nathaniel's oldest brother, Aaron, married Sarah Lincoln. Certainly, Grigsby knew the Lincoln story.[4]

Grigsby moved to Carroll County, Missouri, in 1855 and by 1860 became a Lincoln supporter in a slave state. On July 19, 1860, Grigsby wrote Lincoln to ask if the Republican Party candidates would be on the ballot in Missouri. Lincoln responded on September 20. After an update on his immediate family, Lincoln wrote, "There is now a Republican electoral ticket in Missouri, so that you can vote for me if your neighbors let you. I would advise you not to get into any trouble about it."[5] Family tradition holds that Grigsby narrowly escaped being murdered by southern sympathizers early one morning and wisely decided to move back to Indiana in spring 1861.[6]

In the fall of 1863, as the call came for more Union troops, Grigsby and William Jones, a son of Gentryville storekeeper William Jones, canvassed the county to raise a cavalry unit. This was a difficult task since many of the men were already in the army; but on December 31, 1863, Grigsby mustered into Company G, Tenth Indiana Cavalry, the 125th Regiment, as a second lieutenant. He received an honorable discharge at Decatur, Alabama, on November 18, 1864, after the unit's assistant surgeon found the fifty-three-year-old Grigsby "incapable of performing the duties of an officer. Because of disability caused by old age."[7]

By the 1880s Grigsby returned to Missouri and later moved to Kansas, where he died in 1890. He was a loyal Union man and Republican to the end. To Grigsby the problems of the nation were the result of the Democratic Party from its founding by Andrew Jackson to southern political leadership during the Civil War. Grigsby requested the following notice on his tombstone:

> Through this inscription I wish to enter my dying protest against what is called the Democratic Party. I have watched it closely since the days of Jackson and know that all the misfortune of our nation has come to it through this so called party therefore beware of this party of treason.[8]

Nathaniel Grigsby, Lincoln's friend and William H. Herndon's guide, late in his life.

Grigsby was the first resident Herndon met in his September 1865 visit to Spencer County. By the end of that visit Herndon referred to Grigsby as "my old guide and Companion," and perhaps he stayed with the Grigsby family.[9] Prior to Herndon's visit, Grigsby wrote another letter to Herndon on September 4, 1865, so that Herndon came with specific questions when the two met on September 12.[10] Here is Herndon's record of that visit:

> Gentryville Ind. Septr 12th 1865
> My name is N. Grigsby — am 54 years of age — Knew Abm Lincoln well — My father Came from Ky in the fall of 1815 and settled in what is called now Spencer Co — once a part and portion of Perry — Thomas Lincoln moved to this State in the year 1816 — or 1817 — He came in the fall of the year and Crossed the Ohio River at what is Called Ephraim Thompson's Ferry about 2½ miles west of Troy — The Country was a wilderness and there were no roads from Troy to the place he settled which place is about 1½ miles East of Gentryville — the town in which I now live and you are writing. Thomas Lincoln Lincoln was a large man—Say 6 feet or a little up — strong & Muscular — not nervous —. Thomas Lincoln was a man of good morals — good habits and Exceedingly good humored — he could read and sign his name — write but little. Mrs. Lincoln the mother of Abraham was a woman about 5 ft — 7 inches high — She had dark hair — light hazel Eye — complexion light or Exceedingly fair —. Thomas Lincoln & his wife had 2 children — one Sally and one Abraham — Sally was about 10 ys when she landed in Indiana — Abe was about 8 or 9 years of age. Thomas Lincoln when he landed in Indiana Cut his way to his farm with the Axe felling the forest as he went which was thick & dense — no prairies from the Ohio to his place —. I am informed that he came in a horse waggon to his farm — don't know but have heard this said in the family —: Abm Lincoln & Sally & myself all went to school — we 1st went to school to Andy Crawford in the year 1818, in the winter — the same year that Mrs Lincoln died she having died in Octr — Abe went to school nearly a year say — 9 mo — I was going to school all this time and saw Lincoln there most, if not all the time — The 2d School Master we went to was a Mr Hazel Dorsy — Abe Lincoln went to school to Hazel about 6 months — I went to school all the time — saw Lincoln there all or at least most

of the time. We had to go about 2 miles to school — The 3d time we went to School was to a Mr Swaney who taught 6 mo. Lincoln did not go to school to him all the time Lincoln had to walk about 4 miles — Lincoln was, about, the 1st school 9 or 10 ys of age — The 2d school, he was about 14 or 15 and the 3d School he was about 16 or 18. Lincoln was Large of his age — Say at 17 — he was 6 & 2 inches tall — weighed about 160 pounds or a little more — he was Stout — withy-:wirey—. When we started to School we had Dilworths' Spelling book and the American Spelling book — not Websters I think — Lincoln ciphered at Crawfords school — Dorsys & Swanys — He used Pikes arithmetic —. Ray's was sometimes used —. We only wrote — spelled & ciphered —. We had Spelling Matches frequently — Abe always ahead of all the classes he Ever was in — When we went to Crawford he tried to learn us manners. &c. He would ask one of the schollars to retire from the School room — Come in and then some schollar would go around and introduce him to all the Schollars — male & female. Lincoln was a Studious. Lincoln while going to School to Crawford would write short sentences against cruelty to animals. We were in the habit of catching Turrapins — a Kind of turtle and put fire on their back and Lincoln would Chide us — tell us it was wrong — would write against it — Lincoln wrote Poetry while he was going to School to Dorsy —. Essays & Poetry were not taught in the school — Abe took it up of his own accord. He wrote a good Composition against Cruelty to animals whilst going to Dorsy and Swany. He wrote Poetry when going to these men. These things I remember & Know —. Cannot remember of his reading — any book — or books Excepting Esops fables — Bunyan's Pilgrim's Progress — the Bible — Robinson Crusoe Life of Washington — Dupee's Hymn book — Our libraries consisted of Spelling books — Bibles — Arithmetics — Song books. Lincoln was Kindly disposed toward Every body and Every thing — He scarcely Ever quarreled — was prompt & honorable —He never was an intemperate lad: he did drink his dram as well as all others did, preachers & Christians included — Lincoln was a temperate drinker. When he went out to work any where would Carry his books with and would always read whilst resting —

We wore buckskin pants — and linsey wolsey hunting coat to school. This was our school dress — our Sunday dress and Every day dress. Mr Lincoln was long & tall and like the balance of us he wore low shoes — short socks, wool being Scarce — between the shoe and Sock & his britches — made of buckskin there was bare & naked 6 or more inches of Abe Lincoln shin bone. He would always come to school thus — good humoredly and laughing — He was always in good health — never was sick — had an Excellent Constitution — & took Care of it —

Lincoln did not do much hunting — sometimes went Coon hunting & turkey hunting of nights — Whilst other boys were idling away their time Lincoln was at home studdying hard — would cipher on the boards — wooden fire shovels — &c — by the light of the fire — that burnt on the hearth — had a slate sometimes — but if not handy would use boards — He would shave boards bright and cipher on them — dirty them — re-shave them   Abe would set up late reading & rise Early doing the Same

Mrs Lincoln Abes Mother was born _____ and died in the fall — Octr 1818 — leaving her 2 children — Sally Lincoln was older than Abe — and Abraham — Sally married Aaron Grigsby — my brother — in Aug. 1826 — she died in about 2 years, &c — in 1828 —[11]

Grigsby gave a peer's description of Lincoln's youth. His account of the future president's schooling, appearance, and behavior best portrays the young man out of his family's view. Although "Lincoln was a temperate drinker" appears an honest comment, Grigsby hastens to place the comment into an 1820s pioneer context, "all others did, preachers & Christians included." William Wood, another neighbor, told Herndon basically the same.[12] Certainly Lincoln's protection of animals and lack of interest in hunting were not typical of the frontier.

Next Grigsby describes the Lincoln family:

Mrs Lincoln the mother of Abe Lincoln — was a woman Know for the Extraordinary Strength of her mind among the family and all who knew her: she was superior to her husband in Every way. She was a brilliant woman — a woman of great good sense and Modesty.

Those who Knew her best — with whom I have talked say she was a woman of pale Complexion — dark hair — sharp features — high forehead — bright Keen gray — or hazle Eyes —. Thos Lincoln & his wife were really happy in Each others presence — loved one an other. Thomas Lincoln was not a lazy man — but a [tinker?] — a piddler — always doing but doing nothing great — was happy — lived Easy & contented. had but few wants and Supplied these. He wanted few things and Supplied them Easily — His wants were limited by wanting few things. Sally was a quick minded woman & of extraordinary Mind — She was industrious — more so than Abraham — Abe worked almost alone from the head — whilst she labored both. Her good humored laugh I can see now — is as fresh in my mind as if it were yesterday. She could like her brother Abe meet & greet a person with the very Kindest greeting in the world —make you Easy at the touch & word — He mind, though my brothers wife — was an intellectual & intelligent woman — However not so much as her mother —[13]

Grigsby knew the Lincoln family well and provides a positive view of Thomas and Nancy Hanks Lincoln—Thomas's good morals, good habits, and good humor and Nancy's extraordinary strength of mind, good sense, and modesty. Nancy was superior to her "piddler" husband, but they were happy, loved one another, and provided for the family. Lincoln's sister Sarah had an extraordinary mind, but could not be called lazy.

Grigsby continued:

My brother Wm Grigsby and John D Johnston a step brother of Abe had a severe fight — it was [attended?] from all around the neighborhood — Coming 18 Miles — strong men Came — bullies Came — Abe was there — Abe & my brother first had the quarrel — Abe being large & stronger than my brother turned over his Step brother to do his fighting — so they met — fought — fought ½ mile from Gentryville. There was a store here & probably a grocery — and a blacksmith Shop — This was the town then, of Gentryville — Johnson was badly hurt, but not whipt — My brother was un-hurt seriously so — Johnson & my bro were brave Strong men.[14]

The fight between William Grigsby and John Johnston probably resulted from insults the Grigsbys felt from Lincoln's biting satire. Since he was larger and older than Grigsby, Lincoln asked his stepbrother to fight in his place. Herndon learned more about the fight from Green B. Taylor and relates it this way in the Herndon-Weik Lincoln biography:

> They had a terrible fight . . . and it soon became apparent that Grigsby was too much for Lincoln's man, Johnston. After they had fought a long time without interference, it having been agreed not to break the ring, Abe burst through, caught Grigsby, threw him off and some feet away. There he stood, proud as Lucifer, and swinging a bottle of liquor over his head swore he was "the big buck of the lick." "If any one doubts it," he shouted, "he has only to come on and whet his horns." A general engagement followed this challenge, but at the end of hostilities the field was cleared and the wounded retired amid the exultant shouts of their victors.[15]

The subject of politics and Lincoln's employment are the next topics considered in Grigsby's interview. In his notes, Herndon mistakenly wrote Carlin Township instead of *Carter* Township.

> A. Lincoln came here in 1844 and made a speech. for Clay: He was a Clay Elector in Ills for the race between Polk & Clay. Lincoln Spoke here — once — once at Rockport — and one Carlin township about ¾ of a mile from the home farm. Lincoln in Early years — say from 1820 to 25 was tending towards Democracy — He afterwards Changed — Parties at this time ran Jackson — Adams and others. What changed Lincoln I dont remember — we were all Jackson boys & men at this time in Indiana —
> Lincoln did go to New Orleans: he went to NO about 1828 with a man by the name of Allen Gentry who took — as well as owned the supercargo to New Orleans — The good were sold down on the river — Abe went as a bow hand — working the foremost oars — getting $8.00 per month — from the time of starting to his returning home. Gentry paid his way back on a boat. This I Know. He made rails for Crawford — take jobs of work sometimes — would go to the river — the Ohio — 13 or 16 miles distant and there work. It is 60 miles to the Wabash — he did work on the Wa-

bash — but on the Ohio — Lincoln did not work on the Louisvill Can, but he may have done it nevertheless —[16]

When recording Grigsby's comments on Lincoln's work he probably meant to say, "he did *not* work on the Wabash."[17] The reference to "Louisville Can" addressed whether Lincoln and John Johnston worked on the Louisville and Portland Canal at Louisville, Kentucky, in 1827. Augustus H. Chapman, Dennis Hanks's son-in-law, provided Herndon this information in a written statement on September 8, 1865.[18]

Lincoln's ability to entertain and communicate with his peers concludes the Grigsby interview.

> Lincoln did write what is called "The book of Chronicles" — a Satire on the Grigsby's & Josiah Crawford — not the School Master, but the man who loaned Lincoln the Life of Washington —. The Satire was good — sharp — cutting and showed the Genius of the boy: it hurt us then, but its all over now. There is now no family in the broad land who after this loved Lincoln so well and who now look upon him as so great a man. We all voted for him — all that could — children and grand children — I was for Lincoln & Hamlin, first, last, & always — 2d Election I was at Decatur Alabama in the service of the US —
>
> We had political discussions from 1825 to 1830 the year Lincoln left for Ills. We attended them — heard questions discussed — talked Evry thing over & over and in fact wore it out — We learned much in this way.
>
> I said heretofore that Abe made his mark of manhood Even while in Indiana. His mind & the Ambition of the man soared above us. He naturally assumed the leadership of the boys — He read & thoroughly read his books whilst we played —. Hence he was above us and became our guide and leader & in this position he never failed to be the leader. He was Kind — jocular — witty — wise — honest — just — human full of integrity — Energy — & acting. When he appeared in Company the boys would gather & cluster around him to hear him talk. He made fun & cracked his jokes making all happy, but the jokes & fun were at no mans Expense — He wounded no mans feelings
>
> Mr Lincoln was figurative in his Speeches — talks & conversa-

tions. He argued much from Analogy and Explained things hard for us to understand by stories — maxims — tales and figures. He would almost always point his lesson or idea by some story that was plain and near as that we might instantly see the force & bearing of what he said

Never heard in the family or out of it that the Lincolns were quakers coming from Pennsylvania —. The History is that they came from Virginia[19]

Even as a young man, Lincoln understood how humor and storytelling was a powerful tool in communicating and confronting his listeners. Amazingly, Grigsby ended his comments on Lincoln's humor by saying that the jokes and fun came at no man's expense and that "he wounded no mans feelings." Yet in an earlier comment about Lincoln's satire in "The book of Chronicles," satire aimed at the Grigsbys, he concluded "it hurt us then, but its all over now." Intrigued by this incident, Herndon sought details in his interview with Elizabeth Crawford, finding the story well remembered in the community.

Before leaving Gentryville, Herndon recorded one last interview with Grigsby on September 16, 1865. The first part of the interview concerns Lincoln's 1844 campaign trip for Henry Clay. William Jones brought Lincoln to the Jones home west of Gentryville, and Lincoln saw a number of old friends and made a speech. Grigsby spent the night at the Jones home. Jones was the primary merchant in the area and was elected to the Indiana House of Representatives in 1838, 1839, and 1840. Still later, during the Civil War, he was commissioned a lieutenant colonel of the Fifty-third Regiment of Indiana and was killed near Atlanta, Georgia, July 24, 1864.[20]

In 1844 Lincoln visited this house, built by William and Rachel Jones in the 1830s.

WILLIAM E. BARTELT

Here is Grigsby's last interview with Herndon:

Gentryville Ind Septr   16th 1865 —
After taking the rounds in Spencer Co Indiana I went with my old
guide and Companion Nat Grigsby down to Wm Thompson who
lived where Col Jones had resided — ½ M west of Gentryville. Col
Jones was Lincoln guide & teacher in Politics — Col J was Killed
at Atlanta — Grigsby showed me where Lincoln Spoke in 1844
— When Lincoln was Speaking Grigsby went into the House where
the Speech was being made — Lincoln Saw G Enter — He stopt
Short — said there is Nat. Lincoln then walked over the benches
and over the heads of his hearers —Came rolling — took G by the
hand Shook it most Cordially — Said a few words — went back —
commenced his remarks where he had Stopt — finished his Speech
— told G that he must stay with him all night — Slept at Col Jones'
— When we had gone to bed and way in the night a Cat Commenced mewing and scratching — making a fuss generally — Lincoln got up in the dark and Said —Kitty — Kitty — Pussy — Pussy.
The cat Knew the voice & manner Kind — went to Lincoln — L
rubbed it down — Saw the Sparkling — L took up the Cat — Carried it to the door & gently rubbed it again and again Saying Kitty
— Kitty &c — then gently put it down closed the doors — Commenced telling Stories & talking over old times —
     As we were going down to Thompsons G told me this Story
— which I had heard before. A man by the name of Chas Harper
was going to mill — had an Extremely long wheat bag on the horse
and was met by sister Gordon — who said to Bro Harper — Bro H
your bag is too long — No said Bro Harper — it is only too long in
the summer. They were Bro and Sister in the church — Mrs Gordon
told her husband of the vulgar — Gordon made a fuss — had a
church trial — Lincoln got the Secret — wrote a witty piece of Poetry on the scenes & Conversations — The Poetry of Abe was good
— witty — &c as said by all who read it.[21]

Naturally Herndon sought stories that captured real life in the community, and Grigsby repeated such a story. Charles Harper was actually
the Reverend Charles Harper whose name appears frequently in the Little
Pigeon Baptist Church minute book. Whether Harper meant his comment

to be vulgar, Nancy Gorden took it as such. Although we find no citation in the church minute book of the Gordens' charge against Harper, on November 13, 1824, the minutes state: "Application was Made by Br Harper by letter to the Church for aletter of Dism but the Church oppear loth to Giv him up and oppoints bretheeran Br Gentry & Br linkhon to talk to him on the acation."[22] Discussion with Harper continues for several months, but eventually Harper maintained membership and appeared to continue in good standing. It is not known if this discussion related to the Gorden incident, and no one has found the poetry with Nancy Gorden as the subject.

10

"Could I only whisper in her Ear— 'Your Son was Presdt'"

William Henry Herndon Visits the Sites

On September 14, 1865, William H. Herndon became one of the first tourists to visit the historic southern Indiana sites associated with Abraham Lincoln, sites that became Lincoln Boyhood National Memorial and Lincoln State Park. The 14th was Herndon's third day in Indiana, but he left no record of interviews for September 13. Rodney O. Davis suggests that Herndon may have been ill on that date, since many residents of the neighborhood were ill at the time. The *Rockport Democrat* reported that, during the week, "In some neighborhoods, whole families are down, and scarcely any family is to be found but what some of its members are down sick. The prevailing diseases are chills and fever and bilious fever. Physicians attribute the sickness to the hot and wet weather we are having."[1]

Herndon's guide was Nathaniel (Nat) Grigsby. Herndon's notes for September 14 fall into six divisions: (1) Lincoln home site; (2) Nancy Hanks Lincoln's grave site; (3) the Baptist church and school site; (4) John Romine's comments; (5) an interview with Joseph Richardson; and (6) S. T. Johnson's comments. (Johnson did not know Lincoln, but related local tradition.)

Herndon's first stop was the Lincoln cabin site:

Lincoln Farm   Septr 14th 1865

I started from Nat Grigsby's house, with him as my guide & friend throughout the trip, Except at Rockport on the Ohio R. Grigsby lives in Gentryville — population about 300 — laid off in 1824

— runs North & South Mostly — Mainly — Started at 8 o'c M. Went to the Lincoln farm about 1½ m East of Gentryville and a little North. The house is a one Story hewed log one — porch in front: it is not the house that L lived in — though he built it. The old houses — the 1st & 2d are gone — fronts South — chimney at East End — has 2 rooms, the East one & west one — Stands on a Knowl or Knob about 50 feet above the road & about 150 yards north of the road. On the Gentryville road leading to the Hoffman Mills. The Country is a heavy timbered one — farms are cleared and cut out of the forests. The woods — the timber is hickory — white oak, called buck-eye and buck lands. The old farm now belongs to Jas Gentry — Son of Jas Gentry for whom, the old man the brother of Allen — Lincoln went to N. Orleans in 1828 or 29. John Heaven or Heavener now lives as tenant on the land: it an orchard on it part of Which Abm Lincoln planted with his own hands — Allen Gentry got drunk and fell off the boat going to Louisville and was drowned — Abe Lincoln hewed the logs of this new house for his father — one door north & one South — 2 rooms — plank partition — one window — 2 rooms: it has been moved from its original position — placed further south than the old ones: it is not as Lincoln left it: it was not completed by Thomas Lincoln. The farm was sold to _____ by Thomas Lincoln in 1829 — went to the place of the old Spring N.W of the house — about 300 yards —: it was dry — Saw the place — Saw various old well all Caved in — it is Said water Could not be had on that hill — pity —Saw 5 or 6 old — old apple trees: the old house and Shelter are gone   I say again and again —[2]

The question of Lincoln cabins is problematic. Clearly someone told Herndon that the Lincolns did not occupy the cabin he saw, even though they built it. Furthermore, Herndon records that the first and second cabins are gone. Does Herndon consider the *first* cabin the half-faced camp? If not, the Lincolns constructed the half-faced camp, a temporary log cabin, a more substantial cabin, and the one the family was building at the time they decided to move to Illinois. Evidence suggests this may be the case.

John Hanks told Herndon the first cabin was a rough, unhewn one; the second was "Sorter" hewn (no longer standing by 1860); and the third hewn, but not occupied by the Lincolns.[3] In the interview Herndon conducted with him on June 13, 1865, Dennis Hanks reported a temporary cabin was built in 1818 and the "new grand old log cabin" was built during winter 1819–20.[4] Sarah (Sally) Bush Johnston Lincoln, who arrived in Indiana during December of 1819, told Herndon that Thomas Lincoln had "erected a good log cabin—tolerably comfortable."[5]

Thanks to John Rowbotham, we have an illustration of the building Herndon saw in 1865. Rowbotham, a Cincinnati artist, illustrated Joseph H. Barrett's biography of Lincoln in 1865. Later during his visit to Indiana, Herndon heard the same story from William Wood, about the Lincolns beginning construction of a cabin, but not finishing it. This is the cabin Herndon and Rowbotham saw in 1865.

After exploring the homesite, Herndon traveled south to Nancy's grave site. Nancy Castleman Richardson and her son, Silas, were the first neighbors Herndon met that day. Nancy and her husband, John, moved to Indiana from Nelson County, Kentucky, in 1817 and settled near the Lincolns. John, who died in 1822, had been a Baptist preacher.

> Started to find Mrs Lincoln's grave — it is on a Knob — hill or Knowl about ½ m S.E of the Lincoln house — passed out of the lane going East — landed at the grave — tied my horse: the grave was — is on the very top or crown of the hill. The Know or Knowl

William H. Herndon saw the "Lincoln Cabin" shown in this 1865 sketch by John Rowbotham. The local residents claimed this cabin was the one that the Lincolns were building at the time they left Indiana for Illinois.

William H. Herndon described "a kind of hollow" as the grave of Nancy Hanks Lincoln. John Rowbotham made this sketch of the site earlier in 1865.

is a heavy timbered one. A Space is cut out of the forest by felling
the trees Somewhat circularly. In the centre of this Small cleared
place about 15 feet from a large white oak tree — rather Somewhat
between 2 of them, lies buried Mrs Lincoln. God bless her if I
could breathe life into her again I would do it. Could I only whis-
per in her Ear — "Your Son was Presdt — of the U.S from 1861 to
1866," I would be satisfied. I have heard much of this blessed, good
woman. I stood bare headed in reverence at her grave. I can't Say
why — yet I felt in the presence of the living woman translated to
another world. "God bless her," said her Son to me once and I repeat
that which Echoes audibly in my Soul — "God bless her." The grave
is almost undistinguishable: it has Sunk down, leaving a Kind of
hollow. There is no fence around the grave yard and no tomb — no
head board to mark where She lies. At her head — close to it I
peeled a dog wood bush and cut or marked my name on it. Mrs
Lincoln is buried between two or more persons — Said to be Hall
& his wife on the one hand and Some Children on her left hand
— There are two hollows or sinks. Nat Grigsby & Richardson were
with me at the time — they said this was the grave. Mrs Richardson
Saw Mrs. Lincoln buried and says it is not the grave —one of these
sinks — graves crumbled in lies a few feet — 10 feet — South of
the other: Mrs is the southern one as I think from Dennis Hanks &
A. Lincoln told me. Mrs Lincolns body — her ashes lie just 15 feet
west of a hollow hickory Stump & just 18 feet from — NE — from
a large white oak tree. After looking at the grave and Contemplating
in Silence the mutations of things — death — immortality — God,
I left, I hope, the grave, a better man — at least if but for one moment

Went to Dennis Hanks old place — N.E from the grave yard
about ¾ of a mile — just East of the old Lincoln farm about the
Same distance. Got Silas Richardson — an old friend of Abes: he
came to Indiana in 1816 — so did Lincoln. His mother Saw Mrs
Lincoln buried; he went to the grave yard with us — Nat & myself
and made certain what was before doubtful: he agrees with Dennis Hanks & A Lincoln. Richardson Says old man & Mrs Sparrow
— Abes Grand Father & Mother lie on one Side of Mrs Lincoln.
2 Bruners — probably children lie on the other side — or an old
Lady and a child. Mrs Lincoln lies in the middle The grave is 6 feet

from Said Shaved dogwood bush. Mrs Richardson is 83 years of age. Says that Mrs Lincolns grave lies 4½ feet South of the one I say is the Correct one. Dennis Hanks — A Lincoln — Silas Richardson — the old lady's Son and myself agree to the place. I only go by recollection & what others say — Mrs Richardson & her son go by what they saw — and Know. One Jno Richardson was the husband of old Mrs Richardson — & father of Silas Richardson. — There is no fence around the grave — no palings — Enclosures of any Kind — no headboard — no footboard to mark the Spot where Abm Lincoln's Mother lies — Curious — and unaccountable is it not? All is a dense forest — wild and grand.[6]

The visit to Nancy's grave had an astonishing impact on Herndon. In Davis's words, "At Lincoln's mother's gravesite, the normally freethinking Herndon seems almost to have been transfigured. A sentimental man in a sentimental time, he nonetheless was never again to record having been so moved during his researches."[7]

Of course, Herndon expected an unmarked grave as a result of a letter from Rowbotham he received in June, "There is no stone to mark the spot, but it is well known."[8] Rowbotham also provided directions to the site, suggested persons who could locate the grave, and even named a man who could drive Herndon from Troy to the site—as long as the driver received no whiskey.[9] By using Rowbotham's sketch and Herndon's description, the then-abandoned graveyard can be visualized.

After Little Pigeon Baptist Church decided "to Lay of[f] the burying ground" in 1825, burials in a small family or neighborhood graveyard became less frequent. A prime example is the burial of Sarah Lincoln Grigsby who lies not by her mother, but next to the church. Nancy's grave certainly received care while the family resided near it; after they left Indiana, the cemetery's wooden markers rotted, and the graves lay forgotten.[10]

Undoubtedly, Lincoln visited his mother's grave during his October 1844 visit, and a local tradition suggests that as president, he expressed a desire to mark the grave properly. After Lincoln's assassination, interest grew in marking the grave. In 1869 some local citizens, including Nat Grigsby, discussed erecting a marker; finally, in the mid-1870s a two-foot-tall marker was placed at the grave site. In 1879 Peter E. Studebaker, second vice president of the Studebaker Company, a carriage-making company in South Bend, Indiana, read a newspaper article on the deplorable condition

Lincoln's sister Sarah Lincoln Grigsby was buried in the Little Pigeon Baptist Church Cemetery. A small obelisk marked Sarah's husband Aaron's grave, but her grave was marked with a small stone until this stone was erected in 1916.

Nancy Hanks Lincoln's grave was not permanently marked until Peter Studebaker of South Bend, Indiana, erected this marble stone in 1879. The fence, funded by fifty Spencer County citizens contributing one dollar each, was added in 1880. The stone remains today, but the fence was removed in 1968.

of the grave site. He instructed Rockport Postmaster L. S. Gilkey to buy the best tombstone available for fifty dollars and place it in the cemetery. That marble, arched marker stands today.[11]

As Herndon's fellow visitors could not agree which grave belonged to Lincoln's mother, those marking the grave in 1879 with the "Studebaker monument" found the same problem. Varying accounts describe the decision, and the stone may lie between a couple of graves.[12]

The "Hall & his wife" refers to more of the confusing, extended Hanks family. Two of Nancy's aunts were buried in this cemetery. The first was Elizabeth Sparrow; she and her husband, Thomas Sparrow, died of milk sickness the same fall Nancy died. The other was Nancy Hanks Hall, mother of Dennis Hanks. She was unmarried at the time of his birth but married Levi Hall in 1802. The Halls were the parents of Squire Hall, who married Lincoln's stepsister Matilda Johnston. Sometime in the mid-1820s Levi and Nancy came to Indiana, and both died from milk sickness before 1830.[13]

Herndon and Grigsby continued their visit:

> I then proceeded to old Saml Howells House — South of the grave yard about ½ m — drank out of a good Spring near the little pigeon meeting house out of which Abe had Kneeled and drank a thousand times. Spring close to the Corner of the old Howell farm — part of which is turned out wild again. I passed the Spring a little East — S.E — up a small rise or swell in the ground and landed at the famous Meeting house, called the little Pigeon Meeting House. It is a Babtist Church now and probably was then, but was free to all Comers of all & Every distinction. The House is a two is a two Storie one entrance, but one inside: it was intended to let the Choir and people set up there when crowded, but remains unfinished. This House is about 1½ m from Lincolns house — South & East. Went through the church, stealing in at the windows —The pulpit was made by Thomas Lincoln. I cut a small piece therefrom as memento. Passed East about 50 yds into the large grave yard — Saw the grave of Sarah Lincoln — Mrs Grigsby — Abe's Sister — God bless her ashes — Mrs Grigsby & her husband Aaron lie side by side — God bless'Em. They lie 10 ft South of Nat Grigsby's wife — 1st & mother. Grave yard Slopes East & North — is in the forest — fenced in — quite a pretty place. Crawfords School House lies East of the church — East of the grave yard about 200 yds.: it is

about 2 M from the Lincoln farm S.E: is now — the place Enclosed in a field — School house long since rotted away & gone.[14]

Curious about Lincoln's relationship with religion as a young man in Indiana, Herndon asked questions of his informants. Perhaps the best response came from his stepmother, Sally, "Abe had no particular religion — didnt think of that question at that time, if he ever did — He never talked about it."[15] But Herndon knew Little Pigeon Baptist Church was significant to members of the community, to the Lincolns, and to Abraham.

The Little Pigeon Baptist Church seen in this John Rowbotham sketch intrigued William H. Herndon.

As mentioned earlier, Little Pigeon Baptist Church was formed in neighboring Warrick County in 1816. On December 11, 1819, the congregation selected the Noah Gorden farm as the site to construct a church building. Members chose this site because of a spring on the neighboring Samuel Howell farm and a nearby road. In 1821 the plan for a building was approved, and Thomas was selected to oversee construction. Abraham certainly helped his father with the work. This was the structure Herndon saw in 1865, and the one Rowbotham illustrated.[16]

Thomas and Sally did not join this church until June 7, 1823. He joined "by letter" from Little Mount Separate Baptist Church in Kentucky, and she joined "by experience." Sarah Lincoln joined "by experience" on April

8, 1826, approximately four months before she married Aaron Grigsby.[17] Abraham did not join the church.

Although Abraham was never a member, nevertheless he had close associations with the church and "went to Church generally."[18] Informants enjoyed telling Herndon of Lincoln's imitating the preacher's sermons. In 1909 Caleb A. Obenshain, a Baptist minister, told a newspaper reporter that in 1866 he found a memorandum book in a church loft crevice that contained a list of supplies ordered by "Abe Lincoln, Sexton." Obenshain replaced the book in the crevice before leaving the church.[19] But neither the book nor any other evidence has verified that Lincoln served as a church official. Though the extent of the church's influence on Lincoln's religious views remains open to debate, his curious nature likely forced him to ponder spiritual issues. Perhaps nothing demonstrates Herndon's interest in this place more than his vandalism in carving a piece of pulpit to take with him as a souvenir.

Noah Gorden came to Indiana from Kentucky at about the same time as the Lincolns. In fact, he claimed land at the Vincennes Land Office the same day as Thomas. In 1829 he sold his land to John Romine and moved to Illinois.[20] Because Herndon wanted to see the site of the mill where a horse kicked Abraham, he proceeded up a lane to the site, about a quarter of a mile from the church.

Along the way he found an informant, John Romine, willing to offer an uncomplimentary account of Abraham's work ethic. Romine had married Hannah Gentry, daughter of James, in 1829. Herndon wrote of the meeting with Romine:

> I then Started for John Romines — SW — met Romine in the road meeting us. his age is 60 ys. Says — I Saw Mr Lincoln hundreds of times — have been in Spencer Co since 1815. Lincoln went to N.O. about '28 or '29 — halled some of the bacon to the River — not for Lincoln but for Gentry—Thomas Lincoln was a carpenter by trade — relied on it for a living — not on farming. Abe didn't like to work it — didn't raise more than was Enough for family & stock. Boat Started out of the Ohio in the Spring — Abe about 20 years of age — Started from Rockport — a Short distance below rather — at the Gentry landing — Give about 2 m. Lincoln was attacked by the Negroes — no doubt of this — Abe told me so — Saw the scar myself. — Suppose at the Wade Hampton farm or near by

— probably below at a widows farm. Abe was awful lazy: he worked for me — was always reading & thinking — used to get mad at him — He worked for me in 1829 pulling fodder. I Say Abe was awful lazy: he would laugh & talk and crack jokes & tell stories all the time, didn't love work but did dearly love his pay. He worked for me frequently — a few days only at a time. His breeches didn't & socks didn't meet by 12 inches — Shin bones Sharp — blue & narrow Lincoln said to me one day that his father taught him to work but never learned him to love it.

Saw old Man Gordons Mill — rather the near ruins of it. This is the Mill where Abe got Kicked by a horse — hunted for Lincolns name written in tar & black lead & grease on a shaft of the mill — couldn't find it — got a cog or two of the mill — Romine tells me one verse of the Book of Chronicles — it runs thus —

Reuben & Charley have married 2 girls —

But Billy has married a boy

Billy & Natty agree very well

Mamma is pleased with the match.

The Egg is laid but won't hatch.[21]

Apparently Herndon conducted two more interviews on September 14. Joseph Richardson, another son of Nancy Richardson, had been a partner

with William Jones in his Gentryville store before moving to Rockport in 1854. His obituary called him "an ardent Republican," and he served as county clerk in the 1870s and 1880s. Herndon's notes are in error because the Richardson family arrived in Spencer County in 1817.[22] Richardson provided more anecdotes about Lincoln's sense of humor and

Joseph Richardson's story about boys stealing watermelons demonstrated Lincoln's good nature and sense of humor.

expanded on the "Chronicles." The reference to Lincoln's grandmother may be to Elizabeth Sparrow. The references to Josiah Crawford will become clear when the interview with Elizabeth Crawford is discussed.

Richardson's interview appears in Herndon's notes as follows:

[Sept. 14?, 1865]

My father Came to Spencer Co Indiana in 1828. Lincoln was tall and raw boned at 18. When 16 years of age he was 6 feet high — he was somewhat bony & raw — dark Skinned: he was quick and moved with Energy: he never idled away his time. When out of regular work, he would help & assist the neighbors: he was Exceedingly Studious. I Knew him well — he wrote me a copy in my writing Copy book which runs thus

Good boys who to their books apply

Will make great men by & by.

This Copy was written in 1829. The Weems Washington — the book Story took place in 1829. — one year before Abe went to Ills. Crawford was a close penurious man — probably did not treat Lincoln generously, but Lincoln did not object to what Crawford required. The book Story is correct.

Onc Lincoln & Squire Hall raised some water melons — Some of us boys lit into the melon patch accidentally. We got the melons — went through the Corn to the fence — got over — All at onc to our Surprise and mortification Lincoln Came among us — on us — good naturedly said boys "now I've got you — sat down with us — cracked jokes, told stories & helped to eat the melons.

One day Abe's grand Mother wanted him to read some chapters in the Bible for her. L. did-not want to do it. At last he took up the Bible and read & rattled away so fast that his poor old grand Mother Could not understand it. She good naturedly ran him out of the house with the broom Stick — who being out, the thing he wanted he Kept shy that day — all done in sport & fun.

Lincoln did Keep ferry for Jas Taylor for about 9 mo — at the mouth of Anderson River on the ohio, between Troy & Maxville. The Lincoln & Grigsby family had a Kind of quarrel and hence for some time did not like Each other. Aaron Grigsby had some years before this married Miss Sarah Lincoln — the good & Kind Sister of Abe — Two other Grigsby boys — men rather — got married on the same night at the Same house — though they did-not marry Sisters — they had an infair at old man Grigsbys and all the neighbors, Excepting the Lincoln family were invited — Josiah Crawford the book man helped to get up the infair: he had a long huge blue nose. Abe Lincoln undoubtedly felt miffed — insulted, pride wounded. &c. Lincoln I Know felt wronged about the book transaction. After the infair was Ended the two women were put to bed. The Candles were blown out — up Stairs — The gentlemen — the 2 husbands were invited & shown to bed. Chas Grigsby got into bed with, *by accident* as it were, with Reuben Grigsbys wife & Reuben got into bed with Charles' wife, by accident as it were. Lincoln, I say was mortified & he declared that he would have revenge. Lincoln was by nature witty & here was his Chance. So he got up a witty *poem* — called the Book of Chronicles, in which the Infair — the mistake in partners — Crawford & his blue nose Came in Each for its Share — and this poem is remembered here in Indiana in scraps better than the Bible — better than Watts hymns. This was in 1829, and the first production that I know of that made us feel that Abe was truly & realy some. This called the attention of the People to Abe intellectually. Abe dropt the Poem in the road Carelessly — lost it as it were: it was found by one of the Grigsby boys Satirised who had the good manly Sense to read it — Keep it — preserve it for years — if it is *not in Existence now.*

Grigsby challenged Lincoln to fight. Abe refused. Said he was too big — Johnson — Abe's step brother took Abes part — Shoes — met at the old School house — Johnson got whipt — worsted rather — Richardson Says that Lincoln was a powerful man in 1830 — Could Carry what 3. ordinary men would grunt & sweat at — Saw him Carry a chicken house made of poles pinned together & Covered that weighed at least 600 if not much more. Abe was notoriously good natured — Kind and honest. Men would Swear on his Simple word — had a high & manly sense of honor — was tender — gentle — &c — &c — never seemed to care for the girls — was witty & Sad and thoughtful by turns — as it Seemed to me.

God bless Abe's Memory forever[23]

Another September 14 interview involved thirty-four-year-old S. T. Johnson. Though not born until after the Lincolns left Indiana, Johnson told Herndon a story related to him by a man named Summers. According to Johnson, Lincoln attended court in Boonville and "paid strict attention to what was said and done." In Boonville Lincoln became acquainted with John A. Brackenridge, an early Indiana attorney. According to Johnson's account, Lincoln saw Brackenridge perform in an 1828 murder trial in Boonville. Years later, in 1862, Lincoln met Brackenridge in Washington, D.C. Referring to the 1828 trial, the president told Brackenridge, "It was the best speech that I, up to that time, Ever heard. If I could, as I then thought make as good a speech as that, that my soul would be satisfied."[24]

A local history calls Brackenridge "perhaps the ablest local attorney that ever practiced at the Warrick County bar."[25] He was born in 1800, educated at Princeton University (then College of New Jersey), and came to Indiana to practice law. Certainly he was a locally prominent person with whom Lincoln was familiar. Brackenridge practiced law in Spencer and Warrick counties and appears in the 1830 census as a resident of Spencer County.[26]

Warrick County judge, Roscoe Kiper, wrote in 1924 that although the trial tradition dates to before the Civil War, "The story of Lincoln attending the murder case in which Brackenridge acted as prosecuting attorney is also a matter of pure tradition, unsupported by any record and cannot be traced to any eye witness who saw the incident as related."[27] Louis A. Warren also found problems with the story's detail, including the absence of a murder trial in Warrick County in 1828. Perhaps the trial occurred in Spencer County, but a courthouse fire in 1833 destroyed all its court records. In addition, Warren questioned the local legends about Lincoln borrowing books from Brackenridge while the lawyer lived in Boonville.[28]

11

"A boy of Extraordinary mind"
David Turnham

William H. Herndon spent one day of his Indiana interviews in the northern part of the old Lincoln neighborhood, stopping first in the town of Elizabeth to see David Turnham. Elizabeth was platted in 1843, but the name was changed to Dale (in honor of Congressman Robert Dale Owen of New Harmony) in 1866.[1] Turnham was born in Tennessee in 1803. He was sixteen years old when his family moved to Indiana in March 1819. The family settled on a quarter section of land that bordered the northeast section of the Lincoln claim. The Lincoln and Turnham homes sat about a mile apart.

David Turnham's father, Thomas, led an interesting life. He served two enlistments in the Revolutionary War and saw action at the battles of Brandywine, Germantown, Monmouth, Savannah, Cowpens, and Yorktown. He certainly could tell stories that interested the citizens of the neighborhood, especially a curious boy such as Abraham Lincoln. Thomas was married five times and lived in the same area of Kentucky as the Lincolns before he moved his family to Tennessee. Nancy Castleman Richardson (another Spencer County informant for Herndon) was the daughter of one of his wives.[2]

David Turnham proved a good source of information about the schooling and personality of Abraham, the character of the Lincoln family, and activities of the neighborhood. Herndon respected Turnham's comments and corresponded with him during the next year and a half. There are ten letters from Turnham to Herndon in the Herndon collection.[3]

Here are Herndon's notes from his visit with David Turnham:

The first law book Lincoln read was David Turnham's copy of the *Revised Laws of Indiana*. Turnham is seen here with his wife Nancy.

Septr 15 1865

I went to David Turnhams after leaving the town of Gentryville — T — lives in Elizabeth — a town about 4 ½ M North East — Elizabeth has a population of about 300 hundred people — same size as Gentryvill — Mr Turnham Commenced —

I came to Ind in the year 1819. Mch — settled in Spencer Co — settled about 3 M south of this and about 1 M North East of Thomas Lincolns — am now 62 years. I Knew Abm Lincoln well — Knew his father — didn't Know his Mother — immediately on landing in Ind I became acquainted with Mr Lincon. My father and his were acquainted in Ky — Abe was then about ten years of age. —I being 16 ys of age — Abe was a long tall dangling award drowl looking boy — went hunting and fishing together — Abe was a boy of Extraordinay mind I think — went to School to-gether — Hazel Dorsy & Andw Crawford — Dorzey Kept first, I think: he kept school near the Pigeon Meeting house — about 1¼ miles from Thos Lincolns and south or SE of his his. Crawford (Andw) taught school next: he taught about ¼ East of the Pigeon School Meeting house. Dorsey Keept School before the Marriage of Aaron Grigsby — So did Crawford — Crawford Kept soon after Dorsey — say the next year. Our School were Kept in the fall and winter, working in the Summer. Lincoln went to school to these 2 men about four winters — didn't go steady — I didn't go to school to Swany — Lincoln had a strong mind. I was older than he was by 6 years and further advanced — but he soon outstript me. We Studied 1st in Dilworths Spelling book — 2d in Websters — Lincoln Studied arithmetic — no geography — nor grammar — Lincoln read the life of Washington — the Pilgrims Progress Robinson Crusoe — the Bible — the new Testament — hymn Books — Watts hymns & Dupuy's. — think that news papers as Early as 1828–30 — Saw Sarah Lincoln many times — she was a woman of ordinary size — Have seen Mordecai Lincoln — he came to Indiana on a visit about 1822 or 3 — he was the oldest brother — Sarah Lincoln had a good mind, but I did not Know her so well as I did Abe: She married Aaron Grigsby —. We had but few books at that time and our opportunities were poor —

Abe Lincoln was a moral boy — was temperate — Sometimes he took his dram as Every body did at that time: he was honest: he was an industrious boy — he didn't love physical work — wouldn't do it if was agreeable to all — always was reading, studying, & thinking — Taking all in all he was not a lazy man. Lincoln Sometimes hunted on Sundays — What Lincoln read he read and re-read — read & Studied thoroughly —. He was generally at the head of all his classes whilst at school — in fact was nearly always so — He loved fishing & hunted Some — not a great deal — He was naturally Cheerful and good natured while in Indiana: Abe was a long tall raw boned boy. — odd and gawky — He had hardly attained 6 ft - 4 in when he left Indiana — weighed about 160 — I bought the hogs & corn of Thomas Lincoln when he was leaving for Ills — Bought about 100 and about 400 or 5 hundred bushes of corn — paid 10 c per bushel for the Corn — hogs lumped — Lincoln when a boy wore buckskin — for pants — wore Coon skin Caps — Sometimes fox Skin & possum Skin Caps — Buckskin was a Common dress at that time. When Lincoln was going about he read Everything that he could lay his hands on and it is more than probable that he read the Louisville Journal as well as other papers before he left Indiana and as before remarked what he read he read well and thoroughly — Never forgetting what he read —

Mr. N. Grigsby — says he now remembers that L. read newspapers — That they were Introduced about the time Col Jones came to Gentryville The Lincoln's moved to Ills in an oxe waggon — 2 yoke of oxen — waggon Ironed — Lincoln sold his farm to Gentry— Jas Gentry Sen — the old man — Mr Lincoln wrote a book of Chronicles — Satirizing the Grigsby and Josiah Crawford — The production was witty & showed talent — it marked the boy — as a man. Grigsby & Johnson had a fight — Grigsby would have whipt Johnson, had no foul play been used — Bill Boland showed foul play — the fight took place after the marriage of Chas & Reuben Grigsby were married — Thomas Lincoln had about 40 acres of land under cultivation when he left for Ills — he planted a young orchard on his old farm — Mr Thos Lincoln was a Carpenter & Cabinet Make. I have a Cupboard now in my house which Mr Thomas Lincoln made for me about 21. (1821 or 1822) Abe Lincoln has worked for my father some — worked at farming work —

To show Lincolns — Abes Humanity let me tell you a short story — One night when Lincoln & I were returning home fromg Gentryville we were passing along the road in the night. We saw something laying near or in a mud hole and Saw that it was a man: we rolled him over and over — waked up the man — he was dead drunk — night was cold — nearly frozen — we took him up — rather Abe did — Carried him to Dennis Hanks — built up a fire and got him warm — I left — Abe staid all night — we had been threshing wheat wheat — had passed Lincolns house — Lincoln stopt & took Care of the poor fellow— Smith —This was in the year 1825   There was one Store in Gentryville. Don't publish the mans name: he was an honorable man having now near us Excellent, dear & near relatives —

Went and took dinner with Mr Turnham — good dinner, good man. Abe Lincoln — was not fond of the Girls. Lincoln went to Gordons mills to grind We had hand Mills here

I knew Thomas Lincoln very well — have Studied his make & his form: he was not tall — was dark skinned — was Stout — muscular — not nervous — nor Sinewy — He weighed about 165. lbs.: he was Somewhat raw boned —   Abe favored him in many particulars. Both were humerous — good natured — Slow in action Somewhat. Sarah Lincoln favored Abe: she dark Skinned — heavy built —favored Abe very much — looked alike

I Knew Dennis Hanks: he was not the truest man in the world — would dodge — Equivocate and Exagerate: the idea that he taught Lincoln to read and write is to me preposterous —. The Hanks were a peculiar people — not chaste — Dennis Hanks was a bastard — was the son of _____ His mother married Levi Hall — Dennis Hanks married Miss Johnson Abe Lincoln's Step Sister — Squire Hall married Matilda Johnson — Squire Hall Hall was ½ brother to Hanks. Squire Hall was the Son   Levi Hall. These people were all good clever people I assure you, but they were peculiar —

Abe Lincoln preached the Sermon Jerimiah Cash. Cash had preached a sermon and Abe Said he could repeat it and we boys got him at it Abe mounted a log and proceeded to give the text and at it he went. He did preach almost the identical Sermon. It was done with wonderful accuracy — This was in 1827. Abe did not much like the girls — didn't appear to —

We had here in Early days hand mills on which — rather with which we ground our corn into meal[4]

Turnham was six years older than Lincoln and was admired by Lincoln as an older friend. Turnham was constable of Squire William Wood's court—Wood was interviewed on the same day. After Herndon left, Turnham found a book he used as constable and one Lincoln "read and re-read" when visiting Turnham: *Revised Laws of Indiana, Adopted and Enacted by the General Assembly at Their Eighth Session.* It was published in Corydon, the state capital, in 1824. Turnham sent the book to Gentryville, but Herndon was no longer there; Nathaniel Grigsby forwarded the book to Herndon.[5]

Revised Laws of Indiana was the first law book that Lincoln saw. It contained not only the state's laws but also the Declaration of Independence, the U.S. Constitution, and the Northwest Ordinance of 1787. All of these documents became important to Lincoln not only in practicing law, but also in formulating his view on slavery.

Unlike Lincoln, who "did not much like the girls" in Indiana, Turnham found a girl to marry in 1824. His first child was born on Christmas Day 1825. A family legend holds that the child was named Nancy on Lincoln's recommendation.[6] Lincoln may have been thinking of this child years later when on October 23, 1860, he replied to a letter from Turnham. In the letter, with the salutation of "My dear old friend," the presidential candidate wrote:

> Your kind letter of the 17th. is received. I am indeed very glad to learn you are still living and well. I well remember when you and I last met, after a separation of fourteen years, at the cross-road voting place, in the fall of 1844. It is now sixteen years more and we are both no longer young men. I suppose you are a grandfather; and I, though married much later in life, have a son nearly grown
>
> I would much like to visit the old home, and old friends of my boyhood, but I fear the chance for doing so soon, is not very good.
>
> Your friend & sincere well-wisher.
>   A. Lincoln[7]

Turnham and his family lived on the land purchased by his father within a mile of the Lincoln home, and it is likely that Lincoln frequently visited the family. Turnham's account of purchasing hogs and corn from Thomas in 1830 indicates that Thomas's farm was fairly successful by then.

It appears that Thomas was not only a productive farmer but also a skillful carpenter and cabinetmaker. Several neighbors repeated stories of Thomas building furniture and doing carpentry work for them. Thomas

William H. Herndon learned more about the carpentry work of Thomas Lincoln from David Turnham and probably saw Turnham's corner cabinet with its "star and streamer" and "hole and tooth" designs. The cabinet is in the Evansville Museum of Arts, History, and Science.

EVANSVILLE MUSEUM OF ARTS, HISTORY, AND SCIENCE

worked on this trade during winter and slack farming times. The work provided additional income for the family and allowed him to barter for the items the family needed in the cash-scarce community. Museums today treasure pieces of his furniture made in Kentucky and Indiana. In fact, the corner cabinet Turnham mentions is on display at the Evansville Museum of Arts, History, and Science. This piece, like many others, is both utilitarian and decorative. Inlaid strips of the "star and streamer" design on the jambs beside the doors and a "hole and tooth" design across the top indicate the work of a skilled craftsman.[8]

Turnham credits Thomas with contributing the sense of humor and good nature in Abraham; in appearance Abraham apparently favored Nancy Hanks Lincoln. Turnham complimented the Lincoln family, but reinforced comments Herndon heard from other sources about Dennis Hanks and the Hanks family.

Turnham provided names of some books used in the schools and discussed the importance of newspapers toward the end of Lincoln's stay in Indiana. Sarah (Sally) Bush Johnston Lincoln told Herndon that "Abe was a Constant reader of them — I am sure of this for the years of 1827–28–29–30."[9] Both mentioned the *Louisville Journal* as one such paper. William Wood's interview will detail the importance of newspapers in Lincoln's education. Titles of the papers provided by the neighbors, however, are not necessarily correct; the *Louisville Journal*, for example, did not begin publication until November 1830.[10]

As with all historians who conduct oral histories, Herndon later thought of many questions not asked during his interviews. Indeed, he wrote Turnham a number of times with follow-up questions. In early February 1866, the questions posed to Turnham dealt with local mills, the development of Gentryville, and Lincoln's possible troubles with the law. Here is Turnham's reply:

Dale Ind Feb 21st 66

Dear Sir.

Yours of the 5th inst is at hand. as you wish me to answer several questions, I will give you a few items of the early settlment of Ind. when my father Came here in the spring of 1819 he settled in spencer County with in one mile of Thomas Lincoln then a Widdower. the Chance for schooling was poor, but such as it was   Abraham

and myself attended the same schools, we first had to go seven miles
to mill and then it was a hand mill that would Grind from ten to
fifteen bushels of Corn in a day. there was but little wheat Grown
at that time and when we did have wheat we had to grind it on the
mill described and use it without bolting as there was no bolts in
the Country. in the Course of two or three years a man by the name
of Hufman built a mill on Anderson River about 12 miles distant
Abe and I had to do the milling on horse back, frequently going
twice to get one grist. then they Commenced building horse mills
of a little bitter quality than the hand mill

the Country was verry rough especiely in the low lands, so thick
with brush that a man Could scarcely git through on foot, these
places were Called Roughs, the Country abounded in game such as
bears deers turkies and the smaller game. about the time Huffman
built his mill there was a Road laid out from Corydon to Evansville,
runing by Mr Lincolns farm and through what is now Gentryville.
Corydon was then the state Capital.

About the year '23 there was another Road laid from Rockport
to Bloomington Crossing the aforesaid at right angles where Gentryville now stands   James Gentry Entered the land and in about a
year Gidian Romine brought Goods there and shortly after succed-
ed in geting a post ofice by the name of Gintryville post office. then
followed the laying of lots and selling — and a few were improved
but from some Cause the lots all fell back to the original owner. the
lots were Sold in 24 or 25. Romine kept goods there a short time
and sold out to Gentry. but the place kept on increasing slowly. Wm
Jones came in with a store, that made it improve a little faster but
Gentry bought him out. Jones bought a track of land ½ mile from
Gentryville moved to it went into buisness and drew the po and
nearly all the Custom. Gentry saw that it was ruining his town he
Compromised with Jones and Got him back to Gentryville, and
about the year 47 or 48 there was another survey and sale of lots,
which remains

This is as good a history of the rise of Gentryville as I Can give
after Consulting several of the old setlers, at that time there was a
great many dear licks and Abe and myself would go to those licks
sometimes and wach of nights to kill deer, though Abe was not so

fond of a gun as I was, there was 10 or 12 of those licks in a small Prarie on the Creak lying between Mr Lincolns and Mr Woods the man you Call More. This gave it the name of the Prarie fork of Pigeon Creak, the people in the first settling of this County was verry sociable. kind and accomidating, more so than now, but there was more drunkenness and stealing on a small scale, more immorality, less Religeon, less well placed Confidence.

you wish me to inform you if Abraham Lincoln was ever arested in Indiana. I was well and intimately acquainted with Mr Lincoln, from March 1819 until he left for Illinois having lived in one mile of him all that time and went to school with him, hunted game with him. worked on the farm with him, worked on the River fiting up a flat boat with him where the surrounding influance was verry bad. I believe I knew as much of Abraham Lincoln until he left Indiana as any other man living, and I never knew any thing disonerable of him, nor was he ever arrested to my knowladge or belief, nor did I ever hear of such a Charge until lately, the source of such a falshood Can well be immagined.

I believe I have answered your questions substansielly, if there if there remains any thing in which I Can be of service to you all you have to do is to drop me a few lines, and when you are ready, my son, T R Turnham wishes an Agency for Spencer County, I want a Coppy of your book an I know several that is wating and will buy no other til yours is out. Thomas had Just got home when you was at my house his is impared by being in the army he is not able to work and if he Can git an agency I think he Can sel a good many books, and as soon as he Can git a Canvasing book he will go to work

yours respectfully
D. Turnham[11]

Turnham related to Herndon that the development of Gentryville resulted from road construction. The first road mentioned actually ran along the southern boundary of the Lincoln farm. It is more frequently referred to as the Corydon-Boonville Road or the Corydon-New Harmony Road. It was a major east-west road and provided Abraham with an opportunity to see and talk with travelers.

Because this road was contiguous to James Gentry's farm, he began to sell items out of his house, just east of present-day Gentryville. When the Rockport-Bloomington Road was built (a major north-south road), the ideal location for a store lay at the intersection of the two roads. Gentry moved his store there. Although the early relationship between Gideon Romine and Gentry remains unclear, on June 15, 1826, a U.S. Post Office was established called Gentry's Store with Romine as postmaster. In 1828 Gentry sold a piece of land "where the state road leading from Rockport to Bloomington, intersects the state road from Corydon to Boonville"; the deed uses G. W. Romine's storehouse as a reference point.[12]

William Jones's role in the early commercial history of the area is problematic. Turnham correctly implies that Jones is important in Gentryville's later history, but his business activities during the Lincoln period are not obvious. One account states that "during the year 1828 William Jones was employed as clerk in the store of Gideon Rominie [*sic*], one of the pioneer merchants of that section. The following year he purchased a stock of goods and began business on his own account."[13] Romine had worked for Jones's father in Vincennes. This connection explains why a young man from Vincennes, who worked in business in Kentucky, came to Spencer County, Indiana. Whether Jones actually had a store while Lincoln lived here is not clear. The Gentry Store Post Office closed in 1829 but was reestablished in 1831 with Jones as postmaster. Jones owned property in the Gentryville area beginning in 1831.[14]

This commercial development allowed Lincoln to earn money and created a place for local citizens to gather and discuss concerns and interests. Lincoln worked for Gentry in his store. Gentry hired Lincoln to go with his son, Allen, on the flatboat trip to New Orleans. Apparently Lincoln performed other physical labor for Jones. John Tuley remembered years later, "Abe worked for awhile in a pork house for Bill Jones. I saw him several times cutting up pork and salting in and rendering lard."[15] When Herndon talked with John R. Dougherty and John S. Hougland, two Spencer County residents too young to remember Lincoln, they reported hearing similar stories of Lincoln cutting pork for Jones.[16] And Dennis Hanks maintained that Jones influenced Lincoln's political development.

12

"Abe was always a man though a boy"
William Wood

Most of William H. Herndon's interviewees in Spencer County were Abraham Lincoln's contemporaries, who remembered him as a schoolmate or friend. Three belonged to Lincoln's parents' generation. Nancy Castleman Richardson recalled the burial of Nancy Hanks Lincoln. Unfortunately, Absolom Roby, interviewed on September 17, 1865, did not offer new information. Herndon recorded that Roby said, "my memory is gone & I myself am fast going."[1]

The third older-generation contact was William Wood. Wood was born in Maryland in 1784 and lived in Daviess County, Kentucky, before moving to Spencer County, Indiana. If his information is correct, Wood's arrival in 1809 makes him one of the early settlers in this area; he did not, however, register a land claim with the Vincennes Land Office until years later.[2]

Wood settled on a ridge north of Little Pigeon Creek, about a mile and a half north of the Lincoln farm, putting him on the extreme northern edge of the Lincoln neighborhood. Apparently Wood was an adult with whom Lincoln discussed issues of the day and from whom he sought guidance. Evidently Lincoln referred to him as "uncle." Wood was forty years old when the Lincolns left Indiana.

Wood provided Herndon information on the Lincoln family and on a young Lincoln formulating and expressing opinions on the issues of the day:

Septr 15th 1865

Wm Wood

My Name is Wm Wood — Came from Ky in 1809., March, and settled in Indiana — now Spencer Co — Settled on the hill "yonder" — about l½ m north of the Lincoln farm — am now 82 ys of age. Knew Thomas and Abm Lincoln & family well. Thomas Lincoln & family Came from Ky Hardin Co, in 1816 according to my recollection. Mrs Thomas Lincoln — Abes mother was sick about 1½ years after she came. I sat up with her all one night. Mrs Lincoln, her mother & father were sick with what is called the milk Sickness. Sparrow & wife — Mrs Lincoln's father & Mother as well as Mrs L all died with that sickness — the Milk Sickness. Thomas Lincoln often and at various times worked for me — made cupboards &c other household furniture for me — he built my house — made floors — run up the stairs — did all the inside work for my house. Abe would Come to my house with his father and play and romp with my children

Abe wrote a piece Entitled the Book of Chronicles — a satire on a marriage —, Infair and putting the pairs to bed &c —: it showed the boy — this was in 1829. A wrote a piece on National politics — Saying that the American government was the best form

William Wood lies buried in a family cemetery overlooking Little Pigeon Creek near his homesite. His grave is marked by the broken stone in the foreground.

of Government in the world for an intelligent people — that it
ought to be Kept sound & preserved forever: that general Education Should   fostered and Carried all over the Country: that the
Constitution — should be saved — the Union perpetuated & the
laws revered — respected & Enforced &c (Mr Wood Said much
more which I can recollect)   This was in 1827 — or 8. Abe once
drank as all people did here at that time. I took news papers —
some from Ohio — Cincinnatie — the names of which I have now
forgotten — One of these papers was a temperance paper. Abe used
to borrow it — take it home and read it & talk it over with me: he
was an intelligent boy — a Sensible lad I assure you. One day Abe
wrote a piece on Temperance and brought it to my house. I read
it Carefully over and over and the piece Excelled for sound sense
anything that my paper Contained. I gave the article to one Aaron
Farmer, a Babtist Preacherr: he read it — it Struck him: he said he
wanted it to send to a Temperance paper in Ohio for publication:
it was sent and published   I saw the printed piece — read it with
pleasure over and over again. This was in 1827 — or 8. The political
article I Showed to John Pitcher an attorney of Posey Co Indiana
who was travelling on the circuit — on law business — and stopt
at my house over night: he read it carefully and asked me where I
got it. I told him that one of my neighbor boys wrote it: he couldn't
believe it till I told him that Abe did write it. Pitcher lived in Mt
Vernon Indiana. Pitcher in fact was struck with the article and Said
to me this — "The world can't beat it." He begged for it — I gave
it to him and it was published — can't say what paper it got into
— Know it was published. Abe was always a man though a boy. I
never knew him to swear: he would say to his play fellows and other
boys — Leave off your boyish ways and be more like men. Abe got
his mind and fixd morals from his good mother. Mrs Lincoln was a
very smart — intelligent and intellectual woman: She was naturally
Strong minded — was a gentle, Kind and tender woman — a Christian of the Babtist persuasion — She was a remarkable woman truly
and indeed. I do not think she absolutely died of the Milk Sickness
Entirely. Probably this helped to seal her fate.

   Abe came to my house one day and stood around about timid
& Shy. I Knew he wanted Something. I said to him — Abe what

is your Case. Abe replied — "Uncle I want you to go to the River
— (the Ohio) and give me Some recommendation to some boat." I
remarked — "Abe — your age is against you — you are not 21. yet."
"I Know that, but I want a start said Abe." I concluded not to go
for the boys good — did not go. I saw merchants in Rock-Port and
mentioned the Subject to them. In 1829 — this was

Abe read the news papers of the day — at least such as I took.
I took the Telescope. Abe frequently borrowed it. I remember the
paper now. I took it from about 1825. to 1830 — if not longer.
Abe worked for me on this rigde — (on this road leading from
Gentryville to Elizabeth — Dale P. Office place.). Abe whip sawed
— Saw him cutting down a large tree one day: I asked him what he
was going to do with it: he said he was going to saw it into plank
for his fathers new house The year was 1828 or 9. Abe could sink an
axe deeper in wood than any man I Ever Saw. Abe cut the tree down
and he and one Levi Mills whip sawed it into plank. As I Said the
plank was for Lincoln's new house: the house was not Completed
till after Lincoln left for Ills. The house that Lincoln lived in is gone.
Abe sold his plank to Crawford, the book man. The book story is
substantially Correct. Josiah Crawford put the lumber in his house
where it is now to be seen in the South East room (I Sat on this
plank myself — ate a good dinner at Mrs. Crawford's: Mrs C is a
lady — is a good woman — quite intelligent)   Abe wrote Poetry. a
good deal, but I can't recollect what about Except one piece which
was Entitled the "Neighborhood broil"   Abe always brought his
pieces — prose or Poetry to me straight. I thought more of Abe
than any boy I Ever Saw: he was a strong man — physically powerful: he could strike with a mall a heavier blow than any man: he was
long, tall and strong.

Mr Woods told me an axe story about Abe's bravery — which I
can recollect *'Tell* it.[3]

Wood's comments confirmed much of what others told Herndon.
Thomas Lincoln was indeed a carpenter and cabinetmaker. Again there are
details of the Lincolns starting construction on a house left unfinished when
they departed for Illinois. Thomas sold the planks prepared for the new
house to Josiah Crawford, owner of a book Lincoln accidentally ruined,
thus the reference to the book man.

Most importantly, Wood was present during the illness of Nancy Hanks Lincoln and Thomas and Elizabeth Sparrow. Like many in the community, he mistakenly assumed the Sparrows were Nancy's parents rather than her aunt and uncle. He implies Nancy was not a well person and milk sickness "helped to seal her fate." Although she died young, she was clearly important to her son's intellectual and moral development.

Lincoln's intellectual development is what Herndon found most interesting in the Wood conversation. Lincoln read newspapers and wrote essays on temperance and politics that impressed educated individuals and proved worthy of publication. Unfortunately, no such article has been located. Certainly the two men Wood mentions as arranging for publication had the contacts to accomplish this undertaking.

John Pitcher was one of the most respected attorneys in southwestern Indiana. Born in Connecticut and admitted to the bar there in 1815, Pitcher soon moved to Indiana and lived at Rockport for the last ten years of the Lincolns' stay in Indiana. Later he lived in Princeton, Indiana, and ended his days in Mount Vernon, Indiana. No doubt Lincoln saw Pitcher perform in court and in other legal activities in Spencer County. In 1888 Oliver C. Terry told Herndon collaborator Jesse W. Weik that Pitcher said he was well acquainted with Lincoln and that he lent law books to the Spencer County lad. Also Pitcher was in Rockport when Lincoln gave his speech in 1844 and visited President Lincoln in the White House in 1862. Pitcher does not mention having Lincoln's political article published and responds that "neither he, nor Lincoln ever wrote any thing upon the subject of temperance at any time, they both had mor[e] sense than to meddle with something they knew nothing about as the question was not agitated at that time."[4]

Herndon mistakenly recorded that Aaron Farmer was a "Babtist Preacherr." No Baptist preacher by that name appears in local records. Yet, a United Brethren in Christ preacher by that name worked in Indiana at the time, and Wood was associated with that church later in life. Although the United Brethren Church was active among German-speaking communities, it was open to working among English-speaking citizens as well.[5]

Farmer lived the life of the stereotypical circuit rider of the day, which may explain his death at an early age. He began his home missionary work in 1824 and traveled throughout much of southern Indiana. His best-known achievement—and the one most important in the Lincoln story—is that in 1829 he started publishing the first United Brethren periodical,

Zion's Advocate, from his home in Salem, Indiana. This paper stayed in print for a few years. In 1834 a new church paper was created, the *Religious Telescope*; and it may be the *Telescope* Wood remembered, not realizing it was unavailable while Lincoln lived in Indiana.[6]

Other than Wood's testimony, there is no evidence that the Lincoln articles ever appeared in print. The other interesting fact learned from Wood—Lincoln's desire to work on the river—is plausible. After returning from the New Orleans trip, Lincoln was acquainted with the opportunities that the river could provide. Understandably, a Spencer County farm community was limiting to an ambitious and curious twenty-year-old and the river was a way to escape the frontier. Perhaps Lincoln agreed with Wood, but in another year he turned twenty-one and could pursue his own course.

13

"Said that he would be Presidt of the US"
Elizabeth Crawford

The account of Abraham Lincoln borrowing a George Washington biography from Josiah Crawford widely circulated during the 1860 presidential campaign. The story appeared in the *Evansville Daily Journal* on May 23—less than a week after Lincoln won the Republican nomination. "Anecdote of Abe Lincoln" related this story:

> A man named Crawford owned a copy of "Weem's Life of Washington"—the only one in the whole neighborhood. Young Lincoln borrowed that interesting book (not having money to spare to buy one), and while reading it; by a slight negligence left it in a window, when a rain-storm came up and wet the book so as to ruin it. Young Lincoln felt very badly, but like an honest boy, he went to Mr. Crawford with the ruined book, acknowledged his accountability for its destruction, and his willingness to make due compensation. He said he had no money, but would work out the value of the book.
>
> The owner of the book said to him, "Well Abe, being as it's you, I won't be hard on you. If you will come over and pull fodder for two days I'll let you off."
>
> Abe went over accordingly, and pulled fodder the requisite time; and so tall and handy a lad was he, that Crawford required him to pull the fodder off of the tallest stalks, while he took the shortest ones himself.[1]

Reprints of this article appeared in many newspapers including the *Illinois State Journal*. John L. Scripps included the story in his 1860 biography and, as a result, "Mr. Crawford" became the best-known Indiana neighbor of the Lincolns. Scripps changed the book to Ramsey's *Life of Washington* and the necessary time to three days.

Surely William H. Herndon wanted to learn more about this story, but unfortunately Crawford, also known as "Old Blue Nose," had recently died. Crawford's grandson, William F. Adams, wrote in 1925 that he heard about Lincoln's assassination in a store on April 15, 1865, and hurried to share the news with his family. "When I told Grandfather Crawford, he slumped down and sat for some time as one stunned. He seemed to feel that all was lost. He had always been a strong, robust man, but from that day he began to fail, and on May 2, 1865, in his sixty-third year, he entered the eternal rest, three days less than a month after the death of his idol."[2]

Crawford married Elizabeth Anderson in Nelson County, Kentucky, in 1823. In October 1826 they purchased eighty acres of land southeast of the Lincolns' Indiana farm.[3] Elizabeth's grandson remembered that "she was a midwife by profession, having several medical works in which she was well read, and practices not only in accouchements but also in general practice, being frequently called in consultation by neighboring physicians."[4] Josiah's sister, Sarah, and her husband, William Barker, purchased the nearby Samuel Howell farm. One of William's sisters, Nancy, and her husband, Reuben Grigsby, arrived in the neighborhood before the Lincolns.[5]

Near noon Nathaniel Grigsby went with Herndon to the Crawford place. Since he could not talk to Josiah, Herndon interviewed Elizabeth. Herndon found Elizabeth an excellent source of information:

Sept 16th 1865

I went to Josiah Crawfords — the book man — not the School teacher as represented. The School teacher was a different man — landed there about 11. o'c AM — hitched my horse — Nat Grigsby with me, as he went all the rounds with me & to all places and was present at all interviews & conversations. Mrs Crawford was absent — at a sons house, distant about ¾ m attending to her sick grand child. I called for dinner. Mrs Crawfords daughter got us a good dinner — Sent for Mrs Crawford — her daughter rather would send for her. Before Mrs Crawford Came I looked over the "Library" — counted the Vols. There were 2 Bibles, 4 Hymn

Josiah Crawford is best known as owner of a book Lincoln borrowed and accidentally ruined. Crawford admired Lincoln and died a few weeks after hearing of the president's assassination.

Elizabeth Crawford was considered one of the best informants to William H. Herndon and later interviewers.

John Rowbotham made this sketch of Elizabeth Crawford's house shortly before William H. Herndon's visit. The Crawfords' house was built after the Lincolns left Indiana, and some of the flooring was reportedly prepared by the Lincolns for use in the new house they were building when the decision was made to move to Illinois.

books — Grahams History of the U.S. abridged —, "Great events
of America" — "Pioneers: of the New world" — a Testament
— "Grace Truman" "Websters Dictionary"— a small one — Some
News papers — mostly Religious. There was 12 or 15 books in
all — Mrs Crawford Came — is aged about 59 ys — She is good
looking — is a lady at first blush — is Easily approached quite
talkative — free — and generous. She Knew Abm Lincoln well.
"My husband is dead — died May 1865. Abm was nearly grown
when he left Indiana. Abe worked for my husband — daubed our
Cabin in 1824 or 5 in which we lived — The second work he did
for us was work done for the injured book — Weems life of Washington — Lincoln in 1829 borrowed this book and by accident got
it wet. L came & told honestly & Exactly how it was done —   the
story of which is often told. My husband said "Abe — as long as it
is you — you may finish the book and keep it." Abe pulled fodder
a day or two for it. We brought the book from Ky. Abe worked in
the field yonder — north of the house. Our house was there the
same little log cabin which Abe had *"daubed"*: it was made of round
logs "unhewn & unbarked"   The old Cabin, which Stood here by
this Cotton wood tree, was pulled down and this new one Erected
there. We had cleared about 18 acres of land when Abe first worked
for us. Abe made rails for us. Our first house was about 15 square
— one room — low   Thomas Lincoln made my furniture — Some
of it was sold at my husbands admr Sale. Thomas Lincoln was at
my house frequently — almost Every week — Sarah Lincoln Abe's
Sister worked for me: She was a good, kind, amiable girl, resembling
Abe. The Lincoln family were good people — good neighbors —:
they were honest & hospitable and very — very sociable. We moved
to Indiana in 1824 — Came from Ky. I Knew as a matter of Course
Sarah & Sally Lincoln very well. and I say to you that she was a
gentle, Kind, smart — shrewd — social, intelligent woman — She
was quick & strong minded: She had no Education, Except what
She gathered up herself. I Speak more of what she was by nature
than by culture. I never was a politician in all my life, but when such
men ran as Abe Lincoln — as in 1860 I as it were took the Stump:
he was the noblest specimen of man I Ever saw. Gentryville lies 4
m from here NW. Abe worked for us at various times at 25c per

day — worked hard & faithful and when he missed time would not charge for it. I took some of the rails which Abe cut and Split for us and had Canes made from them. They were white oak — cut from this Stump here — some one got into my house and Stole my cane.

Can't say what books Abe read, but I have a book called "The Kentucky Preceptor," which we brought from Ky and in which & from which Abe learned his school orations, Speeches & pieces to recite. School Exhibitions used to be the order of the day — not as now however. Abe attended them — Spoke & acted his part — always well free from rant & swell: he was a modest and Sensitive lad — never coming where he was not wanted: he was gentle, tender and Kind. Abe was a moral & a model boy, and while other boys were out hooking water melons & trifling away their time, he was studying his books — thinking and reflecting. Abe used to visit the sick boys & girls of his acquaintance. When he worked for us he read all our books — would sit up late in the night — kindle up the fire — read by it —cipher by it. We had a broad wooden shovel on which Abe would work out his sums — wipe off and repeat till it got too black for more: then he would scrape and wash off. and repeat again and again — rose Early. went to work — Come to Dinner — Sit down and read — joke — tell Stories &c. &c — Here is my husbands likeness — you need not look at mine. My husband was a substantial Man (and I say a cruel hard husband, Judging from his looks —). Sarah Lincoln was a strong healthy woman — was Cool — not Excitable — truthful — do to tie to —Shy Shrinking. Thomas Lincoln was blind in one Eye and the other was weak — so he felt his way in the work much of the time: his sense of touch was Keen — Abe did wear buck Skin pants — Coon Skin — opossum skin Caps. Abe ciphered with a coal or with red Keel got from the branches: he smoothed and planed boards — wrote on them — ciphered on them. I have seen this over and over again. Abe was Sometimes Sad — not often — he was reflective — was witty & humorous.

Abe Lincoln was one day bothering the girls — his sister & others playing yonder and his Sister Scolded him — Saying Abe you ought to be ashamed of yourself— what do you Expect will become of you "Be Presdt of the U.S," promptly responded Abe. Abe wrote a good Composition — wrote prose and poetry. He wrote 3 or 4 Satires — one was Called the Book of Chronicles. He said that he would be Presdt of the US told my husband so often — Said it jokingly — yet with a Smack of deep Earnestness in his Eye & tone: he Evidently had an idea —a feeling in 1828 that he was bound to be a great man — No doubt that in his boyish days he dreamed it would be so. Abe was ambitious — sought to outstrip and override others. This I Confess.

One of Abes pieces — the Book of Chronicles — ran about thus —

> "I will tell you a joke about [Josiah?] & Mary
> Tis neither a joke nor a story
> For Reuben & Charles have married 2 Girls
> But Billy has married a boy
> He tried ———— (Mrs Crawford blushed)
> The girls on Every Side
> He had well tried
> None could he get to agree
> All was in vain
> He went home again
> And since that he's married to Natty

I don't pretend to give the Exact words — nor its rhyme — nor metre now —will think it over — recall it and write to you in Ills. The Poem is Smutty and I can't tell it to you — will tell it to my daughter in law: she will tell her husband and he shall send it to you.

I left Mrs Crawford about 3 o'cl. P.M. Before leaving She gave me the American Preceptor and a cane made from one of Abes rails — for both of which I thanked her: I really felt proud of the gift and felt a gratitude for them — Mrs Crawford is a Lady of the Ky Stamp[6]

There is documentation that rails from Crawford's farm were used in the 1860 campaign. On June 2, 1860, the *Evansville Daily Journal* reported that William Jones of Gentryville sent the paper a rail from the Crawford farm that was proudly displayed in the office next to a picture of Henry Clay. The Library of Congress holds the letter that Jones sent to Evansville banker George Rathbone with the rails. He informed Rathbone, "I send you enough for several canes—one to be expressed to Abe himself with my

THE
KENTUCKY PRECEPTOR,

CONTAINING

A NUMBER OF USEFUL LESSONS

FOR READING AND SPEAKING.

COMPILED FOR THE USE OF SCHOOLS.

BY A TEACHER.

Delightful task ! to rear the tender thought,
To teach the young idea how to shoot,
To pour the fresh instruction o'er the mind,
To breathe the enlivening spirit, and to fix
The generous purpose in the glowing breast.
THOMPSON.

THIRD EDITION, REVISED, WITH CONSIDERABLE ADDITIONS.

COPY-RIGHT SECURED ACCORDING TO LAW.

LEXINGTON, (Ky.)

PUBLISHED BY MACCOUN, TILFORD & CO.

1812.

Elizabeth Crawford gave William H. Herndon this copy of *The Kentucky Preceptor*. Lincoln used this book for school recitations. Today it is back in Indiana as part of the collection of the Lilly Library.

compliments & sincere wishes for his success."[7] Rathbone quickly complied with Jones's wishes and, on June 1, 1860, sent a cane and a copy of Jones's letter to Lincoln.[8]

Curiously Elizabeth told Herndon someone stole *her* cane; yet, she gave Herndon a cane in addition to *The Kentucky Preceptor*. Printed in Lexington, Kentucky, the text was purchased in 1819 while the Crawfords lived in Kentucky. Since 1953 it has belonged to the collection of the Lilly Library at Indiana University. Obviously, this volume was popular for school orations; one description notes it "contains essays selected from various sources relating to industry, magnanimity, remorse of conscience, Columbus, Demosthenes, the Scriptures as a rule of life, credulity, and liberty and slavery."[9]

Eventually Herndon returned to questions about the Book of Chronicles or the "Chronicles of Reuben," Lincoln's story recalling marriages of Reuben Grigsby's sons on April 16, 1829: Reuben Jr. to Elizabeth Ray in Spencer County and Charles to Matilda Hawkins in neighboring Dubois County. The family held a wedding feast at the Grigsby home. They invited many of the neighborhood but evidently not the Lincolns. Perhaps this was because the Lincolns blamed the Grigsbys for not getting help for Sarah Lincoln Grigsby during her pregnancy. Following the dinner, the brides entered separate bedrooms upstairs to await their new husbands. As the story goes, Lincoln arranged for the "waiters" to show these bridegrooms the wrong darkened rooms. The story concluded, in the words from *Herndon's Lincoln*, "But the mother, being fearful of a mistake, made enquiry of the waiters, and learning the true facts took the light and sprang upstairs. It came to pass she ran to one of the beds and exclaimed 'O Lord, Reuben, you are in bed with the wrong wife.' The young men, alarmed at this, sprang up out of bed and ran with such violence against each other they came near knocking each other down."[10]

Years later one of the brides, Elizabeth Grigsby, recalled, "Yes, they did have a joke on us. They said my man got into the wrong room and Charles got into my room. But it wasn't so. Lincoln just wrote that for mischief. Natty Grigsby told us that 'it was all set down; all put on record.' Abe and my man often laughed about that."[11] Lincoln was not concerned with the truth but a good story. Yet, at this time, the family probably displayed less than good humor. As Nathaniel said in his interview, "It hurt us then, but its all over now."[12]

Elizabeth felt uncomfortable telling the story to a stranger and said, "The Poem is Smutty and I can't tell it to you — will tell it to my daughter in law: she will tell her husband and he shall send it to you." She did so, and Herndon received the following letter from one of her sons, S. A. Crawford, early the next year. Although Crawford's letter is difficult to read and his spelling confusing (*waters* for *waiters* for instance), it is easily seen why Elizabeth refused to repeat the story:

January the 4th 1866

Dear Sir

i received your letter of September the 28 and also another of December the 15   i beg to excuesed for not ancern your first letter as i was very buissy ageting ready to Sart to nelson County ky to See about my fathers estate and as you did not Say eny thing about us riting to you we neglected as we Concluded t[hat] you had got all the information that you wanted   thair was one thing th[at] i did not think of teling you   when you was here that was the flore you was Setting on when you was here was   plank that abraham lincoln whip Sawed about the year 1830

We moved to this Country in 1824 and Soon after become aquainted with the lincoln famly   when abraham was a strap of a boy and his play mats would fall out with him he would laugh and make rimes and Sing them and tell the boys that he intended to be presedent yet   while other boys would quarl he would apper to be a pese maker and while others would romp and lafe he would be engaged in the arithmetic or asking questions about Som history heard or red of

first Chronicles of ruben now thair was a man in those days whose name was ruben and the Same was very grate in substance in horses and Cattle and Swine and avery grate house hold and it Came to pass that when the Sons of ruben grew up that thay ware desirus of taking to them Selves wives and being too well known as to onor in ther own Country So thay took to them Selves a Journy in to a far Country and procured to them Selves wives   and it Came to pass that when thay ware about to make the return home that thay Sent a messenger before them to bare the tidines to there parents So thay inquired of the mesengers what time there Sones and there wives wood Come   So thay made a grate feast and Cald all ther kinsmen and neighbors in and maid grate preperations   So when the time drew near thay sent out two men to meet the grooms

and ther brids with a treet to welcom them and to acompny them
So when thay Came near to the house of ruben there father the
mesengers Came on before them and gave a Shout and the whole
multitude ran out with Sho[uts of] Joy and musick playing on all
kinds of instruments of musick Some playing on harps and Some on
vials and Some blowing on rams hornes Some Casten dust and ashes
tourd heaven and amongst the rest Josiah bloing his buble making
Sound So grate that it maid the neighborin hills and valys eco with
the resonding aclamation So when thay had played and harped
Sounded tell the grooms and brides approched the gate the father
ruben met them and welcomed them in to his house and the weding
dinner being now ready thay ware all invited to Set down to dinner
placing the bridegroomes and ther wives at each end of the table
waters ware then apointed to Carve and wate on the guests So when
thay had all eaten and ware ful and mary thay went out and Sang
and played tell evening and when thay had made an end of feasting
and rejoising the multitude dispersed each to his one home the family then took Seat with

ther waters to Converse awhile which time preperations ware
being maid in an upper Chamber for the brids to be first Convayed
by the waters to ther beds this being done the waters took the two
brids up stares to ther beds placing one in a bed at the rite hand
of the Stares and the other on the left the   waters Come down
and nancy the mther inquired of the waters which of the brids was
paced on the rite hand and thay told her   So She gave directions to
the waters of the bridegrooms and thair thay took the bridegrooms
and placed them in the rong beds and Came down Stares but the
mother being fearful that thair mite be a mistake inquired again of
the waters and learning the fact took the light and Sprang up tares
and running to one of the beds exclaimed ruben   you are in bed
with Charleses wife   the young men both being alarmed Sprang
out of bed and ran with such violance against each other that thay
Came very near nocking each other down which gave evidence to
those below that the mistake was Ceartain   thay all Came down
and had a Conversation about who had maid the mistake but it
Could not be decided

So ended the Chapter

i will tell you a Joke about Jouel and mary
it is neither a Joke nor a tory
for rubin and Charles has maried two girles
 but biley has maried a boy
the girles he had tried on every Side
but none could he get to agree
all was in vain he went home again
and sens that he is maried to natty

so biley and naty agreed very well
and mamas well pleased at the matc[h]
the egg it is laid but Natys afraid
the Shell is So Soft that it never will hatc[h]
but betsy She Said you Cursed ball head
my Suiter you never Can be
besids your low Croch proclaimes you a botch
and that never Can anser for me

this is memorised by Mrs elizeabeth Crawford an oald blind
lady that Can hardly See
ritten by her Son and farweded
S A Crawford[13]

While some see significance in the homosexual conclusion to the Chronicles, the members of the community saw this addition as a way for more members of the Grigsby family to experience Lincoln's fabricated ridicule. The Grigsby family was angry with the Chronicles, but most others saw the work as witty and funny. Perhaps the most telling lesson from the story is that the young Lincoln gained a greater appreciation for the power of words. Herndon concluded, "These crude rhymes and awkward imitations of scriptural lore demonstrated that their author, if assailed, was merciless in satire. In after years Lincoln, when driven to do so, used the weapon of ridicule with telling effect."[14]

Elizabeth wrote five more letters answering Herndon's questions over the next nine months. In these letters she discussed social customs of the community, flowers grown, songs sung, even a song sung at Sarah Lincoln Grigsby's wedding. In one letter Elizabeth described how the "Linkerns," she spelled the name as she pronounced it, passed around a plate of raw potatoes, for eating like apples, at a religious meeting in the Lincoln home.[15]

14

"I hit him with an Ear of Corn"
Green B. Taylor

Green B. Taylor witnessed an important time during Abraham Lincoln's Indiana years—his work at Troy on the Ohio River. Troy lies about a half mile east of the mouth of the Anderson River, sometimes called Anderson Creek. Troy was laid out in lots in 1815, and some twenty log cabins were erected. Perhaps the most prominent entrepreneur of the town was James Taylor, Green's father. A county history written in 1885 said of Taylor, "He was a farmer and flatboatman. He did a very large business as pork-packer at the mouth of Anderson Creek. He also shipped beef, corn, and other grains, hay, etc. His son, Green B. Taylor, succeeded him in the forties and continued the business on a much larger scale."[1]

As is seen in this interview with Green, the Taylor business drew Lincoln to the river:

Septr 16th 1865

My name is Green B. Taylor — aged 46 — am the son of James Taylor — I Knew Abe Lincoln well — He worked for my father 6 or 9 Months worked on the farm — run the ferry for my father from the Ky shore to the Indiana shore — The ferry crossed the Ohio — & crossed the Anderson River — Abe would ferry from one side to the other and land in Perry or cross the Ohio and Anderson and land in Spencer Co — Abe lived with my father in the year 1825 and worked about 6 or 9 mo — he plowed — ferried, ground Corn on the hand mill — grated Corn — My mother was Kind to Abe and Abe to her — he Abe went after the Doctress when my sister was born [*illegible*] my sister was born in 1825 — so it is no guess

IDA TARBELL, *THE EARLY LIFE OF ABRAHAM LINCOLN* (NEW YORK: S. S. MCLURE, 1896)

Green B. Taylor was known until his death as the boy who hit Lincoln with an ear of corn. This picture was taken in the 1890s.

— Abe helped to Kill hogs for — John Woods — Jno Duthan & Stephen McDaniel — Barrells of hot water — blankets — clubs — were used in the process. Abe Lincoln was honest — industrious — social — Kind & courteous — I hit him with an Ear of Corn once — cut him over the Eye — he got mad — My mother whipt me severely as she should have done — Abe Lincoln got $6 per mo — and 31 c per day for Killing hogs as this was rough work — He and I slept up stairs —   He usually read till near midnight reading — rose Early — would make a fire for my mother — put on the water & fix around generally — John Johnson & Wm Grigsby had a pitched fight — at or near Hoskins   Near the Spring or close to Gentryville — My father was the second for John Johnson — Wm Whitten was the second for Wm Grigsby — They met and had a terrible fight — Wm Grigsby was too much for Lincoln's man — Johnson. After they had fought a long time — and it having been agreed not to break the ring, Abe burst through, caught Grigsby — threw him off some feet — stood up and swore he was the big buck at the lick — (It was here, says Hoskins, says that Abe waived

a bottle of whiskey over his head and said as above). After Abe
did this — it being a general invitation for a general fight they all
pitched in and had quite a general fight.

¼ M below Troy.[2]

When Spencer County split off from Perry County in 1818, the
Anderson River became the dividing line between the two. The river not
only divided the counties but also obstructed land transportation along the
Ohio River. Taylor remedied this situation by starting a ferry over the river;
Lincoln operated the ferry and butchered hogs.

JOSEPH H. BARRETT, *LIFE OF ABRAHAM LINCOLN* (CINCINNATI: MOORE, WILSTACH, AND BALDWIN, 1865)

In 1865 John Rowbotham made this illustration of the area where Lincoln ran a ferry for
James Taylor.

The well-known story of Taylor hitting Lincoln with an ear of corn
served as the headline in Taylor's obituary in the *Evansville Courier* in 1899:

> When Lincoln was about 18 years old and Captain Taylor was a boy
> of 10 or 11 Lincoln ran a ferry across Anderson creek, near Troy, for
> young Taylor's father, James Taylor. Lincoln was a great tease and
> one day while a flatboat was being loaded with corn near the ferry,
> began to plague the boy about some youthful sweetheart. Young
> Taylor soon lost his temper, and picking up an ear of corn threw it
> at the gaunt ferryman. The aim was true and the ear struck Lincoln

just above the eye, cutting a gash which left a scar that Lincoln carried to his grave.[3]

The fight story related in Taylor's interview also appears in the obituary.

Interestingly, Taylor states that the ferry crossed both the Anderson and the Ohio rivers. As president, Lincoln told William Seward, secretary of state, about using a small boat to ferry on the Ohio. In his 1866 Lincoln biography, J. G. Holland relates the story told Seward this way:

> As he [Lincoln] stood at the landing, a steamer approached, coming down the river. At the same time two passengers came to the river's bank that wished to be taken out to the packet with their luggage. Looking among the boats at the landing, they singled out Abraham's, and asked him to scull them to the steamer. This he did, and after seeing them and their trunks on board, he had the pleasure of receiving upon the bottom of his boat, before he shoved off, a silver half dollar from each of his passengers. "I could scarcely believe my eyes," said Mr. Lincoln, in telling the story. "You may think it was a very little thing," continued he, "but it was a most important incident in my life. I could scarcely believe that I, a poor boy, had earned a dollar in less than a day. The world seemed wider and fairer before me. I was a more hopeful and confident being from that time."[4]

In the 1920s Kentucky attorney William H. Townsend discovered another story about Lincoln and the Ohio, this time a legal matter with Lincoln as defendant. If true, this trial is Lincoln's first experience pleading a case. According to Townsend, Lincoln rowed some passengers to meet a steamboat in the river. John Dill and his brothers, who held legal right to operate a ferry across the river, summoned Lincoln to the Kentucky shore. At first, the Dill brothers threatened to harm Lincoln for violating their exclusive ferry rights; but then they decided to take the young Lincoln to court. Court was held at the home of Squire Samuel Pate (the home still stands today between Lewisport and Hawesville, Kentucky). The Dills presented their case, and Lincoln admitted he ferried passengers to the steamboat, but maintained he did not know it was illegal and had no criminal intent.

The young man from Indiana impressed Pate with his sincerity, and the judge found in Lincoln's favor. Pate found that indeed there was a penalty

The Pate House in Kentucky was the site of a court case against Lincoln by the Dill brothers, who claimed Lincoln had illegally ferried passengers to a steamboat. The original log building is a portion of the home seen today.

for anyone who "for reward, set any person over any river or creek, whereupon public ferries are appointed." But in Pate's opinion taking passengers only partway did not meet the definition of *across* the river, and Lincoln had not violated the law. [5]

According to Townsend, Pate took a special interest in Lincoln and took time to discuss legal matters with the young man.[6] One postscript to this story is the legend that Lincoln made frequent trips to the Pate home not only to observe the law in action, but also to visit Pate's niece, Caroline Meeker.[7]

15

"Learned boy among us unlearned folks"
Anna Caroline Roby Gentry

As important as the Gentry name is to the Indiana Abraham Lincoln story, the only person bearing that name interviewed by William H. Herndon was Allen Gentry's wife, Anna. Perhaps these omissions originate in the Gentry family's loyalty to the Democratic Party. Herndon sought to interview only individuals politically friendly to President Lincoln. Ada Gentry Rhoades, great-granddaughter of James Gentry, told this family version of the relationship with candidate Lincoln in 1935:

> "We frequently corresponded," grandfather told me, and when the Gentry family heard that Lincoln was elected president we were overjoyed, although there was not a Gentry cast a vote for him. And when Spencer county friends visited the president after he was inaugurated and he inquired about the Gentrys he was told how happy they were over his election. Lincoln laughed and said, "Yes I know; but they were too good democrats to vote for me and I'll bet on it."[1]

Though it is not known when the Absolom Roby family moved to Spencer County, the 1820 census lists a family of four in the area at that time. Anna Caroline Roby (born in 1807) married Allen Gentry on March 20, 1828. Their first child, born on December 18, 1828, was named James in honor of his grandfather. Anna was a widow when Herndon visited her; Allen had died on September 24, 1862.[2]

Herndon asked Anna about her school days and her husband's trip to New Orleans with Lincoln:

James Gentry was considered the richest man in the neighborhood and the man for whom Gentryville was named. Lincoln accompanied Gentry's son Allen on a flatboat trip in 1828 to New Orleans.

Rockport Ind Septr 17th 1865

My name is Mrs. Gentry — wife of Allen Gentry with whom Mr Lincoln went to NO for Jas Gentry Sen in April 1828 — I knew Mr L well — he and I went to school together — I was 15 ys old — Lincoln about the same age — we went to school to Crawford in 1822 or 3 I think — I used Websters Spelling book— Lincoln the same — One day Crawford put a word to us to Spell: the word to Spell was *defied*. Crawford said if we did not spell it he would keep us in school all day & night — we all missed the word — Couldn't Spell it. We spelled the word Every way but the right way —. I saw Lincoln at the window: he had his finger On his *Eye* and a smile on his face. I instantly took the hint that I must change the letter y into an I. Hence I Spelled the word — the class let out. I felt grateful to Lincoln for this Simple thing. Abe was a good — an Excellent boy. Speaking about the boat & the trip let me say to you that I saw the boat — was on it — saw it start and L with it. It started from yonder landing — Gentrys Landing — My husband was Allen Gentry — They went down the Ohio & Mississippi for Jas Gentry Sen — they Came back in June 1828. — flat boat started from Gentrys landing yonder — say ½ a mile from this house due South & ¾ of a M below Rockport. Abe read many books — cant say what they were — regret it — he worked and bought his books generally — fought his own way — When my husband & L went down the river they were attacked by Negroes — Some Say Wade Hamptons Negroes, but I think not: the place was below that called *Mdme Bushams Plantation* 6 M below Baton Rouche — Abe fought the Negroes — got them off the boat — pretended to have guns — had none — the Negroes had hickory Clubs — my husband said "Lincoln get the guns and Shoot — the Negroes took alarm and left. Abe did not go much with the girls — didn't like crowds — didn't like girls much — too frivalous &c. The Schools we went to taught Spelling —reading — writing and Ciphering to single rule of 3 — no further —. Lincoln got ahead of his masters — Could do him no further good: he went to school no more — Abe was an honest boy — a good boy — all liked him — was friendly — somewhat Sociable — not so much so as we wanted him — Abe was a long — thin — leggy — gawky boy dried up & Shriveled

One Evening Abe & myself were Sitting on the banks of the Ohio or on the boat Spoken of. I Said to Abe that the Moon was going down. He said "Thats not so — it don't really go down: it Seems So. The Earth turns from west to East and the revolution of the Earth Carries us under, as it were: we do the sinking as you call it. The moon as to us is Comparatively still. The moons sinking is only an appearance." I said to Abe — "Abe — what a fool you are." I Know now that I was the fool — not Lincoln. I am now thoroughly Satisfied that Abe Knew the general laws of Astronomy and the movements of the heavenly bodies — He was better read then than the world knows or is likely to Know Exactly —. No man could talk to me that night as he did unless he had Known something of geography as well as astronomy. He often & often Commented or talked to me about what he read — seemed to read it out of the book as he went along — did so to others — he was the learned boy among us unlearned folks — He took great pains to Explain — Could do it so Simply He was diffident then too — only 17 ys of age —[3]

Obviously Herndon was curious about the flatboat trip, and Anna provided some information, including details on the attack along the way. Furthermore, Anna clearly states that the trip was from April to June 1828.

Anna was the only female schoolmate—other than Lincoln's stepsister Matilda Johnston Hall Moore—that Herndon interviewed. Her comments that "Abe was a long — thin — leggy — gawky boy dried up & Shriveled" are not ones to boost a young man's self-confidence around girls.

The story Anna tells of sitting on the banks of the river sounds romantic until it is remembered that Abraham and Anna sit on the flatboat that will travel to New Orleans; thus the evening occurred while she was engaged or married to Gentry. Louis A. Warren documents eleven stories about Lincoln's involvement with young women in Indiana. One girl, Hannah Gentry, complained that Lincoln was "too fond of onions, as she could not endure them." Of course many of these stories emerged after Lincoln became famous, and women wanted to boast that they rejected him.[4]

Everyone from his stepmother to his boyhood friends tells Herndon that Lincoln was not romantically involved with girls in Indiana. Despite much interest in this topic recently, William E. Gienapp perhaps provided the best conclusion: "he had little interest in girls. While they recognized his great kindness of heart, his homely looks, ill-fitting clothes, and lack of manners and social graces intensified his natural awkwardness in the presence of females."[5]

16

"I want a history written that is all true"
Memories and Interpretations after Herndon

For thirty years after William H. Herndon's visit to Indiana, others collected and published Abraham Lincoln stories and memories. In 1902 an Evansville reporter, speaking of Spencer County, wrote:

> The great mass of tradition that clings about memorable spots and memorable occasions has been winnowed repeatedly, but even now when the failing memories of old men brighten for a moment, a new thing is recalled to add to the authentic biography of the great man or to prove what before was doubtful because of contradictions or hearsay.[1]

The result of Herndon's work first appeared in 1872 in Ward Hill Lamon's *Life of Abraham Lincoln*, ghostwritten by Chauncey Black. Needing money, Herndon sold Lamon, a friend and associate of both Herndon and Lincoln, copies of the collected material. From that time on, the Herndon material became the major source of information about Lincoln's Indiana years.

In 1889 Herndon collaborated with Jesse W. Weik to publish *Herndon's Lincoln: The True Story of a Great Life*. Born in Greencastle, Indiana, and educated at DePauw University, Weik met Herndon in Springfield in 1882 when Weik worked as a pension agent for the U.S. government. Weik wrote the Lincoln story while Herndon provided the facts and interpretations.[2]

As early as 1880, Weik had made several trips to southern Indiana to collect his own stories from those who knew Lincoln.[3] One such account came from John M. Lockwood of Princeton, Indiana. According to Lockwood:

> In the afternoon of a particularly warm, dry day in August, 1827, a tall, beardless long-legged boy about my own age, dressed in a suit of well-worn brown jeans, the trousers of which he had long before outgrown, and wearing a woolen hat and coarse, heavy, plain-cut leather shoes of the style then in vogue among backwoods people, came riding up to the mill. Behind him, tied over the horse's back, was a bunch of wool, which, after dismounting, he carried across the road and dropped at my feet, asking if it could be carded. I answered in the affirmative, but added that people who patronized the wool-carder, like those who carried their grain to the grist-mill, had to await their turn; but, when he told me that he had ridden from a point in the interior of Spencer County almost forty miles away, I relented somewhat and decided that in his case I would be justified in waiving the ordinary rule. On account, therefore, of the long return journey that lay before him, I promised that his work should be done in advance of its turn, and that it would be ready for him before the close of the afternoon—an announcement that seemed to afford him great relief. In response to my request he gave me his name, but, being new to me and one I had never before heard, he looked over my shoulder and carefully spelled it for me as I set it down in the little book which contained the history of the day's transactions. There were two ways, I explained to him, of settling for the work—either by paying cash or taking the requisite toll. "But I have no money," he interrupted in a melancholy tone of voice, "so you will have to keep out wool enough for your pay."[4]

Then, according to Lockwood's narrative, Lincoln carefully examined the equipment of the horse-powered mill and walked around the town before returning to claim the fifteen pounds of wool that remained after Lockwood extracted three pounds for the toll. Lockwood continued his account:

> "I don't want to keep you away from your work," he said, "but before I left town I thought I would like to ask you if you know Julia Evans," mentioning the name of my employer's niece. "Yes, I know

her well," I responded, "and she is not only the handsomest but one of the best girls in town."

It was then he confided to me the fact that he had passed Miss Evans in the street a short time before; that she had bowed to him, as was then customary even between strangers, and that from a passer-by he had learned her name. It was very evident he was thoroughly captivated by her beautiful face and figure, for she was indeed a charming girl and admittedly the village belle.[5]

Either Lockwood had an excellent memory or he could tell a good story—or both. Indeed, he told Weik that he talked with Lincoln thirty-one years later in Mount Carmel, Illinois, and Lincoln remembered the 1827 incident.[6]

Of course, as a near relative, Dennis Hanks continued to be the favorite source of Lincoln information, especially by newspaper reporters writing in February—Lincoln's birth month. On September 22, 1892, Hanks was a guest at the thirtieth anniversary celebration of "Emancipation Day" in Paris, Illinois. The nearly blind ninety-three-year-old man was attempting to walk home when a team of horses pulling a wagon ran him down. He died a month later from injuries received in the accident.[7]

Eleanor Atkinson conducted a well-known interview with the elderly Hanks in January 1889 and published her interview in a fifty-seven-page book some sixteen years after Hanks died.

The Atkinson interview provides anecdotal accounts of Lincoln's life in Indiana, including primitive frontier conditions, young Abe's whittling pegs for his mother's coffin, and his expressing interest in Robert Owen's New Harmony experiment. Hanks told Atkinson a story popular in children's books, "thar was always a passel o' youngsters 'round the place. One day Abe put 'em up to wadin in the mud-puddle by the hoss-trough. Then he tuk 'em one by one, turned 'em upside down, an walked 'em acrost the ceilin', them ascreamin' fit to kill." Lincoln's stepmother thought the prank funny, and Abraham offered to clean up the mess and re-whitewash the ceiling.[8] The interview contains wonderful quotations, including "the things I want to know is in books, My best friend's the man who'll git me one." And, when Hanks, referring to *The Arabian Nights*, told Abraham "them yarns is all lies," Lincoln replied, "Mighty darned good lies." Lincoln then continued reading, "chucklin to hisself."[9]

In 1872 the town of Lincoln City was platted partially on the old Lincoln farm. A rail line soon followed, and travelers heard stories of Lincoln's youth at the town's depot, hotels, and saloons.

William Fortune was a young man in 1881 when he interviewed Lincoln acquaintances.

Newspaper reporters also saw Spencer County as a source of fresh information to sell articles and papers. In 1872 the town of Lincoln City was platted by a group of investors from Cincinnati, and two years later the Cincinnati, Rockport, and Southwestern Railroad was completed along the edge of what had been the Lincoln farm. Thus, depot, stores, restaurants, and hotels sprang up less than a hundred yards from the Lincoln cabin site.[10]

In 1894, Rockport resident General James L. Veatch warned:

> Beware of trusting to the stories of roving newspaper correspondents. Every one of this class who passes Lincoln Station on the Rockport Rail Road must needs send to his paper some thing about Lincoln. The train generally stops 15 or 20 minutes. The . . . correspondent rushes out and finds in the nearest whiskey shop a crowd of old "soakers" who are ready at a word to tell many things about Lincoln that no one else even knew.
>
> I have read many of these productions and corrected some of them, but have not seen one single truthful account coming from such a source.[11]

Veatch, accompanied by young William Fortune, sought to obtain the true stories a few years earlier. Born in Boonville, Indiana, on May 27, 1863, while his father, a corporal in the First Regiment of Indiana Cavalry, was away at war, Fortune became a printer's helper at the age of thirteen, working for the *Boonville Standard*. At fifteen or sixteen years old, he began collecting information for a history of Warrick County, his home county. This work resulted in the 180-page book, *Warrick and Its Prominent People: A History of Warrick County, Indiana*, a remarkable achievement for a teenager whose education, like Lincoln's, was obtained merely by reading books.[12]

Speaking of this book, Fortune later recalled:

> This little book attracted some newspaper attention, and some of this fell under the eye of General James C. Veatch, then living at Rockport. . . . He [Veatch] rose to the rank of Major-General in the Civil War and was a personal friend of Abraham Lincoln and was chosen by the Indiana General Assembly as chairman of the Reception Committee of citizens who officially represented our State in welcoming Lincoln when he crossed the boundary line between Illinois and Indiana on his way to the national capitol to become President of the United States. . . .

General Veatch was in the habit of traveling between Rockport and Evansville over the week end. He wrote a letter proposing to stop at Boonville to see me on one of these journeys and soon afterward he visited me. I think General Veatch was very much astonished when he found he was talking to a boy.[13]

Regardless of Fortune's youth, Veatch proposed a visit to Spencer County to interview residents who remembered Lincoln. Thus, in October 1881, the old soldier and the young author interviewed Polly Egnew, Polly Stapleton, Joseph Richardson, Silas Richardson, David Turnham, Henry Bruner [Brooner], Henry Beeler, Elizabeth Crawford, and Nathaniel Grigsby. Although, sadly, Fortune never published his interviews, he did discuss them in a speech to the Southwestern Indiana Historical Society on November 12, 1925. About these Spencer County residents, Fortune concluded, "They preferred to talk about things mainly interesting to themselves, such, for instance, as that the last bear hunt was in 1821 when a total of nine bears were killed; that there were many snakes in the country and that 'one night Abe found a copperhead under his pillow.'"[14] But like Herndon, Fortune found two of his interviewees, Crawford and Grigsby, "outstanding." He described Crawford as "a very bright woman and quite vivacious. Her memory seemed quite clear and definite."[15] In addition to repeating the story about Lincoln ruining the Washington biography, Crawford discussed the Lincoln family. The following excerpt comes from Fortune's 1881 notes.

His sister was a good girl and pretty much like Abe in her character. She staid with me about a year before she married. She said there were enough at home. She was good girl and her and her fellow done their sparking at our house. She died and is buried in old graveyard at Little Pigeon church.

Lincoln's were very poor folks. First time I called on them I remember it all seemd might funny to me. They scraped sweet potatoes and passed 'em round.

Lincoln's mother was mighty sweet woman. She could read and write. Abe told me that she often read Bible to him. Abe once wrote Chronicles which all settlers knew by memory. He was always writing some rhyme.

Thos. Lincoln was a good man—He was a carpenter and I've got a cupboard in there that he made. When about to move away from here he wanted me to buy it. I told him I would take it to accommodate them if he would take trade. I gave him a quilt.

I want a history written that is all true.

Lincoln would never quarrel and would laugh others out of it. His step brothers were quarrelsome and fractious. Abe would do all he could to please them. I always like the boy and was a good friend to him;

L. was leader even when a boy—stories of his powers of memory—Steam wagons—first to know about them—his essays on cruelty—even composed poetry before he knew anything about the principles of poetry—"natural genius."[16]

Of the Grigsby interview, Fortune said in his 1925 address:

"Uncle Natty" was Lincoln's most intimate boyhood friend. As "Uncle Natty" expressed it, they "often et hominy and fat pork together," they often slept together and they were more nearly chums than any of the other boy friends of Lincoln. When I met him he was quite old and feeble. This particular talk with him was while standing beside the road in Gentryville. I remember he was leaning on a cane. I asked some of the usual questions. One of these was about the books in the neighborhood. He named the same list of books Mrs. Crawford had mentioned. I noticed that he was looking down at the ground, leaning on his cane, rather chuckling to himself. I asked him why he was smiling. "There was another book we boys got a lot of fun out of," he answered in the indistinct voice of a feeble old man.

"What was it?" I asked.

"A book of funny stories," he replied. "Lincoln would read it to us out in the woods on Sundays."

"Do you remember the name of it, Uncle Natty?"

"Oh yes; oh yes; right well."

"What was it?"

I understood him to say "The King's Jester." In my notes I simply have the words, "N. Grigsby—Kings Jester."[17]

After years of searching for the King Jester book, Fortune finally learned that the book was actually *Quin's Jests*, published in London in 1766.

Fortune moved to Indianapolis in 1882, the year after the Spencer County interviews, and became a successful businessman and leader of philanthropic institutions. He moved in the best social circles of the city. Various Lincoln biographers consulted Fortune; and he served as a guide to the Indiana Lincoln country.

Although not a familiar name to students of Lincoln's Indiana years, Anna O'Flynn produced work that became well known. A teacher and school principal in Vincennes, Indiana, O'Flynn wrote "positive history" stories for children. She became interested in Lincoln's boyhood after a friend told her about visiting Nancy Hanks Lincoln's grave. Consequently, O'Flynn began corresponding with people who remembered Lincoln, hired a photographer to take pictures of Spencer County sites, and in the summer of 1895 visited the area for a few days. Among Rockport citizens, she visited Veatch, who, when he met O'Flynn, was shocked to see he had corresponded with a *woman*. Veatch's wife commented, "If he had known you were a lady, he would not have been writing long letters to you." In fact, O'Flynn was the one Veatch warned about not trusting the crowd of old "soakers" around Lincoln City depot. That advice appeared in a letter addressed to Mr. A. C. Flinn [*sic*].[18]

O'Flynn wanted stories to inspire students and found such material in the comments of John Lamar. According to O'Flynn,

> He [Lamar] said the first time he saw Lincoln was when as a small boy he [Lamar] was riding to the mill on a horse behind his father. Lincoln was letting the horse rest from plowing and was reading a book. Lamar's father said, "Son, look at that boy. He will make a mark in the world. He either works or reads. He never wastes a minute!"[19]

Since Lamar was about eight years old when the Lincolns left Indiana, his memories of those years were limited. Nevertheless, he had vivid memories of Lincoln's 1844 visit to Spencer County when Lincoln spoke at the crossroads school. Following the speech, he accompanied Lincoln and Josiah Crawford to see an old saw pit where Lincoln once sawed lumber. Next the trio went to Crawford's house. There, in Lamar's words, as reported by O'Flynn,

LEWIS LIBRARY, VINCENNES UNIVERSITY, VINCENNES, INDIANA

EVANSVILLE MUSEUM OF ARTS, HISTORY, AND SCIENCE

Anna O'Flynn visited the old Lincoln neighborhood to talk with remaining neighbors in the mid-1890s. Under the name A. Hoosier she provided the material on the Indiana years used by Ida Tarbell in her early work on Lincoln.

According to John Lamar, Lincoln made this spice box (also called a cabinet or bookcase) while he was a young man and exchanged it with Josiah Crawford for a knife. It is currently part of the collection of the Evansville Museum of Arts, History, and Science.

> I heard him [Lincoln] and Mr. Josiah Crawford talking about the <u>Spice Box or Cabinet</u>. Uncle Josiah Asked: Have you got the knife I gave you for it Abe? And Abe answered "Yes, here it is but I spent the money for other things long ago." When I heard them talking I asked what kind of a Spice Cabinet he had made. Uncle Josiah Sent me in to look at it. At the sale I bought it & presented it to Capt. Wartman of Evansville.[20]

This spice box is also called a cabinet or bookcase. When J. W. Wartmann wrote Herndon in July 1865, he reported that Abraham assisted Thomas Lincoln with carpentry work and added, "Squire John W. Lamar, one of our country Comrs [Commissioners], has a small book case made by Abraham; The 'Squire' prizes it highly and says it is a 'first rate job.'"[21] Although Herndon expressed no interest in the cabinet, O'Flynn did. She believed Abraham made it for his stepmother, and now citizens "looked upon it as Catholics look up the relics of saints."[22]

O'Flynn wrote her story of Lincoln's boyhood in Indiana and, in 1895, using the pseudonym A. Hoosier, submitted the manuscript to several children's magazines. Although none bought the story, one suggested sending the work to *McClure's Magazine* because S. S. McClure was searching for memories of those who knew Lincoln in Kentucky, Indiana, and Illinois for a new biography he planned to serialize in the magazine. McClure asked O'Flynn to expand her research, and she later estimated that she contacted at least thirty-four people in her quest for information.[23]

Ida Tarbell, a journalist, edited the articles and relied on O'Flynn's material to cover the Indiana years for the November and December 1895 *McClure's Magazine* issues.[24] A unique feature of the articles was illustrations of the places, people, and objects associated with Lincoln—including more than two dozen on just the Indiana period. The first article included a sketch of the small cabinet or bookcase made by Lincoln. In 1896 these articles were expanded into Tarbell's book *The Early Life of Abraham Lincoln*.[25]

By the late 1890s only a few residents remembered the Civil War president as a young man in Spencer County, and J. Edward Murr, a Methodist minister who served churches in Spencer and Perry counties, set out to interview them. Between 1892 and 1902 Murr consulted eleven "associates of the President [who] were in the full possession of their faculties."[26] Murr used this information to write "Lincoln in Indiana," published in three parts in the *Indiana Magazine of History* in 1917 and 1918. One original story Murr heard from Joseph Gentry concerned a dispute between two neighbors over ownership of a gray goose. The neighbors decided to take the case before the justice of the peace, and supporters crowded into the room for the hearing. As the story goes, Lincoln, aged seventeen, entered the room and addressed the crowd before authorities arrived. He told both parties that whoever won the case, all they would win was the goose "worth say, about two bits." But he said the winner will really lose. "And lose what, you say? Well, you have both been neighbors, and you'll lose your friendship for one another for one thing; and not only that, it won't stop there." Lincoln predicted the incident would divide families, friends, and the entire neighborhood all "on account of an old gray goose." According to Gentry, the litigants saw the wisdom of Lincoln's words and settled their dispute before the trial started. Murr believed the story and regarded it as Lincoln's "maiden law case."[27]

By the hundredth anniversary of the Lincolns' 1816 arrival in the state, no one still lived who remembered those years. In Evansville, Indiana, however, lawyer John E. Iglehart believed the history should be written "by the children and grandchildren of those people who knew Lincoln in his boyhood days."[28] Therefore, Iglehart founded the Southwestern Indiana Historical Society in 1920, and soon the society began the "Lincoln Inquiry" project. Fortune, O'Flynn, and Murr all shared their earlier work with this society, and members prepared family biographies of early southern Indiana pioneers.

Biographers expanded their research on Lincoln's Indiana years as well. In 1922 Ida Tarbell visited Kentucky, Indiana, and Illinois in search of more information for her 1924 book, *In the Footsteps of the Lincolns*. In October, Tarbell—along with William Fortune, his daughter Evelyn Fortune Lilly (Mrs. Eli Lilly), Cale Young, and Alice Hegan Rice—began a journey through Kentucky and Indiana. The party traveled in Fortune's Pierce Arrow, driven by his chauffeur, Arthur.[29]

The group departed from Louisville and traveled through West Baden and French Lick to Troy, where they stopped before spending the night in Tell City. The next day, the traveling party returned to Troy and then went to Lincoln City, which Tarbell recorded as "a dreadful little town." At a stop in Boonville, Tarbell first saw the Little Pigeon Baptist Church minute book. The next day the others parted with Tarbell, who took a train for Louisville. After concluding her work at the Filson Club in Louisville, she returned to Boonville to copy information from the minute book and do research in the courthouse at Rockport.[30]

Although Tarbell lacked access to the vast Herndon collection, then under the control of Jesse Weik, he did grant complete rights to his friend, former U.S. senator from Indiana Albert Beveridge. Beveridge worked tirelessly in the 1920s to verify accounts Herndon recorded and, using his Washington and Indiana contacts, to document the Lincoln story. Unfortunately, Beveridge died in 1927 before completing the biography. The work was finished using his notes and was published in 1928. Beveridge's *Abraham Lincoln, 1809–1858* remains one of the most respected treatments of Lincoln's prepresidential years, not only because he documents extensively, but also because he shatters many of the romantic Lincoln myths.[31]

The most complete work on Lincoln's Indiana years appeared in the sesquicentennial year of his birth. In 1959 Louis A. Warren published *Lincoln's*

Youth: Indiana Years Seven to Twenty-one, 1816–1830. An ordained Disciple of Christ minister, Warren began his Lincoln research during his first pastorate in Hodgenville, Kentucky. He scoured Kentucky courthouses to discover details about the Lincoln family and fully documented the period in his 1926 book *Lincoln's Parentage and Childhood.* Next Warren moved to Indiana to do similar work and in 1928 gave up the ministry to devote his time to Lincoln research as an employee of the Lincoln National Life Insurance Company in Fort Wayne, Indiana. In Fort Wayne he built the respected institution later known as the Lincoln Museum.[32] Although some of Warren's interpretations are criticized, his work continues to be the most highly respected reference work on Lincoln's Indiana years.

After thousands of books and articles on Abraham Lincoln, perhaps Lincoln's Indiana youth can best be assessed according to an article in the *New York Tribune* days after his 1860 nomination:

> Thus hard work and plenty of it, the rugged experiences of aspiring poverty, the wild sports and rude games of a newly and thinly peopled forest region—the education born of the log-cabin, the rifle, the axe, and the plow, combined with the reflections of an original and vigorous mind, eager in the pursuit of knowledge by every available means, and developing a character of equal resource and firmness—made him the man he has since proved himself.[33]

Appendix

Books Abraham Lincoln Likely Read in Indiana[1]

Author	Title[2]
	Aesop's Fables (Lancaster, PA, 1804)
	[*The Arabian Nights*] *The Oriental Moralist* (Boston, 1797)
Bailey, Nathan	*A Universal Etymological English Dictionary* (Glasgow, 1802)
Barclay, James	*Dictionary* (1799)
Bunyan, John	*The Pilgrim's Progress* (Philadelphia, 1817)
Daboll, Nathan	*Daboll's School Master's Assistant . . . Being a Plain Practical System of Arithmetic* (Albany, NY, 1817)
Defoe, Daniel	*The Life and Most Surprising Adventures of Robinson Crusoe* (London, 1810)
Dilworth, Thomas	*Dilworth's Spelling-Book, Improved* (Philadelphia, 1796)
Dilworth, Thomas	*The Schoolmaster's Assistant: Being a Compendium of Arithmetic, both Practical and Theoretical* (Wilmington, DE, 1796)
Dupuy, Starke	*Hymns and Spiritual Songs* (Frankfort, KY, 1818)
Franklin, Benjamin	*The Life of Dr. Benjamin Franklin Written by Himself* (Montpelier, 1809)
Grimshaw, William	*History of the United States* (Philadelphia, 1820)
	The Holy Bible (1799)[3]
	The Kentucky Preceptor (Lexington, KY, 1812)[4]
Lowe, Abraham	*The Columbian Class Book* (Worchester, MA, 1824; 2nd ed., 1825)
Murray, Lindley	*The English Reader* (New York, 1815)
Pike, Nicholas	*The New Complete System of Arithmetick* (Boston, 1804)
	Quin's Jests; or, The Facetious Man's Pocket-Companion (London, 1766)

Ramsey, David	*The Life of George Washington* (Boston, 1811)
Riley, James	*An Authentic Narrative of the Loss of the American Brig Commerce* (New York, 1817)
	The Revised Laws of Indiana, 1824 (Corydon, IN, 1824)[5]
Scott, William	*Lessons in Elocution . . .* (Philadelphia, 1801)
Webster, Noah	*The American Spelling Book* (Hartford, 1809)
Weems, Mason L.	*The Life of Benjamin Franklin* (Philadelphia, 1829)[6]
Weems, Mason L.	*The Life of Gen. Francis Marion* (Philadelphia, 1822)
Weems, Mason L.	*The Life of George Washington* (Philadelphia, 1809)

---

1. Louis A. Warren, *Lincoln's Youth, Indiana Years, Seven to Twenty-one, 1816–1830* (New York: Apple-Century-Crofts, 1959); Robert Bray, "What Abraham Lincoln Read—An Evaluative and Annotated List," *Journal of the Abraham Lincoln Association* 28 (Summer 2007): 28–81.

2. The exact edition Lincoln read is usually unknown. The editions listed are ones Lincoln could possibly have seen.

3. Now at Abraham Lincoln Birthplace National Historic Site, Hodgenville, KY.

4. Now in the Lilly Library, Indiana University, Bloomington, IN.

5. Ibid.

6. In the Lincoln Museum Collection, Fort Wayne, IN (as of May 2008).

Abraham Lincoln in Indiana Chronology

1816

Late Summer/Fall   Thomas Lincoln makes a preliminary trip to Indiana to select a site for a new home.

December 11   Indiana becomes a state. Around this time the Lincoln family arrives in Indiana.

1817

February 12   Abraham Lincoln celebrates his eighth birthday—a few days before this date he shoots through a crack in the new cabin and kills a wild turkey.

October 15   Thomas Lincoln travels to Vincennes and enters a claim for southwest quarter of Section 32 T4S, R5W—160 acres at $2.00 per acre. He pays $16.00 in cash (one-twentieth of the price).

Fall   Nancy Hanks Lincoln's aunt and uncle Thomas and Elizabeth Sparrow join the Lincolns in Indiana. Their nephew, Dennis Hanks, comes with the Sparrows

December 26   Thomas Lincoln goes to Vincennes to pay an additional $64.00 on his land.

1818

January 10   Spencer County is created from Perry and Warrick counties, named for Spier Spencer who was killed at the Battle of Tippecanoe.

February 12   AL's ninth birthday.

September 21   Thomas Sparrow makes his will. In late September both Thomas and Elizabeth Sparrow die of milk sickness

October 5   Nancy Hanks Lincoln dies from milk sickness. Thomas Lincoln makes the coffin, and AL whittles pegs to hold the boards together. She is buried on a knoll south of the Lincoln farm.

Winter   Andrew Crawford conducts school near Little Pigeon Baptist Church. (The dates used for Lincoln's schooling are those Nathaniel Grigsby related to William H. Herndon.)

1819

February 12   AL completes his tenth year. Sometime during this year he is "kicked by a horse and apparently killed for a time" at Noah Gorden's horse mill.

July 3   Luther Greathouse assigns Thomas Lincoln 139.36 acres of land touching the southwest tip of the Lincoln farm.

December 2   Thomas Lincoln marries Sarah (Sally) Bush Johnston in Elizabethtown, Kentucky. Thomas, Sarah, and children Elizabeth, John D., and Matilda arrive at the Lincoln cabin later in the month.

December 11   The Little Pigeon Baptist Church decides to build a meetinghouse on land donated by Noah Gorden— 1½ miles south of the Lincoln farm.

1820

February 12   AL observes his eleventh birthday—the first with his stepmother.

1821

February 12   AL's twelfth birthday.

March 10   The final plans for the Little Pigeon Baptist meetinghouse are approved. Thomas Lincoln directs construction.

June 14   Dennis Hanks marries Elizabeth Johnston.

September 11   Thomas Lincoln assigns James Gentry the land obtained from Luther Greathouse in 1819.

September 12   Thomas Lincoln applies for a credit extension for his original 160 acres at the Vincennes Land Office.

1822

February 12   AL becomes a teenager as he celebrates his thirteenth birthday.

1823

February 12   AL's fourteenth birthday.

June 7   Thomas Lincoln joins the Little Pigeon Baptist Church with a letter from Little Mount Separate Baptist Church in Kentucky. Sarah Bush Johnston Lincoln joins by experience.

June 12   Thomas Lincoln becomes a trustee of the Little Pigeon Baptist Church.

1824

February 12 AL turns fifteen; attends Hazel Dorsey's school. During this year Abraham worked math problems in his sum book.

1825

February 12 AL's sixteenth birthday.

For 6–9 months AL operates the ferry for James Taylor at Troy.

December 10 The Little Pigeon Baptist Church members decide to establish a cemetery on the church property.

1826

February 12 Seventeenth birthday, AL is 6'2" and weighs about 160 pounds; attends Swaney's school around this time.

March 1 AL dates a page in his sum book. The problems deal with discounting debts.

April 8 AL's sister Sarah joins the Little Pigeon Baptist Church on experience by grace.

June 15 A post office is established at Gentry's Store with Gideon Romine as postmaster.

August 2 Sarah Lincoln marries Aaron Grigsby.

August AL, Dennis Hanks, and Squire Hall earn money by cutting firewood for steamboats on the Ohio River.

1827

February 12 AL's eighteenth birthday.

April 5 Thomas Lincoln is assigned land (N½, NW¼ of Sec. 3, T5S, R12W) in Posey County, Indiana.

April 30 Thomas Lincoln travels to Vincennes to relinquish the east 80 acres of his Spencer County farm, plus 80 acres of land he acquired in Posey County. This settles his obligation to the United States government for the west 80 acres of the Spencer County farm.

June 6 Thomas Lincoln is issued a patent for the 80 acres he retained.

1828

January 20 Sarah Lincoln Grigsby dies in childbirth and is buried in the Little Pigeon Baptist Church cemetery along with her stillborn child.

February 12   AL's nineteenth birthday.

April–June   Allen Gentry and AL make the flatboat trip down the Ohio and Mississippi rivers to New Orleans. Some Lincoln biographers maintain that the trip took place from December 1828 to March 1829.

1829

February 12   AL's twentieth birthday. Some time during 1829 Lincoln works for John Romine, James Gentry, and William Jones.

April 16   Reuben Grigsby Jr. marries Elizabeth Ray, and Charles Grigsby marries Matilda Hawkins. AL writes "The Chronicles of Reuben."

Late summer   AL borrows the Washington biography from Josiah Crawford, the book is damaged, and AL pulls fodder to pay for it.

Fall   The Lincolns start construction of a new cabin.

October 29   Gentry's Store post office is discontinued.

November 26   Charles Grigsby secures a bond from Thomas Lincoln for the Spencer County farm.

December 12   The Little Pigeon Baptist Church grants a letter of dismissal to Thomas and Sally Lincoln.

1830

February 12   AL reaches his twenty-first birthday and becomes an independent citizen.

February 20   Thomas and Sally Lincoln deed the farm to Charles Grigsby for $125.

March 1   The extended Lincoln family leaves Spencer County for Illinois.

1844

October–November   AL campaigns in southern Indiana for Whig presidential candidate Henry Clay. He visits Vincennes, Bruceville, Washington, Rockport, and Boonville.

1846

February 24   AL writes Illinois lawyer Andrew Johnston with a first draft of his "My Childhood-Home I See Again" poem.

April 18   AL sends Johnston another version of the poem.

September 6   AL sends Johnston his "Matthew Gentry" and "Bear Hunt" poems.

1855

September 17   AL travels across Indiana on his way to Cincinnati to be a counsel in the McCormick Reaper Case.

September 26   AL leaves Cincinnati and probably crosses Indiana on his return to Springfield, IL.

1859

September 19   AL delivers a speech at the Masonic Hall in Indianapolis. A tradition says AL went home by way of Terre Haute to see a lady who possessed a "mad stone" after son Robert was bitten by a dog.

1860

February 22   AL passes through Lafayette and Logansport before changing trains in Fort Wayne on his way to deliver the Cooper Union speech in New York.

March 14   The return trip crosses Indiana.

1861

February 11   On the way to Washington to assume the presidency, AL passes through State Line, Lafayette, Thorntown, Lebanon, and Zionsville, before spending the night in Indianapolis. He makes two speeches in the capital city.

February 12   The trip continues by way of Greensburg, Shelbyville, Morris, and Lawrenceburg.

1865

April 30   AL's funeral train crosses the state passing through Richmond before arriving at Indianapolis on a rainy morning at 7:00 a.m. The body lay in state in the capitol during the day and leaves for Chicago at midnight.

May 1   The funeral train moves slowly to Chicago by way of Lafayette, making an hour-long impromptu stop in Michigan City.

June 5   William Herndon addresses a letter to "Some good Union Lawyer" in Rockport, Indiana, to solicit information about Lincoln in Indiana.

June 8   Attorney J. W. Wartmann responds to Herndon's letter with some contacts and information.

June 13   William Herndon interviews Dennis Hanks in Chicago.

September 8   William Herndon interviews Dennis Hanks, Sarah (Sally) Bush Johnston Lincoln, and Matilda Johnston Hall Moore in Charleston, IL.

September 12–17   William Herndon interviews citizens of Spencer County.

Notes

1: "There I grew up"

1. Mark E. Neely Jr., *The Abraham Lincoln Encyclopedia* (New York: McGraw Hill, 1982), 107–8.

2. Abraham Lincoln to Jesse W. Fell, "Enclosing Autobiography," December 20, 1859, in Roy P. Basler et al., eds., *The Collected Works of Abraham Lincoln*, 9 vols. (New Brunswick, NJ: Rutgers University Press, 1953–55), 3:511.

3. Ibid., 3:511–12.

4. R. Carlyle Buley, *The Old Northwest: Pioneer Period, 1815–1840*, 2 vols. (Indianapolis: Indiana Historical Society, 1950), 1:58–66.

5. Charles Kettleborough, *Constitution Making in Indiana*, 3 vols. (Indianapolis: Indiana Historical Commission, 1916), 1:68–69; John D. Barnhart and Dorothy L. Riker, *Indiana to 1816: The Colonial Period* (Indianapolis: Indiana Historical Bureau and Indiana Historical Society, 1971), 427. Barnhart and Riker quote additional sources that state the figures as 12,211 for white males and 62,697 total inhabitants.

6. Barnhart and Riker, *Indiana to 1816*, pp. 439–62; James H. Madison, *The Indiana Way: A State History* (Bloomington: Indiana University Press; Indianapolis: Indiana Historical Society, 1986), 50–51.

7. Madison, *Indiana Way*, 59, 63.

8. William H. Herndon interview with Dennis Hanks, June 13, 1865, in Douglas L. Wilson and Rodney O. Davis, eds., *Herndon's Informants: Letters, Interviews, and Statements about Abraham Lincoln* (Urbana: University of Illinois Press, 1998), 40, 251.

9. Charles J. Kappler, comp. and ed., *Indian Treaties, 1778–1883* (New York: Interland Publishing, 1972), 70–73.

10. Barnhart and Riker, *Indiana to 1816*, pp. 339–40.

11. *History of Warrick, Spencer, and Perry Counties, Indiana* (Chicago: Goodspeed Brothers, 1885), 251–54; Louis A. Warren, *Lincoln's Youth: Indiana Years, Seven to Twenty-one, 1816–1830* (New York: Appleton-Century-Crofts, 1959), 35; William Fortune, ed., *Warrick and Its Prominent People* (Evansville: Courier Company, 1881), 10–13.

12. *History of Warrick, Spencer, and Perry Counties*, 251.

13. Abraham Lincoln, "The Bear Hunt," Basler et al., eds., *Collected Works of Abraham Lincoln*, 1:386.

14. *History of Warrick, Spencer, and Perry Counties*, 271.

15. "Brief Autobiography," Basler et al., eds., *Collected Works of Abraham Lincoln*, 2:459.

16. Donald F. Carmony, *Indiana, 1816–1850: The Pioneer Era* (Indianapolis: Indiana Historical Bureau and Indiana Historical Society, 1998), 363.

17. *History of Warrick, Spencer, and Perry Counties*, 409.

18. Frank M. Gilbert, *History of the City of Evansville and Vanderburg[h] County, Indiana*, 2 vols. (Chicago: Pioneer, 1910), 1:255.

19. David Herbert Donald, *Lincoln* (New York: Simon and Schuster, 1995), 29.

20. Madison, *Indiana Way,* 108.

2: "The old homestead in Indiana"

1. Mark E. Neely Jr., *The Abraham Lincoln Encyclopedia* (New York: McGraw Hill, 1982), 14, 271. See also John Locke Scripps, *Life of Abraham Lincoln*, Roy P. Basler and Lloyd A. Dunlap, eds. (Bloomington: Indiana University Press, 1961).

2. Roy P. Basler et al., eds., *The Collected Works of Abraham Lincoln*, 9 vols. (New Brunswick, NJ: Rutgers University Press, 1953–55), 4:61–63.

3. C. Edward Skeen, *1816: America Rising* (Lexington: University Press of Kentucky, 2003), 1, 6.

4. William H. Herndon (hereafter cited as WHH) interview with Dennis Hanks, June 13, 1865, in Douglas L. Wilson and Rodney O. Davis, eds., *Herndon's Informants: Letters, Interviews, and Statements about Abraham Lincoln* (Urbana: University of Illinois Press, 1998), 38.

5. Louis A. Warren, *Lincoln's Youth: Indiana Years, Seven to Twenty-one, 1816–1830* (New York: Appleton-Century-Crofts, 1959), 16.

6. Louis A. Warren, *Lincoln's Parentage & Childhood* (New York: Century Company, 1926), 121, 290, 329–30.

7. Skeen, *1816*, p. 1.

8. Basler et al., eds., *Collected Works of Abraham Lincoln*, 7:281.

9. Warren, *Lincoln's Parentage & Childhood*, 289, and *Lincoln's Youth*, 13.

10. Warren, *Lincoln's Parentage & Childhood*, 270–71; David Herbert Donald, *Lincoln* (New York: Simon and Schuster, 1995), 24.

11. James H. Madison, *The Indiana Way: A State History* (Bloomington: Indiana University Press; Indianapolis: Indiana Historical Society, 1986), 47–50, 53–54.

12. John D. Barnhart and Dorothy L. Riker, *Indiana to 1816: The Colonial Period* (Indianapolis: Indiana Historical Bureau and Indiana Historical Society, 1971), 458–59. Barnhart and Riker list Spencer County as having a slave entry. Reading the 1820 Spencer County census is confusing. Column headings are only used on the first page, and there are so few African American entries that most pages do not have columns for those entries. In examining the census on microfilm the author concluded there were no slaves recorded for Spencer County. For the complete Indiana census see W. Heiss, comp., *1820 Federal Census for Indiana* (Indianapolis: Indiana Historical Society, 1966). Heiss shows twelve slaves in Perry County in 1820, but does not include four additional slaves entered only under the name Ben. There are no such slave listings in Sharon Patmore and Kristine Manley, *1820, 1830, 1840 Spencer, Warrick, Perry Counties, Indiana Census Returns* (Chrisney, IN: Newspaper Abstracts, 1995), 1–10. Patmore and Manley list six "colored" residents of Spencer County in 1820, while the census taker reported five.

13. Patmore and Manley, *1820, 1830, 1840 Spencer, Warrick, Perry Counties*, 71.

14. For the most recent and authoritative treatment of the Lincoln Kentucky land transactions, see Kent Masterson Brown, *Report on the Title of Thomas Lincoln to, and the History of, the Lincoln Boyhood Home along Knob Creek in LaRue County, Kentucky* (U.S. Department of Interior, National Park Service, 1997).

15. R. Carlyle Buley, *The Old Northwest: Pioneer Period, 1815–1840*, 2 vols. (Indianapolis: Indiana Historical Society, 1950), 1:94–95.

16. Edwin Coles Bearss, *Lincoln Boyhood—As a Living Historical Farm* (Springfield, VA: National Park Service, National Technical Information Service Report PB 200500, 1967), 43–48.

17. Quoted in Warren, *Lincoln's Youth*, 20.

18. Dennis F. Hanks to WHH, March 22, 1866, Wilson and Davis, eds., *Herndon's Informants*, 235.

19. The controversy was fueled by two state commissions investigating the migration for a possible Lincoln Way highway to be built on the same route. These investigations, one authorized in 1915 and the other in 1930, combined historical research with a desire by many communities to obtain the highway for their region. See Arthur F. Hall et al., *The Lincoln Memorial Way through Indiana* (Indianapolis, 1932).

20. R. Gerald McMurtry, "The Lincoln Migration from Kentucky to Indiana," *Indiana Magazine of History* 33 (December 1937): 412.

21. Wilson and Davis, eds., *Herndon's Informants*, 38, 78–79, 93, 111, 228; McMurtry, "Lincoln Migration from Kentucky to Indiana," 412.

22. Bearss, *Lincoln Boyhood*, 11–16.

23. Ibid., 16; McMurtry, "Lincoln Migration from Kentucky to Indiana," 415; Warren, *Lincoln's Youth*, 19–20.

24. Henry J. Raymond, *The Life and Public Services of Abraham Lincoln* (New York: Derby and Miller, 1865), 19.

25. McMurtry, "Lincoln Migration from Kentucky to Indiana," 394.

26. Hanks interview, June 13, 1865, Wilson and Davis, eds., *Herndon's Informants*, 38–39; Hanks to WHH, March 7, 1866, ibid., 226.

27. William H. Herndon and Jesse W. Weik, *Herndon's Lincoln*, ed. Douglas L. Wilson and Rodney O. Davis (Galesburg, IL: Knox College Lincoln Studies Certer; Urbana: University of Illinois Press, in association with the Abraham Lincoln Bicentennial Commission, 2006), 26.

28. Erastus Wright interview with Dennis F. Hanks, June 8, 1865, Wilson and Davis, eds., *Herndon's Informants*, 28.

29. Bearss, *Lincoln Boyhood,* 73–74; Wilson and Davis, eds., *Herndon's Informants*, 28.

30. Hanks interview, June 13, 1865, Wilson and Davis, eds., *Herndon's Informants*, 39.

31. Charles B. Strozier, *Lincoln's Quest for Union: Public and Private Meanings* (New York: Basic Books, 1982), 25–26.

32. Herndon and Weik, *Herndon's Lincoln*, 27. Also see John G. Nicolay and John Hay, *Abraham Lincoln: A History*, 10 vols. (New York: Century, 1886) 1:29. Dennis Hanks reported to Herndon that the turkey incident actually happened in the half-faced camp. Hanks interview, June 13, 1865, Wilson and Davis, eds., *Herndon's Informants,* 39.

33. Benjamin P. Thomas, *Abraham Lincoln* (New York: Alfred A. Knopf, 1952), 10.

34. Hanks to WHH, March 7, 1866, Wilson and Davis, eds., *Herndon's Informants*, 226. The scientific name for white snakeroot changed over time. Now known as Ageratina altissima (*Eupatorium rugosum*), it was also called *Eupatorium urticaefolium* and *Eupatorium ageratoides.*

35. James Fitton Couch, *Trembles (or Milk Sickness)*, Circular 306 (U.S. Department of Agriculture, November 1933). William D. Snively Jr., "Discoverer of the Cause of Milk Sickness," *The Journal of the American Medical Association* 196 (June 20, 1966): 1055–60.

36. *Evansville Journal*, October 14, 1840; Warren, *Lincoln's Youth*, 52.

37. Daniel Drake, *A Memoir of the Disease Called by the People the Trembles and the Sick Stomach or Milk-Sickness: As They Appear in the Virginia Military District in the State of Ohio* (Louisville: James Maxwell, 1841), 28, 29. A copy of this publication can be found

in the William Henry Smith Memorial Library, Indiana Historical Society, Indianapolis, Indiana.

38. Ibid., 48.

39. Ibid., 51–53. See also Walter J. Daly, "The 'Slows': The Torment of Milk Sickness on the Midwest Frontier," *Indiana Magazine of History* 102 (March 2006): 29–40.

40. Snively, "Discoverer of the Cause of Milk Sickness," 1055, 1058–60.

41. Ibid., 1058.

42. "White Snakeroot Poisoning," Circular 436, University of Illinois College of Agriculture Experiment Station and Extension Service in Agriculture and Home Economics.

43. Couch, *Trembles (or Milk Sickness)*, 2, 8.

44. J. T. Hobson, *Footprints of Abraham Lincoln: Presenting Many Interesting Facts, Reminiscences, and Illustrations Never before Published* (Dayton: Otterbein Press, 1909), 18, 19. Hobson interviewed a number of Spencer County residents during the 1890s. Among those were Nancy Brooner's sons Henry and Allen. Henry told Hobson that Sophia Hanks was also living with the Sparrows at the time of their deaths.

45. Warren, *Lincoln's Youth*, 51; William Wood interview with WHH, September 15, 1865, Wilson and Davis, eds., *Herndon's Informants*, 123.

46. Couch, *Trembles (or Milk Sickness)*, 4.

47. Warren, *Lincoln's Youth*, 53.

48. Ibid., 55. Hobson, *Footprints of Abraham Lincoln*, 19.

49. Herndon and Weik, *Herndon's Lincoln*, 30–31.

50. Eleanor Atkinson, *The Boyhood of Lincoln* (New York: McClure Company, 1908), 16–17.

51. Hobson, *Footprints of Abraham Lincoln*, 18. Henry Brooner told this story in about 1888. See also Warren, *Lincoln's Youth*, 55.

52. J. G. Holland, *The Life of Abraham Lincoln* (Springfield, MA: Gurdon Bill, 1866), 29. Holland, an eastern moralist, writes in great detail about the funeral conducted by Elkin. See also Hanks interview, June 13, 1865, Wilson and Davis, eds., *Herndon's Informants*, 40.

53. Charles H. Coleman, *Abraham Lincoln and Coles County, Illinois* (New Brunswick, NJ: Scarecrow Press, 1955), x–xi.

54. Warren, *Lincoln's Youth*, 58.

55. Atkinson, *Boyhood of Lincoln*, 19–20.

56. Warren, *Lincoln's Youth*, 59–63; Warren, *Lincoln's Parentage & Childhood*, 332n29. Warren provides the most detail on Daniel Johnston and his family.

57. Warren, *Lincoln's Youth*, 63–64.

58. Ibid.

59. Coleman, *Abraham Lincoln and Coles County*, x–xii. Warren records Matilda's age as younger than John D. The author accepts Coleman's work.

60. WHH interview with Sarah Bush Lincoln, September 8, 1865, Wilson and Davis, eds., *Herndon's Informants*, 106.

61. Ibid., 107; Warren, *Lincoln's Youth*, 66–70.

62. For a complete treatment of Thomas Lincoln's Indiana land activities, see William E. Bartelt, "The Land Dealings of Spencer County, Indiana, Pioneer Thomas Lincoln," *Indiana Magazine of History* 87 (September 1991): 211–23.

63. Ibid., 212–13.

64. Ibid., 215, 218–20.

65. The documents of this transaction are in the National Archive file, Indiana, Vincennes Land Office, Credit Under 2578, National Archives, Washington, D.C.

66. Lowell H. Harrison, *Lincoln of Kentucky* (Lexington: University Press of Kentucky, 2000), 25.

67. Nathaniel Grigsby to WHH, September 4, 1865, Wilson and Davis, eds., *Herndon's Informants*, 93; WHH interview with Grigsby, September 12, 1865, ibid., 112; WHH interview with David Turnham, September 15, 1865, ibid., 121.

68. Warren, *Lincoln's Youth*, 81.

69. Anthony Gross, ed., *Lincoln's Own Stories* (New York: Harper and Brothers, 1912), 113–15. See also Warren, *Lincoln's Youth*, 83.

70. Allen Thorndike Rice, ed., *Reminiscences of Abraham Lincoln by Distinguished Men of His Time* (New York: North American, 1888), 237–38.

71. WHH interview with Anna Caroline (Roby) Gentry, September 17, 1865, Wilson and Davis, eds., *Herndon's Informants*, 131.

72. Grigsby interview, September 12, 1865, Wilson and Davis, eds., *Herndon's Informants,* 112. For more information on Crawford and his school, see Warren, *Lincoln's Youth*, 81–83.

73. Grigsby interview, September 12, 1865, Wilson and Davis, eds., *Herndon's Informants*, 112. For more information on Dorsey see Warren, *Lincoln's Youth*, 125–28. Warren accepts the order given in Lincoln's autobiographical statement and concludes the Dorsey school was the third one attended. David Turnham told Herndon it was before the Crawford school.

74. Grigsby interview September 12, 1865, Wilson and Davis eds., *Herndon's Informants*, 112; WHH interview with John Oskins, September 16, 1865, ibid., 128; Warren, *Lincoln's Youth*, 99–103.

75. David A. Morgan, "Early Schools of Spencer County." A copy of this 1921 paper may be found in the Southwestern Indiana Historical Society notebooks, Evansville–Vanderburgh Public Library, Central Library, Evansville, Indiana.

76. Joshua F. Speed to WHH, December 6, 1866, Wilson and Davis, eds., *Herndon's Informants*, 499.

77. Sarah Bush Lincoln interview, September 8, 1865, ibid., 106, 108.

78. Ibid., 107.

79. Grigsby to WHH, September 4, 1865, Wilson and Davis, eds., *Herndon's Informants*, 93.

80. Warren, *Lincoln's Youth*, 131. Warren gives a description of all pages. Images of the pages may be seen in Basler et al., eds., *Collected Works of Abraham Lincoln*, 1: preceding page 1.

81. Rice, ed., *Reminiscences of Abraham Lincoln by Distinguished Men of His Time*, 458.

82. Herndon and Weik, *Herndon's Lincoln*, 51.

83. Ibid., 50–51.

84. Robert L. Reid, ed., *Always a River: The Ohio River and the American Experience* (Bloomington: Indiana University Press, 1991), xiii.

85. Richard F. Nation, *At Home in the Hoosier Hills: Agriculture, Politics, and Religion in Southern Indiana, 1810–1870* (Bloomington: Indiana University Press, 2005), 94, 99. See chapter 3 of this work, titled "'Surplus Produce' and Market Exchange" for a detailed

discussion of the topic. Hominy is corn soaked in lye water.

86. Ibid., 78.

87. Hanks to WHH, January 6, 1866, Wilson and Davis, eds., *Herndon's Informants*, 154.

88. Hanks to WHH, January 26, 1866, ibid., 176.

89. Turnham interview, September 15, 1865, ibid., 121.

90. Warren, *Lincoln's Youth*, 177.

91. Bess V. Ehrmann, *The Missing Chapter in the Life of Abraham Lincoln* (Chicago: Walter M. Hill, 1938), 20; Buley, *Old Northwest*, 1:532.

92. Gentry interview, September 17, 1865, Wilson and Davis, eds., *Herndon's Informants*, 131.

93. Ehrmann, *Missing Chapter in the Life of Abraham Lincoln*, 8; Warren, *Lincoln's Youth*, 178–79.

94. W. D. Howells, *Life of Abraham Lincoln* (Bloomington: Indiana University Press, 1960), 23.

95. See Warren, *Lincoln's Youth*, 173–86, for descriptions of possible sites Lincoln might have visited on this trip.

96. Ibid., 152, 173.

97. For a treatment of the Cave-In-Rock bandits see W. D. Snively and Louanna Furbee, *Satan's Ferryman: A True Tale of the Old Frontier* ([New York]: Frederick Ungar, 1968).

98. Gentry interview, September 17, 1865, Wilson and Davis, eds., *Herndon's Informants*, 131.

99. Albert J. Beveridge, *Abraham Lincoln*, 2 vols. (Boston: Houghton Mifflin, 1928), 1:88.

100. Phillip Shaw Paludan, "Lincoln and Negro Slavery: I Haven't Got Time for the Pain," *Journal of the Abraham Lincoln Association* 27 (Summer 2006): 8–9.

101. Warren, *Lincoln's Youth*, 185–86.

102. Ibid., 84, 209. For Hanks's land transactions, see Vincennes Land Office Records, Credit Under Final Certificate 2573 and Cash Final Certificate 23.323, National Archives.

103. Warren, *Lincoln's Youth*, 154, 209.

104. Ibid., 203–6. William Wood told Herndon of the new Lincoln house in his September 15, 1865, interview, Wilson and Davis, eds., *Herndon's Informants*, 124. For the traditional negative Thomas Lincoln treatment see Nicolay and Hay, *Abraham Lincoln*, 1:45.

105. Hanks to WHH, March 7, 1866, Wilson and Douglas, eds., *Herndon's Informants*, 226.

106. Ibid.

107. Warren, *Lincoln's Youth*, 205.

108. Ibid., 207.

109. Ibid., 266n14.

110. Ibid., 208.

111. Hall et al., *Lincoln Memorial Way*, 62.

112. Ibid., 63.

113. Ida Tarbell, *The Early Life of Abraham Lincoln* (South Brunswick, NJ: A. S. Barnes, 1974), 87. The reference occurs in a caption on the page in this reprint.

3: "My childhood's home I see again"

1. Roy P. Basler et al., eds., *The Collected Works of Abraham Lincoln*, 9 vols. (New Brunswick, NJ: Rutgers University Press, 1953–55), 1:367.

2. Ibid.

3. Ibid., 1:370.

4. Ibid., 1:378.

5. Ibid.

6. Ibid., 1:367.

7. Douglas L. Wilson, "Abraham Lincoln's Indiana and the Spirit of Mortal," *Indiana Magazine of History* 87 (June 1991): 166. See this article for a discussion of the relationship between Lincoln's poetry and his favorite poem "Mortality."

8. Ibid., 167.

9. Basler et al., eds., *Collected Works of Abraham Lincoln*, 1:378–79.

10. Ibid., 1:384–86.

11. Ibid., 1:386–89.

12. The author is indebted to Doctor Sherry Bevins Darrell, director of humanities and professor of English at the University of Southern Indiana, for the technical analysis of Lincoln's poetry.

13. Basler et al., eds., *Collected Works of Abraham Lincoln*, 1:392n3.

14. Jay M. Shafritz, *The Dorsey Dictionary of American Government and Politics* (Chicago: Dorsey Press, 1988), 186–87.

15. Anna O'Flynn is quoted in Ida M. Tarbell, *The Life of Abraham Lincoln*, 2 vols. (New York: Lincoln Memorial Association, 1900), 1:198. For information on the 1844 trip see *Lincoln Lore* 271, 811, 1496.

16. This is from a speech given by Anna O'Flynn to the Southwestern Indiana Historical Society on November 17, 1925. A copy may be found in the Southwestern Indiana Historical Society notebooks in the Evansville–Vanderburgh Public Library, Central Library, Evansville, Indiana, and the John Iglehart Papers, William Henry Smith Memorial Library, Indiana Historical Society, Indianapolis.

17. *Rockport Herald*, November 1, 1844.

18. William Jones's son, also named William, told this account. See William L. Barker et al., *Brief* (Warrick County Lincoln Route Association, 1931), 23.

19. *Evansville Journal*, June 7, 1860.

20. Dorothy Riker and Gayle Thornbrough, *Indiana Election Returns, 1816–1851* (Indianapolis: Indiana Historical Bureau, 1960), 38–47. The town and counties Lincoln visited in 1844 are Vincennes (Knox County), Washington (Daviess County), Rockport and Gentryville (Spencer County), and Boonville (Warrick County). Only Warrick County cast more votes for Polk.

4: "The inner life of Mr. L."

1. David Herbert Donald, *Lincoln's Herndon* (New York: Alfred A. Knopf, 1948), 181.

2. Mark E. Neely Jr., *The Abraham Lincoln Encyclopedia* (New York: McGraw Hill, 1982), 145.

3. Donald, *Lincoln's Herndon*, 167.

4. Ibid., 169.

5. Ibid., 368.

6. Douglas L. Wilson made this point in a presentation at the fourth Lincoln Institute for Teachers, held at the University of Southern Indiana on June 15–16, 2006. See Rodney O. Davis, "William Herndon, Memory, and Lincoln Biography," *Journal of Illinois History* 1 (Winter 1998): 99–112, for a discussion of the reliability of oral history.

7. The birth and death dates are taken from Douglas L. Wilson and Rodney O. Davis, eds., *Herndon's Informants: Letters, Interviews, and Statements about Abraham Lincoln* (Urbana: University of Illinois Press, 1998), 744–77; death date for Dennis Hanks is in Charles H. Coleman, *Abraham Lincoln and Coles County, Illinois* (New Brunswick, NJ: Scarecrow Press, 1955), 232; for Green B. Taylor, see *Evansville Courier*, May 1, 1899.

5: "He was the best boy I ever saw"

1. Louis A. Warren, *Lincoln's Youth: Indiana Years, Seven to Twenty-one, 1816–1830* (New York: Appleton-Century-Crofts, 1959), 60–61.

2. Ibid., 62.

3. Ibid., 62–63.

4. Charles H. Coleman, *Abraham Lincoln and Coles County, Illinois* (New Brunswick, NJ: Scarecrow Press, 1955), 2, 19.

5. William H. Herndon (hereafter cited as WHH) interview with Sarah Bush Lincoln, September 8, 1865, in Douglas L. Wilson and Rodney O. Davis, eds., *Herndon's Informants: Letters, Interviews, and Statements about Abraham Lincoln* (Urbana: University of Illinois Press, 1998), 109.

6. Ibid., 106–9.

7. Coleman, *Abraham Lincoln and Coles County*, 61, for details of Lincoln's concern for his relatives, 61–78.

8. Lincoln to John D. Johnston, November 25, 1851, in Roy P. Basler et al., eds., *The Collected Works of Abraham Lincoln*, 9 vols. (New Brunswick, NJ: Rutgers University Press, 1953–55), 2:113.

9. Coleman, *Abraham Lincoln and Coles County*, 156.

10. WHH interview with John Hanks [1865–66], Wilson and Davis, eds., *Herndon's Informants*, 455.

11. For a detailed account of John D. Johnston, see Stanley O. Harris, "John D. Johnston" (master's thesis, Southern Illinois University, n.d.), John D. Johnston File, Lincoln Boyhood National Memorial, Lincoln City, Indiana.

12. John Y. Simon, "House Divided: Lincoln and His Father" (Tenth Annual R. Gerald McMurtry Lecture, Lincoln National Life Foundation Inc., Fort Wayne, Indiana, 1987), 3.

13. Dennis F. Hanks to WHH, January 26, 1866, Wilson and Davis, eds., *Herndon's Informants*, 176.

14. Simon, "House Divided," 8–10.

15. Rodney O. Davis, "Abraham Lincoln: Son and Father" (The Edgar S. and Ruth W. Burkhardt Lecture Series, Knox College, 1997), 20.

6: "He loved us all"

1. Charles H. Coleman, *Abraham Lincoln in Coles County, Illinois* (New Brunswick, NJ: Scarecrow Press, 1955), 201–2.

2. Ibid., 203. See also David Kent Coy, *Recollections of Abraham Lincoln in Coles County, Illinois* (Charleston, IL: Looking for Lincoln Committee, 2000), 5–6.

3. William H. Herndon (hereafter cited as WHH) interview with Matilda Johnston Moore, September 8, 1865, in Douglas L. Wilson and Rodney O. Davis, eds., *Herndon's Informants: Letters, Interviews, and Statements about Abraham Lincoln* (Urbana: University of Illinois Press, 1998), 109–10.

4. WHH interview with Dennis Hanks, September 8, 1865, ibid., 105. This issue will be covered in more detail in the next chapter.

7: "[I] knew him intimately and well"

1. William H. Herndon (hereafter cited as WHH) interview with Dennis F. Hanks, June 13, 1865, in Douglas L. Wilson and Rodney O. Davis, eds., *Herndon's Informants: Letters, Interviews, and Statements about Abraham Lincoln* (Urbana: University of Illinois Press, 1998), 38. For an outline of the confusing Hanks family, see Paul Verduin's work, ibid., 779–83.

2. David Herbert Donald, *Lincoln's Herndon* (New York: Alfred A. Knopf, 1948), 177.

3. Rodney O. Davis, "William Herndon, Memory, and Lincoln Biography," *Journal of Illinois History* 1 (Winter 1998): 107. For a transcript of the Wright interview see Wilson and Davis, eds., *Herndon's Informants*, 27–29.

4. Donald, *Lincoln's Herndon*, 177.

5. WHH interview with Hanks, September 8, 1866, Wilson and Davis, eds., *Herndon's Informants*, 103.

6. Donald, *Lincoln's Herndon*, 352.

7. Wilson and Davis, eds., *Herndon's Informants*, 779–83.

8. Donald, *Lincoln's Herndon*, 179–80.

9. Hanks interview, June 13, 1865, Wilson and Davis, eds., *Herndon's Informants*, 37. The entire interview may be found on, 35–43.

10. Donald, *Lincoln's Herndon*, 178–79.

11. Hanks interview, June 13, 1865, Wilson and Davis, eds., *Herndon's Informants*, 38.

12. William E. Bartelt, "Dennis Hanks and His Indiana 'Pre-emption Rights,'" unpublished report, July 1989, Dennis Hanks File, Lincoln Boyhood National Memorial, Lincoln City, Indiana.

13. Hanks interview, June 13, 1865, Wilson and Davis, eds., *Herndon's Informants*, 38–43.

14. Hanks interview, September 8, 1865, ibid., 103–6.

15. For the impact of the development on Indiana see James H. Madison, *The Indiana Way: A State History* (Bloomington: Indiana University Press; Indianapolis: Indiana Historical Society, 1986), 131–34.

16. WHH interview with Nathaniel Grigsby, September 12, 1865, Wilson and Davis, eds., *Herndon's Informants*, 114.

17. Dorothy Riker and Gayle Thornbrough, *Indiana Election Returns, 1816–1851* (Indianapolis: Indiana Historical Bureau, 1960), 5, 7, 9.

18. Ibid., 11, 13.

19. For the view that the Lincolns never supported Jackson see Louis A. Warren, *Lincoln's Youth: Indiana Years, Seven to Twenty-one, 1816–1830* (New York: Appleton-Century-Crofts, 1959), 189–91.

20. William E. Bartelt, "'Keeping Up with the Jones[es]': A Research Report Prepared for the Jones House State Historic Site," 9–20, unpublished report, 1995, the files of the William Jones House State Historic Site, now administered by Lincoln State Park, Lincoln City.

21. Ward H. Lamon, *The Life of Abraham Lincoln: From His Birth to His Inauguration as President* (Boston: James R. Osgood and Company, 1872), 21.

22. Hanks to WHH, December 24, 1865, Wilson and Davis, eds., *Herndon's Informants*, 146.

23. Hanks to WHH, January 6, 1866, ibid., 153–54.

24. Donald, *Lincoln's Herndon*, 180.

8: "Old friends of my boyhood"

1. Roy P. Basler et al., eds., *The Collected Works of Abraham Lincoln*, 9 vols. (New Brunswick, NJ: Rutgers University Press, 1953–55), 4:130–31. The original letter is on display at the Evansville Museum of Arts, History, and Science.

2. For a more detailed discussion of Indiana emigration, see James H. Madison, *The Indiana Way: A State History* (Bloomington: Indiana University Press; Indianapolis: Indiana Historical Society, 1986), 58–62.

3. Edwin Coles Bearss, *Lincoln Boyhood—As a Living Historical Farm* (Springfield, VA: National Park Service, National Technical Information Service Report PB 200500, 1967), 40.

4. Louis A. Warren, *Lincoln's Youth: Indiana Years, Seven to Twenty-one, 1816–1830* (New York: Appleton-Century-Crofts, 1959), 100. O. V. Brown of Dale, Indiana, a local Lincoln buff, who drew maps of the area for interested visitors in the mid-twentieth century, also used this description. The legal description of the land is

    Sections 4, 5, 6, 7, 8, 9, 16, 17, 18, 19, 20, 21, T5S, R5W
    Sections 28, 29, 30, 31, 32, 33, T4S, R5W
    Sections 1, 12, 13, 24, T5S, R6W
    Sections 25, 36, T4S, R6W

5. The land was sold in quarter sections; thus there are ninety-six-quarter sections in the twenty-four-section area. By 1830 thirty-two of the quarters were claimed. Fifteen quarters were claimed in 1817, and 12.5 in 1818. Vincennes Land Office Books 7, 8, 9, Bureau of Land Management, Springfield, Virginia. Land records are also available in the Indiana State Archives, Indianapolis, Indiana.

6. Lowell H. Harrison, *Lincoln of Kentucky* (Lexington: University Press of Kentucky, 2000), 29.

7. This information comes from viewing the Vincennes Land Office records, Bureau of Land Management. Additional documentation comes from Family History Files, Lincoln Boyhood National Memorial, Lincoln City, Indiana, Spencer County Public Library, Rockport, Indiana, and the Nelson County Public Library, Bardstown, Kentucky.

8. Warren, *Lincoln's Youth*, 98–99, reaches the same conclusion that a large number of children lived in the neighborhood. Warren's numbers, however, seem inflated. He included families such as the Bruners, who were no longer living in Spencer County, and John Jones and David Casebier, who no longer owned land within a mile of the Lincolns in 1820. He also included John Romine, who does not appear in the 1820 census and did not marry until 1829. Warren's figures may reflect those children living in the area at some time

between 1816 and 1820, but not at any one time such as 1820.

9. Gentry, Grigsby, Turnham, Wood, Gontramann, and Whittinghill appear in the 1830 census. There is a Thomas Carter in the 1830 census, but information in the Carter Family File, Nelson County, Kentucky, Public Library indicates that Lincoln's neighbor was in Illinois in 1825. David Edwards Sr. died in 1822. See Edwards File, Spencer County Public Library.

10. J. Edward Murr, "Lincoln in Indiana," *Indiana Magazine of History* 13 (December 1917): 337.

11. Albert J. Beveridge, *Abraham Lincoln*, 2 vols. (Boston: Houghton Mifflin, 1928), 1:50.

12. Warren, *Lincoln's Youth*, 86–87. Several clarification deeds were necessary over the years because some of the land deeded by Gorden was actually on the Samuel Howell property. There is a general confusion on the spelling of the name Gorden/Gordon. Land records and the Little Pigeon Baptist Church Minute Book use both spellings. However, the author accepts Gorden as the correct spelling. There are two extant 1829 deeds with, what appear to be, original signatures. In both cases the signature is clearly Noah Gorden. He is buried in Polk County, Missouri, where the tombstone uses the Gorden spelling. See Gorden/Gordon File, Lincoln Boyhood National Memorial; *Cemetery Directory of Polk County, Missouri* (Bolivar, MO: Historical Society of Polk County, Missouri), 70.

13. Thomas F. Schwartz to Norman Hellmers, September 23, 1987, "Little Pigeon Baptist Church Minute Book" File, Lincoln Boyhood National Memorial.

14. Bess V. Ehrmann, "Old Pigeon Creek Minute Book Sold," *Lincoln Herald* 45 (December 1943): 25–28.

15. *Minute Book of Little Pigeon Creek Baptist Church* (Rockport, IN: Spencer County Historical Society, n.d.), 2–3. Warren, *Lincoln's Youth*, 113, lists the articles of faith. There are some spelling, wording, and capitalization variations in the two versions.

16. "Little Pigeon Baptist Church, 150th Anniversary," pamphlet, Rockport Branch of the Spencer County Library.

17. Little Pigeon Baptist Church Minute Book, January 10, 1830; Warren, *Lincoln's Youth*, 207.

18. Frank M. Gilbert, *History of the City of Evansville and Vanderburg[h] County Indiana*, 2 vols. (Chicago: Pioneer, 1910), 1:68–69. While Gilbert describes such activities a couple of counties away from the Lincolns, the facts hold true for most of southern Indiana.

19. Dennis Hanks to William H. Herndon (hereafter cited as WHH), January 6, 1866, in Douglas L. Wilson and Rodney O. Davis, eds., *Herndon's Informants: Letters, Interviews, and Statements about Abraham Lincoln* (Urbana: University of Illinois Press, 1998), 154.

20. R. Carlyle Buley, *The Old Northwest: Pioneer Period, 1815–1840*, 2 vols. (Indianapolis: Indiana Historical Society, 1950), 1:227.

21. Hanks to WHH, March 22, 1866, Wilson and Davis, eds., *Herndon's Informants*, 235; A. H. Chapman statement [Ante Sept. 8, 1865], ibid., 100.

22. *History of Warrick, Spencer, and Perry Counties, Indiana* (Chicago: Goodspeed Brothers, 1885), 272; Warren, *Lincoln's Youth*, 187.

23. Buley, *Old Northwest*, 1:235.

24. *Minute Book of Little Pigeon Creek Baptist Church*, 91, 101–2. This list appears in the book following an entry dated January 4, 1835. Obviously the list was made years earlier

because a number of the men, such as Noah Gorden and Thomas Lincoln, no longer lived in the community at that time.

25. *Evansville Courier*, February 12, 1933. The article concerns Eli Grigsby, and many details of his Lincoln story disagree with accounts Herndon collected. It may be significant that Nathaniel Grigsby did not mention the Grigsby still to Herndon.

26. *History of Warrick, Spencer, and Perry Counties*, 272.

27. Ibid., 274.

28. Warren, *Lincoln's Youth*, 44–45.

29. *History of Warrick, Spencer, and Perry Counties*, 271, 366.

30. Ibid., 271, 373; Buley, *Old Northwest*, 1:228.

9: "The man soared above us"

1. J. W. Wartmann to William H. Herndon (hereafter cited as WHH), June 8, 1865, in Douglas L. Wilson and Rodney O. Davis, eds., *Herndon's Informants: Letters, Interviews, and Statements about Abraham Lincoln* (Urbana: University of Illinois Press, 1998), 29.

2. Wartmann to WHH, June 19, 1865, ibid., 47.

3. Nathaniel Grigsby to WHH, July 4, 1865, ibid., 70.

4. Grigsby File, Lincoln Boyhood National Memorial, Lincoln City, Indiana.

5. Abraham Lincoln to Nathaniel Grigsby, September 20, 1860, in Roy P. Basler et al., eds., *The Collected Works of Abraham Lincoln*, 9 vols. (New Brunswick, NJ: Rutgers University Press, 1953–55), 4:116.

6. Elizabeth N. Nicholson, ed., *Memorabilia: The Grigsby Family Reunion Book, 1779–1979* (Chestnut Hill, MA: Nicholson, 1979), 142.

7. Copies of War Department invalid pension papers for Nathaniel Grigsby, Grigsby File, Lincoln Boyhood National Memorial; *History of Warrick, Spencer, and Perry Counties, Indiana* (Chicago: Goodspeed Brothers, 1885), 390–91.

8. Nicholson, *Memorabilia*, 144; David Hann, *Sampling Kansas: A Guide to the Curious* ([Lawrence, KS]: D. Hann, 1990), 60–63.

9. WHH interview with Nathaniel Grigsby, September 16, 1865, Wilson and Davis, eds., *Herndon's Informants*, 127; Rodney O. Davis, "William Herndon's Indiana Oral History Project, 1865," *Indiana Magazine of History* 89 (June 1993): 140.

10. Grigsby to WHH, September 4, 1865, Wilson and Davis, eds., *Herndon's Informants*, 93–94.

11. WHH interview with Grigsby, September 12, 1865, ibid., 111–13.

12. WHH interview with William Wood, September 15, 1865, ibid., 123.

13. Grigsby interview, September 12, 1865, ibid., 113.

14. Ibid., 113–14.

15. William H. Herndon and Jesse Weik, *Herndon's Lincoln*, ed. Douglas L. Wilson and Rodney O. Davis (Galesburg, IL: Knox College Lincon Studies Center; Urbana: University of Illinois Press, in association with the Abraham Lincoln Bicentennial Commission, 2006), 43. This story was so identified with Green Taylor that it was included in his obituary. See *Evansville Courier*, May 1, 1899.

16. Grigsby interview, September 12, 1865, Wilson and Davis, eds., *Herndon's Informants*, 114.

17. Ibid., 114n8.

18. A. H. Chapman statement [Ante Sept. 8, 1865], Wilson and Davis, eds., *Herndon's*

Informants, 100–101, 743.

19. Grigsby interview, September 12, 1865, ibid., 114–15.

20. *Evansville Journal*, February 4, 1889.

21. Grigsby interview, September 16, 1865, Wilson and Davis, eds., *Herndon's Informants*, 127–28.

22. Little Pigeon Baptist Church Minute Book, November 13, 1824, transcript, Spencer County Public Library, Rockport, Indiana.

10: "Could I only whisper in her Ear — 'Your Son was Presdt'"

1. Reprinted in the *Evansville Daily Journal*, September 15, 1865. See also Rodney O. Davis, "William Herndon's Indiana Oral History Project, 1865," *Indiana Magazine of History* 89 (June 1993): 139.

2. William H. Herndon (hereafter cited as WHH) interview with Nathaniel Grigsby et al., September 14, 1865, in Douglas L. Wilson and Rodney O. Davis, eds., *Herndon's Informants: Letters, Interviews, and Statements about Abraham Lincoln* (Urbana: University of Illinois Press, 1998), 116.

3. WHH interview with John Hanks, [1865–66], ibid., 455.

4. WHH interview with Dennis F. Hanks, June 13, 1865, ibid., 39–40.

5. WHH interview with Sarah Bush Lincoln, September 8, 1865, ibid., 106. For a complete discussion of Lincoln Indiana cabins see John E. Santosuosso, "A Survey of Lincoln Boyhood National Memorial and Lincoln City" (unpublished report, 1970), 3–28. This report includes a detailed account of the cabin and grave sites and may be found in the library at Lincoln Boyhood National Memorial, Lincoln City, Indiana.

6. Grigsby et al. interview, September 14, 1865, Wilson and Davis, eds., *Herndon's Informants*, 116–17.

7. Davis, "William Herndon's Indiana Oral History Project," 144.

8. John B. Rowbotham to WHH, June 24, 1865, Wilson and Davis, eds., *Herndon's Informants*, 56.

9. Ibid.

10. Louis A. Warren, *Lincoln's Youth: Indiana Years, Seven to Twenty-one, 1816–1830* (New York: Appleton-Century-Crofts, 1959), 174.

11. Santosuosso, "Survey of Lincoln Boyhood National Memorial and Lincoln City," 83–95.

12. Bess V. Ehrmann, *The Missing Chapter in the Life of Abraham Lincoln* (Chicago: Walter M. Hill, 1938), 124; Santosuosso, "Survey of Lincoln Boyhood National Memorial and Lincoln City," 95–99. See also Jill York O'Bright, *"There I Grew Up . . . ": A History of the Administration of Abraham Lincoln's Boyhood Home* ([Washington, D.C.]: National Park Service, 1987), 7–11.

13. See the work of Paul H. Verduin, in Wilson and Davis, eds., *Herndon's Informants*, 781–82.

14. Grigsby et al. interview, September 14, 1865, ibid., 117–18.

15. Lincoln interview, September 8, 1865, ibid., 107.

16. Warren, *Lincoln's Youth*, 86–87.

17. "The Minute Book of Little Pigeon Babtist [*sic*] Church 1816–1840," Abraham Lincoln Presidential Library, Springfield, Illinois. See also Warren, *Lincoln's Youth*, 114–15, 151.

18. John Hanks interview, [1865–1866], Wilson and Davis, eds., *Herndon's Informants*, 455.

19. Warren, *Lincoln's Youth*, 121–22, 241n30.

20. Gorden Family File, Lincoln Boyhood National Memorial.

21. Grigsby et al. interview, September 14, 1865, *Herndon's Informants*, 117–18.

22. *Rockport Journal*, August 5, 1892.

23. WHH interview with Joseph C. Richardson, September 14, 1865, Wilson and Davis, eds., *Herndon's Informants*, 119–20.

24. WHH interview with S. T. Johnson, September 14, 1865, ibid., 115.

25. *History of Warrick, Spencer, and Perry Counties, Indiana* (Chicago: Goodspeed Brothers, 1885), 66.

26. Warren, *Lincoln's Youth*, 198. See also "The Brackenridge Family," Biography Files of the Southwestern Indiana Historical Society, Willard Library, Evansville, Indiana.

27. Roscoe Kiper to Albert J. Beveridge, September 25, 1924. The original letter is in the Beveridge Collection, Library of Congress, Washington, D.C. A copy is in the Lincoln Collections, Albert J. Beveridge File, Lincoln Boyhood National Memorial.

28. Warren, *Lincoln's Youth*, 197–99.

11: "A boy of Extraordinary mind"

1. *History of Warrick, Spencer, and Perry Counties, Indiana* (Chicago: Goodspeed Brothers, 1885), 359.

2. See the Nila Michel Papers and the Turnham Family File, Lincoln Boyhood National Memorial, Lincoln City, Indiana. Some sources record Turnham's birthplace as being in Kentucky.

3. David Turnham's letters to William H. Herndon (hereafter cited as WHH) in Douglas L. Wilson and Rodney O. Davis, eds., *Herndon's Informants: Letters, Interviews, and Statements about Abraham Lincoln* (Urbana: University of Illinois Press, 1998), 129, 138, 142, 147–48, 216–18, 334, 356, 376, 403, 518.

4. WHH interview with David Turnham, September 15, 1865, Wilson and Davis, eds., *Herndon's Informants*, 120–23.

5. David Turnham to WHH, September 16, October 12, 1865, ibid., 129, 138. Turnham's book is now in the collection of the Lilly Library, Indiana University, Bloomington, Indiana.

6. Michel Papers.

7. Roy P. Basler et al., eds., *The Collected Works of Abraham Lincoln*, 9 vols. (New Brunswick, NJ: Rutgers University Press, 1953–55), 4:130–31. The original letter is on display at the Evansville Museum of Arts, History, and Science.

8. "Thomas Lincoln's Corner Cupboards," *Lincoln Lore* 1476 (February 1961): 1–3.

9. WHH interview with Sarah Bush Lincoln, September 8, 1865, Wilson and Davis, eds., *Herndon's Informants*, 107.

10. Ibid.

11. Turnham to WHH, February 21, 1866, Wilson and Davis, eds., *Herndon's Informants*, 216–18.

12. Louis A. Warren, *Lincoln's Youth: Indiana Years, Seven to Twenty-one, 1816–1830* (New York: Appleton-Century-Crofts, 1959), 187–88.

13. *Evansville Journal*, February 4, 1889.

14. For general background on Jones, see William E. Bartelt, "Colonel William Jones of Spencer County" (unpublished report, Lincoln Boyhood National Memorial, 1992). Bartelt also wrote several unpublished reports for the Jones House State Historic Site (now part of Lincoln State Park), "Keeping Up with the Jones[es]': A Research Report Prepared for the Jones House State Historic Site" (1995) and "William Jones and Mainstream Culture" (1996).

15. *Rockport Journal*, February 12, 1897.

16. WHH interviews with John S. Hougland and John R. Dougherty, September 17, 1865, Wilson and Davis, eds., *Herndon's Informants*, 130, 133.

12: "Abe was always a man though a boy"

1. William H. Herndon (hereafter cited as WHH) interview with Absolom Roby, September 17, 1865, in Douglas L. Wilson and Rodney O. Davis, eds., *Herndon's Informants: Letters, Interviews, and Statements about Abraham Lincoln* (Urbana: University of Illinois Press, 1998), 132. See 768 for a short biographical statement on Roby.

2. See the Nila Michel Papers and the Wood Family File, Lincoln Boyhood National Memorial, Lincoln City, Indiana. His tombstone in the family cemetery on the farm records his death date as December 1867 at age eighty-three years, six months, twenty-four days, which would make his year of birth 1784. Herndon records that Wood told him he was eighty-two years old in September 1865, which would make the birth year 1783. Perhaps Wood said he was in his eighty-second year in 1865.

3. WHH interview with William Wood, September 15, 1865, Wilson and Davis, eds., *Herndon's Informants*, 123–25.

4. Oliver C. Terry to Jesse W. Weik, July 14, 1888, ibid., 659. See 658–59 and 662–63 for additional Pitcher comments. See also *Evansville Courier*, August 3, 1892. An assessment of the Lincoln-Pitcher relationship appears in Louis A. Warren, *Lincoln's Youth: Indiana Years, Seven to Twenty-one, 1816–1830* (New York: Appleton-Century-Crofts, 1959), 199–201.

5. L. C. Rudolph, *Hoosier Faiths: A History of Indiana Churches and Religious Groups* (Bloomington: Indiana University Press, 1995), 245–55.

6. W. M. Weekley, H. H. Fout, and G. M. Mathews, *Our Heroes; or, United Brethren Home Missionaries*, 2 vols. (Dayton: United Brethren Missionary Society, [1908–11]), volume 2, chapter four deals with Aaron Farmer.

13: "Said that he would be Presidt of the US"

1. *Evansville Daily Journal*, May 23, 1860. What became of Lincoln's copy of Weem's *Life of Washington* is not known. However, a copy of another book he reportedly read in Indiana, Weem's *Life of Benjamin Franklin*, is in the collection of the Lincoln Museum, Fort Wayne, Indiana. This book contains Lincoln's signature.

2. Bess V. Ehrmann, *Lincoln and His Neighbors* (Rockport, IN: Spencer County Historical Society, 1948), 15. Crawford would have died on May 12, 1865, to make it "three days less than a month" after Lincoln.

3. Vincennes Land Office Book 8, p. 2022, Bureau of Land Management, Springfield, Virginia.

4. Ehrmann, *Lincoln and His Neighbors*, 14. If, in fact, she was a midwife it must be pondered if she assisted Sarah Lincoln Grigsby in her delivery.

5. Crawford, Barker, and Grigsby families, Historical Files, Lincoln Boyhood National Memorial, Lincoln City, Indiana.

6. William H. Herndon (hereafter cited as WHH) interview with Elizabeth Crawford, September 16, 1865, in Douglas L. Wilson and Rodney O. Davis, eds., *Herndon's Informants: Letters, Interviews, and Statements about Abraham Lincoln* (Urbana: University of Illinois Press, 1998), 125–27.

7. William Jones to George Rathbone, May 27, 1860, Series 1, General Correspondence, 1833–1916, Abraham Lincoln Papers, Library of Congress, Washington, D.C.

8. G. W. Rathbone to Abraham Lincoln, June 1, 1860, ibid.

9. Cecil K. Byrd and Ward W. Moore, eds., *Abraham Lincoln in Print and Photograph: A Picture History from the Lilly Library* (Mineola, NY: Dover Publications, 1997), 6.

10. William H. Herndon and Jesse Weik, *Herndon's Lincoln*, ed. Douglas L. Wilson and Rodney O. Davis (Galesburg, IL: Knox College Lincoln Studies Center; Urbana: University of Illinois Press, in association with the Abraham Lincoln Bicentennial Commission, 2006), 47. For a detailed account of this story see ibid., 44–49, or Louis A. Warren, *Lincoln's Youth: Indiana Years, Seven to Twenty-one, 1816–1830* (New York: Appleton-Century-Crofts, 1959), 196–97.

11. *Rockport Journal*, February 12, 1897.

12. WHH interview with Nathaniel Grigsby, September 12, 1865, Wilson and Davis, eds., *Herndon's Informants*, 114.

13. Elizabeth Crawford to WHH, January 4, 1865, ibid., 150–52.

14. Herndon and Weik, *Herndon's Lincoln*, 48–49.

15. Elizabeth Crawford to WHH, April 19, 1865, Wilson and Davis, eds., *Herndon's Informants*, 245. Other letters appear on 215–16, 245–46, 248–50, 261–62, 335–3.

14: "I hit him with an Ear of Corn"

1. *History of Warrick, Spencer, and Perry Counties, Indiana* (Chicago: Goodspeed Brothers, 1885), 668, 671. Louis A. Warren treats Troy history and the Lincoln-Taylor activities in some detail in *Lincoln's Youth: Indiana Years, Seven to Twenty-one, 1816–1830* (New York: Appleton-Century-Crofts, 1959), 145–49.

2. William H. Herndon interview with Green B. Taylor, September 16, 1865, in Douglas L. Wilson and Rodney O. Davis, eds., *Herndon's Informants: Letters, Interviews, and Statements about Abraham Lincoln* (Urbana: University of Illinois Press, 1998), 129–30.

3. *Evansville Courier*, May 1, 1899.

4. J. G. Holland, *The Life of Abraham Lincoln* (Springfield, MA: Gurdon Bill, 1866), 33–34.

5. William H. Townsend, *Lincoln the Litigant* (Boston: Houghton Mifflin Company, 1925), 34–38.

6. Ibid., 38–39.

7. Warren, *Lincoln's Youth*, 156.

15: "Learned boy among us unlearned folks"

1. *Evansville Courier and Journal*, February 10, 1935. In an address to the Southwestern Indiana Historical Society, J. Edward Murr was surely mistaken when he said Herndon stayed in the Joseph Gentry home in Gentryville. See Bess V. Ehrmann, *The Missing Chapter in the Life of Abraham Lincoln* (Chicago: Walter M. Hill, 1938), 89.

2. Ehrmann, *Missing Chapter*, 7–9. Gentry Family File, Spencer County Library, Rockport, Indiana.

3. William H. Herndon interview with Anna Caroline Roby Gentry, September 17, 1865, in Douglas L. Wilson and Rodney O. Davis, eds., *Herndon's Informants: Letters, Interviews, and Statements about Abraham Lincoln* (Urbana: University of Illinois Press, 1998), 131–32.

4. Louis A. Warren, *Lincoln's Youth: Indiana Years, Seven to Twenty-one, 1816–1830* (New York: Appleton-Century-Crofts, 1959), 154–58.

5. William E. Gienapp, *Abraham Lincoln and Civil War America* (New York: Oxford University Press, 2002), 7.

16: "I want a history written that is all true"

1. *Evansville Journal*, October 12, 1902.

2. Douglas L. Wilson and Rodney O. Davis, eds., *Herndon's Informants: Letters, Interviews, and Statements about Abraham Lincoln* (Urbana: University of Illinois Press, 1998), xvii.

3. Jesse W. Weik to Albert J. Beveridge, May 23, 1923, Albert Beveridge Papers, Library of Congress, Washington, D.C. A copy is in the Beveridge File, Lincoln Boyhood National Memorial, Lincoln City, Indiana.

4. *Indianapolis Star*, February 7, 1909.

5. Ibid.

6. Ibid.

7. Charles H. Coleman, *Abraham Lincoln and Coles County, Illinois* (New Brunswick, NJ: Scarecrow Press, 1955), 232. See also David Kent Coy, *Recollections of Abraham Lincoln in Coles County, Illinois* (Charleston, IL: Looking for Lincoln Committee, 2000), 13.

8. Eleanor Atkinson, *The Boyhood of Lincoln* (New York: McClure Company, 1908), 36. See also 12, 16, 31–32.

9. Ibid., 23, 25.

10. John E. Santosuosso, "A Survey of Lincoln Boyhood National Memorial and Lincoln City" (unpublished report, 1970), 116–19.

11. James Veatch to A. C. Flinn [Anna O'Flynn], March 14, 1894, Anna C. O'Flynn-Lincoln Research File, Regional History Collection # 324, Byron R. Lewis Historical Library, Vincennes University, Vincennes, Indiana.

12. Charles Latham Jr., *William Fortune (1863–1942): A Hoosier Biography* (Indianapolis: Guild Press of Indiana, 1994), 1–10. The citation for the Fortune book is William Fortune, *Warrick and Its Prominent People: A History of Warrick County, Indiana* (Evansville: Courier Company, 1881).

13. "Address by William Fortune before the Southwestern Indiana Historical Society at Princeton, Indiana, on November 12, 1925," pp. 7–8, William Fortune Papers, box 4, folder 26, William Henry Smith Memorial Library, Indiana Historical Society, Indianapolis, Indiana. Copies of brief notes from Fortune's interviews (hereafter cited as Fortune's notes) are available in box 4, folder 4, of the collection. The speech is also in Bess V. Ehrmann, *The Missing Chapter in the Life of Abraham Lincoln* (Chicago: Walter M. Hill, 1938), 61–78.

14. "Address by William Fortune before the Southwestern Indiana Historical Society," 11.

15. Ibid., 9–12; Fortune's notes, 8–9.

16. Fortune's notes, 8–9.

17. "Address by William Fortune before the Southwestern Indiana Historical Society," 12–13.

18. Anna O'Flynn, "The Environments of Abraham Lincoln in Indiana, the Best Witnesses," address, Southwestern Indiana Historical Society, November 17, 1925, pp. 1, 2, 5, 11. This address is in the Southwestern Indiana Historical Society Annuals, Central Library, Evansville, Indiana. See also Veatch to Flinn [Anna O'Flynn], March 14, 1894.

19. O'Flynn, "Environments of Abraham Lincoln in Indiana," 5.

20. A. Hoosier (Anna O'Flynn) manuscript, Ida Tarbell Collection, Allegheny College Library, Meadville, Pennsylvania (hereafter cited as Tarbell Papers). The manuscript has been divided, and this section is labeled Lamar and begins "Capt. John Lamar." A copy of this letter and other items from this collection are also in the Ida Tarbell File, Lincoln Boyhood National Memorial. See John Lamar to Anna C. O'Flynn, New Year's Day, 1896, Anna O'Flynn-Lincoln Research File.

21. J. W. Wartmann to WHH, July 21, 1865, Wilson and Davis, eds., *Herndon's Informants*, 79.

22. Anna O'Flynn, "Boyhood Home of Lincoln or Historic Grounds of Indiana," 15, Tarbell Papers.

23. O'Flynn, "Environments of Abraham Lincoln in Indiana," 2–3, 11, 14–15.

24. Ibid., 3.

25. Ida Tarbell, ed., "Abraham Lincoln," *McClure's Magazine* 5 and 6 (November and December 1895); Ida M. Tarbell, *The Early Life of Abraham Lincoln* (New York: S. S. McClure, 1896). Today the cabinet is in the Evansville Museum of Arts, History, and Science, Evansville, Indiana.

26. J. Edward Murr, "Some Pertinent Observations Concerning Abe Lincoln – The Hoosier," 2. This document is part of the unpublished play written by Murr and is in the Archives of DePauw University and Indiana United Methodism, Roy O. West Library, Greencastle, Indiana. See the file "Lincoln History—J. Edward Murr Articles," Lincoln Boyhood National Memorial, for a list of some interviewees with dates.

27. J. Edward Murr, "Lincoln in Indiana," *Indiana Magazine of History* 14 (March 1918): 73–74.

28. Judith Q. McMullen, "Indiana's Lincoln: Oral History Gathered by the Southwestern Indiana Historical Society during the 'Lincoln Inquiry,' 1920–1927," *The Hoosier Genealogist* 43 (Winter 2003): 206.

29. Ida Tarbell to Mr. Phillips, October 23, 1922, I.M.T. [Ida M. Tarbell] "In the Footsteps of the Lincolns," Tarbell Papers. See also William E. Bartelt, "Lincoln Boyhood National Memorial Research Proposal #97," July 12, 1990, p. 2. Alice Hegan Rice is the author of the 1901 work *Mrs. Wiggs of the Cabbage Patch*.

30. Tarbell to Phillips, October 23, November 4, November 16, 1922, Tarbell Papers.

31. Wilson and Davis, eds., *Herndon's Informants*, xix. For a complete treatment of Beveridge, see Benjamin Thomas, *Portrait for Posterity* (New Brunswick, NJ: Rutgers University Press, 1947), 243–66.

32. "Louis Austin Warren (April 23, 1885–June 22, 1983)," *Lincoln Lore* 1733–1736 (July–September 1982).

33. "Honest Old Abe," originally published in the *New York Tribune*, republished in the *Evansville Daily Journal*, May 28, 1860.

Selected Bibliography

Articles

Bartelt, William E. "The Land Dealings of Spencer County, Indiana, Pioneer Thomas Lincoln." *Indiana Magazine of History* 87 (September 1991): 211–23.

Daly, Walter J. "The 'Slows': The Torment of Milk Sickness on the Midwest Frontier." *Indiana Magazine of History* 102 (March 2006): 29–40.

Davis, Rodney O. "William Herndon, Memory, and Lincoln Biography." *Journal of Illinois History* 1 (Winter 1998): 99–112.

_____. "William Herndon's Indiana Oral History Project, 1865." *Indiana Magazine of History* 89 (June 1993): 136–46.

Ehrmann, Bess V. "Old Pigeon Creek Minute Book Sold." *Lincoln Herald* 45 (December 1943): 25–28.

"Louis Austin Warren (April 23, 1885–June 23, 1983)." *Lincoln Lore* 1733–1736 (July–October 1982).

McMullen, Judith Q. "Indiana's Lincoln: Oral History Gathered by the Southwestern Indiana Historical Society during the 'Lincoln Inquiry,' 1920–1927." *The Hoosier Genealogist* 43 (Winter 2003): 206–13.

McMurtry, Gerald R. "The Lincoln Migration from Kentucky to Indiana." *Indiana Magazine of History* 33 (December 1937): 385–421.

Murr, J. Edward. "Lincoln in Indiana." *Indiana Magazine of History* 13 (December 1917): 307–48.

_____. "Lincoln in Indiana." *Indiana Magazine of History* 14 (March 1918): 13–75.

_____. "Lincoln in Indiana." *Indiana Magazine of History* 14 (June 1918):148–82.

Paludan, Phillip Shaw. "Lincoln and Negro Slavery: I Haven't Got Time for the Pain." *Journal of the Abraham Lincoln Association* 27 (Summer 2006): 1–23.

Snively, William D. "Discoverer of the Cause of Milk Sickness." *The Journal of the American Medical Association* 196 (June 1966): 1055–60.

Tarbell, Ida, ed. "Abraham Lincoln." *McClure's Magazine* 5 and 6 (November and December 1895).

"Thomas Lincoln Cupboards." *Lincoln Lore* 1476 (February 1961): 1–3.

Wilson, Douglas L. "Abraham Lincoln's Indiana and the Spirit of Mortal." *Indiana Magazine of History* 87 (June 1991): 155–70.

Books, Reports, and Pamphlets

Abraham Lincoln Portrayed in the Collections of the Indiana Historical Society. Edited and with an introduction by Harold Holzer. Indianapolis: Indiana Historical Society Press, 2006.

Atkinson, Eleanor. *The Boyhood of Lincoln*. New York: McClure Company, 1908.

Barker, William L., et al. *Brief*. Boonville, IN: Warrick County Lincoln Route Association, 1931.

Barnhart, John D., and Dorothy L. Riker. *Indiana to 1816: The Colonial Period*. Indianapolis: Indiana Historical Bureau and Indiana Historical Society, 1971.

Barrett, Joseph. *Life of Abraham Lincoln*. New York: Moore, Wilstach, and Baldwin, 1865.

Barton, William E. *The Women Lincoln Loved*. Indianapolis: Bobbs-Merrill Company, 1927.

Basler, Roy P., et al., eds. *The Collected Works of Abraham Lincoln*. 9 vols. New Brunswick, NJ: Rutgers University Press, 1953–55.

Bearss, Edwin Coles. *Lincoln Boyhood—As a Living Historical Farm*. Springfield, VA: National Park Service, 1967.

Beveridge, Albert J. *Abraham Lincoln*. 2 vols. Boston: Houghton Mifflin, 1928.

Boone, Richard G. *A History of Education in Indiana*. New York: D. Appleton and Company, 1892.

Brown, Kent Masterson. *Report on the Title of Thomas Lincoln To, and the History of the Lincoln Boyhood Home along Knob Creek in LaRue County, Kentucky*. U.S. Department of Interior, National Park Service, 1997.

Buley, R. Carlyle. *The Old Northwest: Pioneer Period, 1815–1840*. 2 vols. Indianapolis: Indiana Historical Society, 1950.

Byrd, Cecil K., and Ward W. Moore. *Abraham Lincoln in Print and Photographs: A Picture History from the Lilly Library*. Mineola, NY: Dover Publications, 1997.

Carmony, Donald F. *Indiana, 1816–1850: The Pioneer Era*. Indianapolis: Indiana Historical Bureau and Indiana Historical Society, 1998.

Coleman, Charles H. *Abraham Lincoln and Coles County, Illinois*. New Brunswick, NJ: Scarecrow Press, 1955.

Couch, James Fitton. *Trembles (or Milk Sickness)*. Circular 306. United States Department of Agriculture, 1933.

Coy, David Kent. *Recollections of Abraham Lincoln in Coles County, Illinois*. Charleston: Looking for Lincoln Committee, 2000.

Davis, Rodney O. *Abraham Lincoln: Son and Father*. Galesburg, IL: Knox College, 1997.

Donald, David Herbert. *Lincoln*. New York: Simon and Schuster, 1995.

———. *Lincoln's Herndon*. New York: Alfred A. Knopf, 1948.

Drake, Daniel. *A Memoir of the Disease Called by the People the Trembles and the Sick Stomach or Milk-Sickness: As They Appear in the Virginia Military District in the State of Ohio*. Louisville: James Maxwell, 1841.

Ehrmann, Bess V. *Lincoln and His Neighbors*. Rockport, IN: Spencer County Historical Society, 1948.

———. *The Missing Chapter in the Life of Abraham Lincoln*. Chicago: Walter M. Hill, 1938.

Esarey, Logan. *Internal Improvements in Early Indiana*. Indianapolis: Edward J. Hecker, 1912.

Etcheson, Nicole. *The Emerging Midwest*. Bloomington: Indiana University Press, 1996.

Fortune, William. *Warrick and Its Prominent People*. Evansville, IN: Courier Company, 1881.

Gienapp, William E. *Abraham Lincoln and Civil War America*. New York: Oxford University Press, 2002.

Gilbert, Frank M. *History of the City of Evansville and Vanderburg[h] County, Indiana*. Chicago: Pioneer, 1910.

Gross, Anthony, ed. *Lincoln's Own Stories*. New York: Harper and Brothers, 1912.

Hall, Arthur F., et al. *The Lincoln Memorial Way through Indiana*. Indianapolis, 1932.

Hann, David. *Sampling Kansas: A Guide to the Curious*. [Lawrence, KS]: D. Hann, 1990.

Harris, Stanley O. *John D. Johnston*. N.p., n.d.

Harrison, Lowell H. *Lincoln of Kentucky*. Lexington: University Press of Kentucky, 2000.

Heiss, Willard, comp. *1820 Federal Census for Indiana*. Indianapolis: Indiana Historical Society, 1966.

Herndon, William H., and Jesse W. Weik. *Herndon's Lincoln*. Edited by Douglas L. Wilson and Rodney O. Davis. Galesburg, IL: Knox College Lincoln Studies Center; Urbana: University of Illinois Press, in association with the Abraham Lincoln Bicentennial Commission, 2006.

History of Warrick, Spencer, and Perry Counties, Indiana. Chicago: Goodspeed Brothers, 1885.

Hobson, J. T. *Footprints of Abraham Lincoln*. Dayton, OH: Otterbein Press, 1909.

Holland, J. G. The Life of Abraham Lincoln. Springfield, MA: Gurdon Bill, 1866.

Howells, W. D. Life of Abraham Lincoln. Bloomington: Indiana University Press, 1960.

Kappler, Charles J., comp. and ed. *Indian Treaties, 1778–1883*. New York: Interland Publishing, 1972.

Kettleborough, Charles. *Constitution Making in Indiana*. Vol. 1. Indianapolis: Indiana Historical Commission, 1916.

Lamon, Ward H. *The Life of Abraham Lincoln: From His Birth to His Inauguration as President*. Boston: James R. Osgood and Company, 1872.

Latham, Charles Jr. *William Fortune (1863–1942): A Hoosier Biography*. Indianapolis: Guild Press of Indiana, 1994.

Madison, James H. *The Indiana Way: A State History*. Bloomington: Indiana University Press; Indianapolis: Indiana Historical Society, 1986.

Nation, Richard F. *At Home in the Hoosier Hills: Agriculture, Politics, and Religion in Southern Indiana*. Bloomington: Indiana University Press, 2005.

Neely, Mark Jr. *The Abraham Lincoln Encyclopedia*. New York: McGraw Hill, 1982.

_____. *Escape from the Frontier: Lincoln's Peculiar Relationship with Indiana*. Fort Wayne, IN: Lincoln National Life Insurance Company, 1983.

Nicholson, Elizabeth N., ed. *Memorabilia: The Grigsby Family Reunion Book, 1779–1979*. Chestnut Hill, MA: Nicholson, 1979.

Nicolay, John G., and John Hay. *Abraham Lincoln: A History*. 10 vols. New York: Century, 1886.

Patmore, Sharon, and Kristine Manley. *1820, 1830, 1840 Spencer, Warrick, Perry Counties, Indiana Census Returns*. Chrisney, IN: Newspaper Abstracts, 1995.

Pence, George, and Nellie C. Armstrong. *Indiana Boundaries, Territory, State, and County*. Indianapolis: Indiana Historical Bureau, 1933.

Raymond, Henry J. *The Life and Public Services of Abraham Lincoln*.

New York: Derby and Miller, 1865.

Reid, Robert L., ed. *Always a River: The Ohio River and the American Experience*. Bloomington: Indiana University Press, 1991.

Rice, Allen Thorndike, ed. *Reminiscences of Abraham Lincoln by Distinguished Men of His Time*. New York: North American Publishing Company, 1888.

Riker, Dorothy, and Gayle Thornbrough. *Indiana Election Returns, 1816–1851*. Indianapolis: Indiana Historical Bureau, 1960.

Rudolph, L. C. *Hoosier Faiths: A History of Indiana Churches and Religious Groups*. Bloomington: Indiana University Press, 1995.

Santosuosso, John E. "A Survey of Lincoln Boyhood National Memorial and Lincoln City." Unpublished report, 1970.

Scripps, John Locke. *Life of Abraham Lincoln*. Roy P. Basler and Lloyd A. Dunlap, eds. Bloomington: Indiana University Press, 1961.

Shafritz, Jay M. *The Dorsey Dictionary of American Government and Politics*. Chicago: Dorsey Press, 1988.

Simon, John Y. *House Divided: Lincoln and His Father*. Fort Wayne, IN: Lincoln National Life Foundation, 1987.

Skeen, C. Edward. *1816: America Rising*. Lexington: University Press of Kentucky, 2003.

Snively, W. D., and Louanna Furbee. *Satan's Ferryman: A True Tale of the Old Frontier*. [New York]: Frederick Ungar, 1968.

Strozier, Charles B. *Lincoln's Quest for Union: Public and Private Meanings*. New York: Basic Books, 1982.

Tarbell, Ida. *The Early Life of Abraham Lincoln*. New York: McClure's, 1896.

———. *The Life of Abraham Lincoln*. 2 vols. New York: Lincoln Memorial Association, 1900.

Thomas, Benjamin P. *Abraham Lincoln*. New York: Alfred A. Knopf, 1952.

Townsend, William H. *Lincoln the Litigant*. Boston: Houghton Mifflin Company, 1925.

Van Natter, Francis Marion. *Lincoln's Boyhood*. Washington: Public Affairs Press, 1963.

Vannest, Charles Garrett. *Lincoln the Hoosier: Abraham Lincoln's Life in Indiana*. St. Louis: Eden Publishing House, 1928.

Warren, Louis A. *Lincoln's Parentage & Childhood*. New York: Century

Company, 1926.

_____. *Lincoln's Youth: Indiana Years, Seven to Twenty-one, 1816–1830.* New York: Apple-Century-Crofts, 1959.

_____. *The Slavery Atmosphere of Lincoln's Youth.* Fort Wayne, IN: Lincolniana Publishers, 1933.

Weekley, W. M., H. H. Fout, and G. M. Mathews. *Our Heroes; or, United Brethren Home Missionaries.* Dayton, OH: Otterbein Press, 1911.

"White Snakeroot Poisoning." Circular 436. University of Illinois College of Agriculture Experiment Station and Extension Service in Agriculture and Home Economics.

Wilson, Douglas L., and Rodney O. Davis. *Herndon's Informants: Letters, Interviews, and Statements about Abraham Lincoln.* Urbana: University of Illinois Press, 1998.

Manuscripts

Abraham Lincoln Presidential Library and Museum. Springfield, Illinois.

Allegheny College Library. Meadville, Pennsylvania.
    Ida M. Tarbell Collection.

Barbara and James Hevron's Spencer County History Collection. Newburgh, Indiana.

Brown-Pusey House. Elizabethtown, Kentucky.
    Family Files.

Bureau of Land Management. Springfield, Virginia.
    Vincennes Land Office Records.

The Byron R. Lewis Historical Collection Library. Vincennes University, Vincennes, Indiana,
    Anna O'Flynn Papers.
    Francis Marion Van Natter Papers.

Evansville–Vanderburgh County Public Library. Evansville, Indiana.
    Southwestern Indiana Historical Society Annuals.

Indiana State Archives. Indianapolis, Indiana.
    Vincennes Land Office Records.

Indiana State Library. Indianapolis, Indiana.
    O. V. Brown Collection.

Library of Congress. Washington, D.C.
    Albert Beveridge Papers.

Lilly Library. Indiana University, Bloomington, Indiana.

Lincoln Manuscript Collection
Lincoln Boyhood National Memorial. Lincoln City, Indiana.
History Files.
Nila Michel Family History Material.
The Lincoln Museum. Fort Wayne, Indiana.
Lincoln Boyhood Files.
National Archives. Washington, D. C.
Land Records.
Nelson County Public Library. Bardstown, Kentucky.
Family History Files.
Spencer County Public Library. Rockport, Indiana.
Family Files.
Roy O. West Library. DePauw University, Greencastle, Indiana.
Albert J. Beveridge Collection.
J. Edward Murr Collection.
Jesse W. Weik Collection.
Willard Library. Evansville, Indiana.
Southwestern Indiana Historical Society Collection.
William Henry Smith Memorial Library. Indiana Historical Society, Indianapolis, Indiana.
William Fortune Papers.
John E. Iglehart Papers.

Newspapers
Evansville Courier.
Evansville Journal.
Rockport Herald.
Rockport Journal.

Index